Growth Points in Cognition

International Library of Psychology

Growth Points in Cognition

Edited by
Guy Claxton

Routledge
London and New York

First published in 1988 by
Routledge
11 New Fetter Lane, London EC4P 4EE

Published in the USA by
Routledge
a division of Routledge, Chapman and Hall, Inc.
29 West 35th Street, New York, NY 10001

Set in Baskerville 10/12 pt.
by Columns of Reading
and printed in Great Britain
by Richard Clay Ltd
Bungay, Suffolk

Library of Congress Cataloging also available

British Library Cataloguing in Publication Data
Growth points in cognition.—(International
    library of psychology).
    1. Cognition
    I. Claxton, Guy   II. Series
    153.4   BF311

ISBN 0 415 00260 5 (c)
        0 415 00261 3 (p)

For Parker,
inspiring underachiever
and excellent friend

Contents

Contributors

Vicki Bruce
Department of Psychology, University of Nottingham

Ruth Campbell
Department of Experimental Psychology, University of Oxford

Guy Claxton
Centre for Educational Studies, King's College London

H. Valerie Curran
Department of Psychology, Institute of Psychiatry, University of London

Alan Garnham
Centre for Research on Perception and Cognition, University of Sussex

David W. Green
Department of Psychology, University College, London

M. Sebastian Halliday
Department of Psychology, University of Manchester

Nigel Harvey
Department of Psychology, University College, London

Graham J. Hitch
Department of Psychology, University of Manchester

Peter Morris
Department of Psychology, University of Lancaster

Preamble: more wood, less trees

'Cognition' is not so much a field as a forest. It presents the newcomer with an immense wealth of detail: theories, models, terms and findings that are entangled and sometimes seemingly impenetrable. There is plenty of new growth – of which some will thrive and much will wither. And a lot of dead wood too, some recognised and some not. Here and there are totem poles: not alive at all, but nonetheless revered and frequently referred to. How is the student to begin to make sense of all this? Certainly it cannot be enough to sit her in a lecture hall for a term, pointing out the monuments, then give her a machete and say 'Off you go'. What is needed is not history but perspective, a climb up to a vantage point from which the lie of the land can be discerned, and a sketch map made that will help guide the exploration. Such a period of reflection and orientation is time well spent, for it reveals not only structure but points of interest. From above you can see where the densest centres of activity and growth are to be found.

Growth Points in Cognition is designed to provide such a vantage point for the student about to set out on a journey into the interior of cognition; and also perhaps a handbook to take along, to check up on local culture and the things to see. It will also, we hope, be of interest to the more seasoned explorer, postgraduate and lecturer, who may enjoy a break from scrutinising trees to take stock of the wood, and may find it worth while to put her own sense of 'The Big Picture' alongside some other people's, and thereby clarify it a little. Many recent commentators on the state of cognitive psychology have bemoaned the plethora of Small Pictures and the absence of a Big one, and this book aims to be a step in the desired direction. The discipline of trying to see the wood for the trees, in order to map it out clearly for students, is itself, I would argue, a timely contribution to knowledge. Even to have helped to open up a little the debate about synthesis and coherence would have been useful. British cognitive psychologists have been, by temperament perhaps as well as by training, more beaver than bird, and such higher-order, reflective discussions have sometimes been treated as signs of grandiosity, or of an unhealthy and unproductive interest in one's own navel. I would argue, on the contrary, that this kind of reflection is a vital precursor to more detailed theorising and experimentation, and that without some sense, albeit hazy, of the Big Picture, such research runs the risk of being neither well-motivated nor cumulative.

As well as being synoptic, the book attempts to be predictive. The contributors have been encouraged not only to provide an overview of their area, but also to have a shot at highlighting the 'new growth' that seems to them to hold promise for the future – whether it be methodological, empirical or conceptual. We may, of course, have got it wrong. But, even if we have, we may nevertheless have helped ourselves, and hopefully you, to think more deeply about what patterns and directions can be spotted in the profusion. And speculation tends to add a little spice to things, as well.

Guy Claxton
King's College London

Acknowledgments

Acknowledgment is gratefully made to the following for permission to reprint previously published material:

To Professor H. K. Nishihara, and The Royal Society, for figures 3, 6, and 8 from D. Marr and H. K. Nishihara (1978) 'Representation and recognition of the spatial organisation of three-dimensional shapes', *Proceedings of The Royal Society of London, Series B, 200*, 269-94; reproduced here as figures 2.13, 2.14 and 2.15.

To Professor F. Parke and The Institute of Electrical and Electronic Engineers, Inc, for figure 2 from F. Parke (1982), 'Parameterised models for facial animation', IEEE: C. G. and A., *2*, 61-8; reproduced here as figure 2.18.

Figures

1 How do you tell a good cognitive theory when you see one?

Guy Claxton

What is cognition all about?

People are theorists: we are theory-holders, theory-users and theory-builders. For example, we have theories about the physical world that enable us to cross busy streets, or to predict the flight of a ball. We have theories about the social world, which provide us with ways of managing encounters at parents' evenings or at family Christmases. We have theories about ourselves – what kind of person we are, and how we will react to other people's aggression. These theories vary in a variety of respects. For example, some of them are very general, like the one that says that something that looks opaque will be solid to the touch[1] (Campbell, 1974). And some are very specific, enabling us to anticipate the taste of a strawberry from its visual impression. In many areas these theories, though often tacit, are extremely sophisticated and successful – only rarely do we walk full tilt into plateglass doors, make social gaffes, or catch ourselves behaving wildly 'out of character'.

One special class of these theories concerns our own mental processes, 'folk psychology', as Churchland (1984) calls it.[2] Perhaps surprisingly, of all our vast array of theories, those that pertain to our own psychology seem often to be the ones that are crude, limited or mistaken. We know very little about how we talk, think, see, remember, attend, understand and select appropriate actions. We don't have much in the way of a theory about ourselves as cognisers. How is our knowledge represented in our minds? How is it organised? How do we get at it? How do we synthesise old theories into creative solutions to new problems? How do we store the records of our own autobiographies? Why is it that memory sometimes seems to work brilliantly and at other times appallingly? How can we recognise the faces of our friends in a flash, yet are hardly able to describe them at all? How can we perform complicated skills like driving, sometimes

I am grateful to Chris Leach, John Morton and John Pickering for their comments and advice.

1

for miles, without seeming to have had any awareness of what we were doing? On questions such as these our personal theories are very often silent.

Cognitive psychology is the systematic attempt to improve on folk psychology. The study of cognition aims to produce theories about our own theories, and about how we use and modify those theories. Put somewhat more technically, 'representation in the widest sense of the term is the central issue in cognitive psychology...the other central concern of cognitive psychology is how thoughts and acts are produced, and the specification of the processes that operate on the representations' (Mandler, 1985). Cognitive psychology, we might say, is the mind trying to represent itself to itself: an enterprise that remains fascinating and sensible despite Ambrose Bierce's (1958) cynical definition of mind as 'a mysterious form of matter secreted by the brain, (whose) chief activity consists in the endeavour to ascertain its own nature, the futility of the attempt being due to the fact that it has nothing but itself to know itself with.'

The question I want to focus on here is not 'How far have we got?' The other chapters in the book provide excellent answers to that. It is 'How do we know we have got anywhere at all?' How do we know whether we have improved on folk psychology? How do we estimate the success or the value of cognitive theories? How do we weigh one theory against another? By what criteria do we, and should we, judge? My argument in brief is that cognitive psychologists have for the last three decades been using criteria to assess their conjectures that have turned out to be too narrow, generating a vast array of theories that, in the light of *other* criteria, which researchers are now beginning to apply, can seem very unsuccessful indeed. As these new criteria for what counts as a valid and interesting theory of cognition come to be accepted, so the hold of the old criteria is being relaxed, and while they remain important, they are no longer prescriptive or preeminent. The new directions in cognition are currently being formed as a result of these shifts in the 'rules' that tell us what rates as a good theory. This chapter is about what these criteria are, and why the shift is taking place.

The criteria

The experimental criterion

Twentieth-century academic psychology has seen itself as above all an experimental science, in which matters of theory are settled by putting them to empirical test. Cognitive psychology, until recently very much a child of this tradition, has therefore sought to evaluate its theoretical conjectures by putting them to the test of practical refutation. This criterion asks of a theory: 'How well does it account for the data?' And by 'data' is meant the results of experiments that have been specifically designed to probe the relative explanatory adequacy of this and other theories that claim to offer accounts of phenomena in the same domain. Laboratory tests are best, it is held, because they enable us to anatomise the organic complexity of 'real life' into its constituents, and thereby allow us to focus on the behaviour of the few variables that are, from the point of view of the theory under consideration, relevant, and ignore the rest. In an under-graduate physiology practical class on neural conduction, we are able to dissect out from the whole frog just the large nerve in its leg and apply our probes to it. The rest of the frog, having been safely 'neutralised', can be forgotten about. We do not have to consider its educational history, or whether it understands the purpose of our clumsy ministrations. The experimental criterion supposes that we can dissect out particular psychological processes – 'working memory', 'problem-solving skills' or whatever – in just the same way, and that we can for the moment, and with equal success, ignore the rest of a person whilst we test a partial theory of a partial function. Having understood the bits, we can then reassemble them into a functioning human being, and at the same time fit the partial understandings together into a working model of that human being. In physiology this approach has proved very successful: we can build models of heart and liver, nerve and muscle, vision and taste separately, at least up to a point, and *then* stick them together.

Thus the requirement to test cognitive theories against laboratory data has forced us to follow the 'fragmentation' approach, and has *ipso facto* led us towards the proliferation of micromodels designed to account for prescribed, laboratory-based ranges of phenomena. Accepting the preemin-ence of the experimental criterion has heavily influenced not only the way we test theories, but also the kinds of theories that have been generated. Good theories are those that are amenable to laboratory testing: they are formulated in such a way that they give rise to logically derived, empirically falsifiable predictions.

Over the last few years people have begun to question the over-riding control over cognitive theorising that this criterion has held. They have looked at the theories that have been produced under its sway, and found them disappointing. Newell (1973) and Allport (1975) have both commented sadly on the way in which these types of micromodels seem often to be neither integrated nor cumulative. They do not fit with each other, and frequently their authors don't seem very interested in fitting them together. In the introduction to *Cognitive Psychology: New Directions* (1980), I summed up the criticisms like this: 'Cognitive psychologists are like the inhabitants of thousands of little islands, all in the same part of the ocean, yet totally out of touch with each other. Each has evolved a different culture, different ways of doing things, different languages to talk about what they do. Occasionally inhabitants of one island may spot their neighbours jumping up and down and issuing strange cries; but it makes no sense, so they ignore it.' And on the subject of the plethora of micromodels, echoing Newell (1973), I said: 'The proliferation of languages and models means that cognitive psychology is full of specialist terminology ("jargon" is perhaps too pejorative a word). Much of it, only a few years old, seems already obsolete: psychologists generate and disgard new models at a rate that the motor trade would envy. Researchers, being the manufacturers, tend to be less confused by this than consumers, the students. Trying to write an essay that "compares and contrasts" models of visual pattern recognition, or short-term memory, or computer simulations of language comprehension, is an awful job, and one whose value, other than as a training of the critical faculties, is open to question.'

Have things improved in the last few years? Not much, if the pessimism of two recent commentators is to be believed. Eysenck (1984) observes that: 'Psychological models proliferate at such a rate that it is rapidly becoming true that every self-respecting cognitive psychologist has his or her own theory and the beleaguered researcher or student finds it almost impossible to compare theories because they are based on different sets of data, using separate constructs and terminology.' (It is sad to note that, since my comment in 1980, the researchers now seem to be no better off than the students. We are all in the same boat, surrounded by the flotsam and jetsam of yesterday's proud, new theories.) While Mandler (1985) is forced to reiterate complaints of ten years earlier: 'Psychologists in every corner of the empirical domain of psychology seem to be in search of quaint minitheories (which) are seldom put to the test against other competing claimants: they rarely attain the age of consent to be tested.'

The predicament in which cognitive psychology finds itself reflects partly the unwanted side effects of an over-zealous adherence to the experimental criterion, and partly the way in which we have chosen to divide cognition up into researchable bits. The rest of this section illustrates the first of these: the 'fragmentation problem' we will return to in the next section.

The practical problem seems to be that conscious human beings are not as much like anaesthetised frogs as we had hoped. The *modus operandi* that delivers good theories in physiology (and other sciences) does not seem to have been so effective in psychology. Why is that? In part because the rest of the 'frog' cannot be 'neutralised' quite so easily. It is true that in the laboratory you can hold variables of feeling, need, mood, interest and attribution relatively still, so that inter and intra-subject variability across different conditions or experiments is reduced, and the effect of chosen independent on chosen dependent variables stands a chance of being observed. But the variables of emotion and motivation are not thereby 'removed': they are merely set or frozen at particular values. Thus the laboratory situation tends to be rather different from 'real life' both in the values at which these variables *are* set, and in the fact that they are set at all, and not allowed to float as freely as they normally do. As a subject you are *supposed* to keep trying, to stay calm, to be serious, to concentrate; you are supposed *not* to get upset when you make mistakes, not to try to outwit the random stimulus generating program, not to try to figure out what's going on, not to be playful or whimsical, not to let your thoughts wander, not to engage the experimenter in conversation in the middle of a 'run', and so on. The first-time subject, in trying to find an analogue to the experimental situation in their previous experience, may tacitly liken it to a cross between a party game, a driving test, and taking 'O' levels. But exactly how he or she construes it is not the point. What is, is the fact that to be a subject is not to put yourself in a situation that is neutral with respect to your feelings, thoughts and needs, or even less, one from which these factors are removed. Rather it is to be in a very particular situation, within which these factors are set at somewhat peculiar values.

Let us note briefly a couple of aspects of the typical experimental situation that make it rather a special one. First, subjects are often required to make timed decisions about whether statements are true, or whether they have been previously presented, or whether they accurately describe a picture, 'as quickly as you can without making mistakes'. However gently worded, this instruction presents subjects with two conflicting demands that have to be integrated in order to find some optimal solution. It is by no means a straightforward demand, but quite a subtle problem that for its solution requires a fair amount of trial and error ('How fast *can* I go before I start to get it wrong?') and intuitive judgement and interpretation ('What do I suppose constitutes an "acceptable" error rate?'). So as well as making a series of decisions about the individual stimuli, subjects are cumulatively learning to solve the higher-order problem of how to meet the task demands. And this process is normally accompanied by a sense of haste, effort and intention, with sporadic blips of feeling either pleased or cross with oneself as one happens to perform particularly well or poorly, or to have hit on a strategy that appears to be a good or bad one.

Now the point of this description is not to accuse experiments of being 'artificial', as if there were something wrong with them *per se*. It is to show that they are representative of a very particular type of mildly stressed problem-solving situation, in which a consistently high level of performance has to be maintained, often over a long period of time, despite the fact that (even given some practice) one is still learning how best to achieve it, and experimenting with different strategies or procedures for so doing: and all this, usually, to achieve a performance that has no intrinsic, personal significance, for reasons of financial gain, educational merit, or friendship. It is not only possible, therefore, but highly likely, that we will be in error if we assume that the characteristics of this performance reflect stable features of a general-purpose cognitive process. As we shall see in more detail later, if we have learnt one thing from experimental work in cognition over the last decade, it is that transfer of one 'skill', 'process' or 'structure' from one test situation to another, even apparently quite similar one, is highly unpredictable and unreliable. We cannot therefore build a psychology of *relaxed* cognition, or *easy* cognition or *stable* cognition from performances that are stressed or difficult or transitional. Any cognitive performance arises from the interaction of a host of variables, many of them not themselves cognitive in nature but emotional or 'systemic', and in such a case the experimental method breaks down. As Oatley (1987) reminds us, 'the methods of natural science are good at uncovering causal chains which operate either one at a time or independently of context, but they are not tuned to discovering influences that are multiple or sensitive to context.'

So unfortunately there is no methodological escape from this problem. If practice is given (the data from which is then discarded), the danger is that the data one uses derive from purpose-built task, content and context-specific strategies. Whereas if little or no practice is given, the data, whilst potentially reflecting more accurately the real-life processes and knowledge-structures that subjects bring with them, also reflect those processes and structures in a labile stage where they are being internally 'customised' to meet the particular demands of the task. And both individuals and more importantly tasks (perhaps different conditions within the same experiment) may take different lengths of time, different numbers of trials, for this customisation of pre-existing resources to take place. In addition, different subjects may arrive at different solutions for meeting the demand characteristics of the task, making it necessary (as researchers are increasingly doing), almost as a matter of routine, to look at individual patterns of performance before throwing them together into the statistical melting-pot (Eysenck, 1984). These considerations, by the way, cannot be dismissed as 'hypothetical'. There is abundant evidence now to show that cognitive processes *are* very often task-specific. Illustrations are provided in this book for vision, where Vicki Bruce argues for different processes of pattern recognition for objects and for faces; for memory, where Peter Morris shows how poorly a range of different memory tasks correlate, for a given individual, with each other; and for problem-solving, where David Green demonstrates that a solution to a problem may not transfer even to a marginally different version of the same problem.

A second way in which experiments are unusual situations is that they make ends out of means. One does not normally recognise objects in order to recognise them. One usually does so in the context of some wider purpose. One does not normally interrogate semantic memory in order simply to bring to mind what one knows. One usually does so in the broader context of having a discussion with a friend, or solving a crossword puzzle. And so on. Here again the point is not that such studies tell us nothing about normal functioning, but that we cannot *assume* that the way these processes operate while they are being foregrounded or highlighted will be the same as when they are embedded within a simultaneously active system of processes that are orchestrated by the intention to achieve a personal goal. We cannot even assume that they will be the same processes (Polanyi, 1967).

One final point needs to be made about the constricting effect that the experimental criterion has on the development of theories when its application excludes all other considerations. In its preemptive form, this criterion says that any theory that does not immediately generate clearly falsifiable predictions is not a good theory. Thus more general attempts to construct 'frameworks' or 'notations' or 'ways of viewing' cognition that have not yet been driven to the point of yielding testable hypotheses have sometimes been undervalued. However, there is a growing body of opinion (e.g. Anderson, 1983; Morton, 1985) that says we have lost something – perhaps rather a lot – by applying this criterion too early and too harshly. Baddeley (1982), in offering for consideration his notion of 'domains of recollection', felt he had to defend himself against just this charge. '(One) question that may be raised with regard to the proposed framework is that it is not directly testable...I suggest, however, that as a blanket criterion for evaluating all kinds of theory, it is misguided. Theoretical concepts can operate at a whole series of levels ranging from the detailed and precise to the very general. The criteria for evaluating an explanatory concept will depend on the level and purpose for which it is devised. In the present instance the purpose of the theoretical concepts in question is to provide a coherent framework to assist in the understanding of a wide range of phenomena. In this view, a theoretical concept should be evaluated not by whether it approximates to some absolute truth, but by the extent to which it performs the useful function of interpreting what we already know while facilitating further discovery.'

By about 1980 many cognitive psychologists were beginning to see that the experimental criterion, applied rigorously and on its own, had exerted something of a stranglehold on the development of cognitive theories. It seemed to be producing, like the seed that fell on stony ground, lots of little shoots that sprang up quickly and withered away equally quickly for lack of root. And it had ruled out of court other kinds of theoretical approach that may have been less well-formulated, less technical, less testable but which, there was a growing suspicion, might prove more robust and sturdy in the long run. It may be that we clung to the experimental criterion, as sole arbiter, for too long for fear that, if we let it go, there might be no other sensible criteria we could draw on, and we would simply be opening the doors to a non-scientific free-for-all. Or it may be that, having staked its claim as a respectable academic discipline on the basis of its being a natural science, psychology's conservatism has been fuelled by the belief that a relaxing of the experimental criterion will lead to a lowering of respect in the academic community at large.

And it may be, too, that we have been trying to run before we could walk. Refined laboratory testing has been a productive criterion when applied within the context of a mature science, where points of detail need to be decided within the bounds of an agreed mythology, a widely accepted core set of frameworks, concepts and guiding metaphors. But cognitive psychology still lacks such a central vision, and I suspect that the attempt to make cumulative progress without it, or worse, to try to find it, through the meticulous application of rigorous experimental procedures, is untimely and, indeed, counter-productive. It is as if we had been feeding psychology a vast diet of details, but without first giving it a stomach with which to digest them. Thus the recent history, and probably the immediate future, of cognitive psychology, are to be characterised more by the search for alternative criteria for what counts as a good theory than by startling empirical discoveries.

J. Anderson (1976), for example, has argued that an experimentally testable hypothesis is the tip of an iceberg of speculation and presupposition, much of which is tacit and/or deeply embedded within the language, metaphor or other notation within which the speculations have been cast. Developing a plausible and integrated *point of view* about cognition is a vital and time-consuming stage on the way to the elaboration of any well-founded technical notation, and the falsifiable hypotheses to which it gives rise. I would suggest further that in this preparatory stage, in psychology as well as in physics or biology, simple images and analogies are invaluable. The more concrete they are the better, both because it is easier to draw out their latent implications (Hesse, 1966) and because it is more difficult to forget that what one is working with *is* a metaphor. The complex, purpose-built models with which cognitive science abounds have the disadvantage of seeming more 'real', thus leading their proponents into believing that memory *must be* a 'store', for example, and resisting too hard their refutation; and secondly they are less easy to pin down. A clear metaphor, such as J. Reitman's (1970) 'waiting room' model of short-term memory, is useful precisely because its limits and limitations are transparent. It is much easier to fudge the specification of a 'response buffer' or a 'working memory'.

In cognitive psychology the need for such conceptual play has not been outgrown. Yet, perhaps impatient with this developmental stage, and over-anxious to look grown up, we seem to have rushed too soon into the elaboration of technical notations and paradigm-specific micromodels, and into attempts to test them, that continue to prove premature and which leave the discipline fragmented.

The global criterion

The global criterion goes hand in hand with the experimental criterion. It says: 'A theory that purports to apply everywhere is better than a theory that only seems to apply to a restricted domain of phenomena.' It represents a pretheoretical stance about how cognition is organised that has been translated, like the experimental criterion, into a principle for guiding and evaluating research. Perhaps misled by the 'cog' in 'cognition', it sees the mind as a complex mechanism, like a watch, that could be 'dismantled' by suitable experimental procedures, allowing each part of the mechanism to be studied in turn. Thus cognition is chopped up into the familiar chapter headings of cognitive psychology: perception, speech production, attention, memory, language comprehension, decision-making and so on. The aim of theory, then, is to further subdivide these categories (memory into long-term and short-term; long-term memory into episodic and semantic; short-term memory into articulatory loop and visuospatial scratch pad...) and to explain 'how they work'. The crucial characteristic of this approach is that the mechanisms it proposes are *general-purpose*. As I said in 1980: 'The assumption is that human beings possess general cognitive abilities, skills and structures that sit around inside the head waiting to be called; that any task, in any context, in any form that "logically" requires those abilities, will make them manifest; and that when they do so their properties will shine through the background haze of extraneous factors clearly and unambiguously. All experiments that are conducted in laboratories using "simple" tasks and "simple" materials rely on this rationale. (No one would want to say that such experiments *only* tell you about how undergraduates make decisions (about words) in darkened rooms...)'

However, the assumption of separability of functions – that you can dismantle cognition into separate processes and study them one by one – queried as long ago as 1970 by Walter Reitman and raised again by Miller and Gazzaniga (1984), appears now to be untenable. It seems increasingly unlikely that such components will ever be capable of being bolted back together into a coherent theory of cognition unless 'The Big Picture' (and the same, or at least compatible Big Pictures) has been borne in mind all along. Norman (1980), for instance, contends that 'the study of cognition requires the consideration of all...different aspects of the entire system...Of course no one can study everything all at the same time, but I argue that we cannot ignore these things either, else the individual pieces that we study in such detail will not fit together in the absence of some thought about the whole.' And if he is right, this means that we will be unable to apply such models to the explanation of everyday cognitive performance, where cognition works as a harmonious, integrated, organic *system*, in the service of a personally meaningful pursuit. Neisser (1976), for example, suggests that 'psychology...may hope to emerge from the laboratory some day with a new array of important ideas, but that outcome is unlikely unless it is already working with principles whose applicability to natural situations can be foreseen.'

Others have argued that it is not so much that we *cannot* break down cognitive processing into constituents, as that the *way* that psychologists have tried to do it may not be the best one. As Clark (1986) says: 'It is an understandable, probably inevitable, tactic in the face of our almost total ignorance of psychological mechanisms, to try to understand the mind by decomposing its activity into a series of individually addressable sub-problems. But, he goes on, I shall criticise the choice of *particular* sub-problems as all too often biologically unsound.' We shall return to Clark's reasons for this criticism later on. But it may serve here to flag a general point. Not only can the strong application of the experimental criterion be faulted for not generating good theories in its own terms – the argument we have been following so far. When we begin to allow the validity of other criteria, such as the 'biological' ones to which Clark alludes, we uncover a range of other, more *a priori*, reasons why the theoretical products of experimental cognitive psychology may not deserve as much respect as they have usually been given.

Fodor (1983) has been particularly responsible recently for dragging the global criterion into the limelight of cognitive psychology, by reminding us of what the alternative way of dismantling the mind is: into 'modules' that have their own relatively autonomous, relatively fixed package of processing operations that are called up by and applied to delimited and specific domains of experience. As Marshall (1984) puts it, we can analyse cognition into bits not according to what they (the bits) do, but what they do it to. Fodor calls these packages 'vertical faculties' (as distinct from perception, memory and so on, which are 'horizontal faculties'), and argues that much of cognition is in fact organised vertically. (In fact, he goes on to argue that there are some cognitive systems that *are* non-modular – what he calls 'central processes' – but even this claim has been disputed by Marshall (1984) and Shallice (1984).)

Certainly much recent evidence supports the modular view. The cognitive processes that seem to be manifest in any situation depend frequently on what the situation is: specifically on the *content* of the task – the way it is instantiated or 'dressed up' (as, for example, with the different versions of the Wason 4 Card problem discussed by Dave Green); on the physical, psychological and emotional *context* within which the task is presented (as shown by the mass of research on 'state-dependent learning' see, e.g., Eich, 1980); and on the internal *purposes* and task *demands* that jointly specify the direction and goal of processing. And this evidence comes not only from laboratory studies of 'normal' adult cognition, but from the fields of developmental and cross-cultural psychology, and neuropsychology, which are reviewed in the present book by Hitch and Halliday, Curran and Campbell respectively.

Thus it seems that theories that postulate general-purpose mechanisms may not after all be preferable to ones that are explicitly local. The attempt to model performance in particular domains seems more limited, but it may reflect the 'functional anatomy' of cognition more accurately, and may ultimately therefore be more productive. The global criterion has all too often led researchers to make an illogical jump from performance in a very restricted range of tasks to the existence of some basic procedure or structure. Then, when this mechanism appears to be altered or absent in some other, perhaps minimally different, situation, there seems to be a problem, which is frequently resolved by contorting the theory to fit (on the assumption that it *must* apply, in some form or other) or by a grudging search for 'procedural differences' or experimental flaws that are used somehow to justify ignoring the awkward data. It may well be that it is uncritical acceptance of the global criterion that has led to the insularity of which Allport, Mandler and others have complained. The alternative methodology is to start from the assumption that 'circumstances alter cases' and to vary the contents, contexts and demands of tasks so as to discover the limits of applicability (or 'range of convenience', as Kelly (1955) called it) of a model that has been accepted, right from the word go, to *be* limited. Increasingly, cognitive research is doing just this: abandoning the global criterion, and focussing instead on developing models of behaviour in situations that are interesting in their own right.

The economic criterion

The third type of criterion that has commonly been used, often in conjunction with the first two, to define what constitutes a good theory, has focussed not on its generality or empirical adequacy, but on features that are intrinsic to it, such as elegance, coherence and parsimony. If you cannot decide between two equally successful theories, so the economic criterion suggests, choose the one that is simpler and neater. Load up Lloyd Morgan's Canon, whet the blade of Occam's Razor and ruthlessly discard the theory that contains the *ad hoc*, the gratuitous or the baroque.

While this seems a sensible rule of thumb, there are those, with an eye on *other* kinds of criteria, who would not give economy and elegance the position and the power in theory-evaluation that they have sometimes enjoyed. The economic criterion is, they would argue, a good servant but a bad master. In particular when we look at cognition from either an evolutionary or a neurophysiological perspective, there is room to doubt whether the simpler is *ipso facto* the more accurate. The author of the most sophisticated and all-embracing cognitive model that we yet have, John

Anderson, starts his 1976 exposition, for example, by quoting with evident approval, from Marvin Minsky: 'I believe that parsimony is still inappropriate at this stage, valuable as it may be in later phases of every science. There is room in the anatomy and genetics of the brain for much more mechanism than anyone today is prepared to suppose, and we should concentrate for a while more on sufficiency and efficiency rather than on necessity.' While Paul Churchland (1984) defends ad hocery and lack of coherence on evolutionary grounds.

> On the computational approach, conscious intelligence does not emerge as having a single unifying essence, or a simple unique nature. Rather, intelligent creatures are represented as a loosely interconnected grab bag of highly various computational procedures, rather in the way a fellow student once characterised my first car as 'a squadron of nuts and bolts flying in loose formation'...The slow accretion of semi-isolated control systems does make evolutionary sense. Nervous systems evolved by bits and pieces, the occasional accidental addition being selected for because it happened to give an advantageous control over some aspect of the creature's behaviour or internal operations. Long-term natural selection makes it likely that surviving creatures enjoy a smooth interaction with the environment, but the internal mechanisms that sustain that interaction may well be arbitrary, opportunistic, and jury-rigged.

We shall return to biology and evolution later in order to explore more fully the grounds for Churchland's claim. The point here is that *if* there is reason to suppose that our mental theories are complex and untidy, we should not try too hard to make our models of those theories simple and neat. Given that fact, however, it obviously makes good sense to search for models that *are* as unitary and coherent as possible. This illustrates again the main argument: that the weight an evaluative criterion is given is a function of what *other* criteria one is willing to accept. And the selection and weighting of a portfolio of criteria which define what counts as a good theory is not itself a scientific – certainly not an empirical – matter. Deciding what goods one wants one's science to deliver is not a problem that science itself can solve. What we are seeing in cognitive science at the moment is a rethinking of what we want out theories to *do*.

The computational criterion

Very popular for the last twenty years has been the computational criterion: it asks of a theory 'can you be turned into a working program that will cause a computer to mimic, in its essentials, the human performance that your creator is interested in?' And a theory that can is better than one that can't. The former is applauded for being explicit, unambiguous and complete; the latter berated for being vague and woolly.

This is an important and valuable criterion. The attempt to simulate aspects of human cognition on a computer has indeed driven theorising forward and has produced a host of elegant and sophisticated models. A fruitful interaction has been promoted between the fields of experimental psychology and artificial intelligence (AI) with empirical data being used to check that the developing stimulations not only do what people do but do it at the same kind of speed, and are prone to the same kinds of errors – in other words that they are aiming to mimic the covert processes as well as the overt products.

There are, however, a number of costs and pitfalls associated with this criterion that should make us chary of applying it in isolation, or with too much enthusiasm. These have been explored by authors such as Dreyfus, Marr and other contributors to Haugeland (1981), and I will focus here on just two. The first is the danger of producing what Dennett (1984a) calls a 'cognitive wheel', which he defines as 'any design proposal in cognitive theory...that is profoundly unbiological, however wizardly and elegant it is as a bit of technology.' Clark (1986) explains (if we need it explaining) that 'the wheel image is intended to convey the fear that the strategies and mechanisms developed in AI may bear as little relation to nature's solutions to problems of cognitive design as the wheel bears to natural solutions to the problem of mammalian locomotion.' In other words the computation criterion is not enough. It allows us to come up with theories that are explicit enough to be programmable, and which will even reproduce the fine structure of an area of human performance, but which need bear no relation, structural or functional, to the way the central nervous system does it. The argument is reminiscent of Broadbent's (1973) rebuttal of Chomsky's oft-repeated claim in the 1960s that because transformational grammar was a 'good' (i.e. elegant, coherent, economical) model of linguistic *competence*, generating all and only the sentences of a language that were judged acceptable by a native speaker, therefore it must also be a model of how people produce and understand language: a model in other words of linguistic *performance*. People must 'know' (in some sense of the word) transformational grammar. Maybe, replied Broadbent, but only in the obscure and unhelpful sense in which Giotto, who could draw perfect freehand circles of an infinite number of sizes – he used to leave them as calling cards for his friends – had to 'know' that $x^2 + y^2 = r^2$ This formula is an elegant rule that described ('generates') his products. But it tells us nothing interesting at all about his astonishing muscular control.

The trouble is that, in being forced to be explicit, unambiguous and complete in formulating our theories, we are also forced into making lots of little decisions – just to get the program to run – that are irrelevant to our main concerns, and often psychologically uninteresting. The only sensible way to make these decisions is to do what is easiest in programming terms – because, by definition, there is no psychological basis for choice. But in so doing we may, unknowingly, have turned our simulation into a wheel. While it is a good thing to be precise, it is a bad thing to be forced to be more precise than you are actually capable of being. We might bear in mind William James's (1890) *caveat* that 'at a certain stage in the development of every science a degree of vagueness is what best consists with fertility'. It is not at all clear that we have yet outgrown this stage. In addition it would help if we could develop further the ability to compute with vagueness – that is to say to find well-formulated ways of represented ill-defined theoretical structures and processes (e.g. Zadeh, 1982).

The other big problem with the computational approach, which is only just beginning to be tackled, is that cognitive mechanisms have developed, over the life of the species and of each individual, on the basis of a vast amount of (mostly non-verbal) experience; while the computer's knowledge arrives codified, ready-made and relatively fixed. Clark (1986) has spelt out the pitfalls inherent in such a modelling procedure. By programming computers with knowledge that is not grown but assembled, we inevitably lose much of the experiential richness that subserves and underpins what we consciously know, and we unnaturally dissociate that knowledge from the tacit procedures that gave rise to it. As psychologists we must be concerned with:

> the strategies that guide (an organism's) learning and its subsequent construction of a store of *secondary* (learnt) presumptive knowledge. On the other hand psych. AI (i.e. computer simulation) seems concerned to model the constructivist strategies of the experienced adult organism, and hence to model the stock of secondary presumptions learnt by interaction with the world...the aim is to give the system the kind of presumptive knowledge ('frames', 'scripts', or whatever) it would have acquired in the course of experience had it been a human being engaged in a certain form of life...(But) the informational content of any frame aimed at encoding secondary presumptive knowledge must always lack the density of items required of an adequate model. The frames lack the rich and varied connections to the overall gamut of human experience which partially determines the semantic content of our assertions on the subject in question.

It is as if we were trying to model the behaviour of icebergs using only the tips, and without allowing for the phenomena of freezing and melting. It begins to look, unfortunately, as if *any* model that relies on preprogrammed secondary knowledge is doomed to be a cognitive wheel.

It may even be that such a deep, pervasive and apparently reasonable assumption as the separation of a passive, 'declarative' store of knowledge from an active 'procedural' system that operates on this knowledge is itself a mistake, and one that has sent a generation of computer modellers off on the wrong track (Claxton, 1978; Miller and Gazzaniga, 1984). The 'connectionist' approach, perhaps best represented for present purposes by McClelland and Rumelhart (1986), has started to experiment very successfully with models that do not start from this distinction, but from a unified representational system within which the momentary processing operations are completely determined by the structural and energetic state of the system. We shall return to these later.

Before we move on to look at some of the newer criteria that are beginning to redirect the study of cognition, this might be the place to say a word about the difference between so-called 'cognitive science' and cognitive psychology. It is nowadays more fashionable to speak of the former: already in some quarters the term 'cognitive psychology' has a slightly dated air about it. 'Cognitive science' is more Where It's At. There is a more substantial difference than mere 'with-it-ness', however, though it is one of emphasis rather than kind. It reflects a tacit agreement to give different prominence to the four criteria that we have discussed so far. A cognitive *psychologist* is a person who steers by the experimental criterion above all else, and who is likely (though this is changing) to accept the global criterion as well. On this definition all the contributions to this book represent cognitive psychology, though the authors vary in how 'global' or 'local' their emphasis is. Cognitive *scientists* on the other hand tend to be more concerned with the computational and economic criteria, and it is not surprising therefore that they show more interest in linguistics and philosophy, as well as artificial intelligence, for it is these disciplines that have traditionally been guided by the consideration of elegance, coherence, logic and parsimony. Though there is considerable variation, cognitive scientists tend to be less concerned with the fine detail of empirical data, and to be more content to build models of performance in local domains (or 'microworlds'). Taken together these four criteria, albeit with different weightings, have represented a consensus about how to evaluate cognitive theories until quite recently.

The evolutionary criterion

Some of the newer criteria have been prefigured in the discussions of the first four, because they have provided the fresh vantage points from which re-evaluations have been made. The evolutionary criterion, one of the most interesting of the new perspectives, was introduced in the last section. It says: 'a good theory is one which contains within itself some indications of how its hypothetical mechanisms evolved.' More specifically, this criterion asks a theory to give a plausible, or at least an interesting, answer to the question of how its mechanisms, strategies or structures arose, in the course of history, as a response to the conditions, problems, needs and opportunities of the time. Put starkly, 'human intelligence has evolved as a means of satisfying our basic survival requirements. It has not been selected for its capacity to achieve the high-level mental feats which so much work in psych.AI is dedicated to modelling' (Clark, 1986). These feats themselves can (and on this criterion at some point must) be given an evolutionary account: we shall examine one such in a moment. But Clark's point is that they are evolutionarily recent, and they can only be sensibly discussed in the context of all the earlier evolution which they presuppose. As Clark continues, 'If we *can* perform such feats...it is only in virtue of our being endowed with a set of low-level capacities which just happen to facilitate the higher level activity...Biological reflection thus suggests that we should conceive of our high-level abilities as almost *accidental* benefits conferred on us by our use of information processing strategies whose primary application is quite elsewhere.' And in similar vein, Norman (1980) asks: 'Did the evolutionary sequence that produced superior cognitive systems do so to permit professors to exist, to publish, to hold conferences? One suspects not, that the regulatory (i.e. survival) system was first, that the cognitive system grew out of the requirements of that system.'

Such a perspective suggests approaches and lines of enquiry that are quite different from the traditional ones: concerns with developmental, anthropological and biological aspects of cognition become relevant, as do the capacities of lower organisms. We shall pick these up later. Here I want to pursue a line of thought that reinforces our already expressed scepticism about the economic criterion. From the evolutionary point of view it is plausible to suppose that, like Churchland's car, cognition has evolved as a loose accretion of purpose-built strategies – not as a coherent framework built according to an elegant blueprint. An example of this untidy-but-effective way of thinking, from the area of perception, is provided by Runeson (1977), with his idea of 'smart perceptual mechanisms'. These he introduces as mechanisms that 'are specialised on a particular (type of) task in a particular (type of) situation and *capitalise on the peculiarities of the situation and the task*, i.e. use shortcuts, etc. They consist of few but specialised components. For solving problems that are repeated very often smart instruments, if they exist, are more efficient and more economical. Do not be confused by this use of the word 'economical' here: he is referring to a *functional* economy, meaning smart mechanisms run smoothly, quickly, reliably and without having to draw on central reserves of attention, effort or decision-making capacity. This is quite different from *descriptive* economy: there is no reason at all to suppose that smart mechanisms should be easy to describe, analyse or explain; if anything the reverse, because they may have embedded (or embodied, perhaps) quite complex operations within a cunningly simple structure.

If Runeson is right, then the rationale of investigating cognition experimentally using 'simple' tasks and 'simple' materials (like judging whether two geometric figures are the same or different) is further undermined. If pattern recognition is not subserved by a hierarchy of progressively more complex arrays of general-purpose feature-detection devices (as many current models suppose), but by an effective patchwork of devices that are designed to solve the normal, repetitive, *complex* problems of everyday perception, then the apparently 'simple' tasks are not simple at all. What our experiments are showing us is not the smooth running of an integrated system, but the way smart perceptual mechanisms can contort themselves to solve rare (and looked at from their point of view by no means simple) perceptual problems. They may in fact have to draw on 'higher-level', more general strategies, that are not usually required at all in the course of everyday perception.

Likewise we may also possess 'smart problem-solving mechanisms' that can deliver solutions to problems correctly recognised as instances of a familiar type in a ready-made, non-reflective fashion. Such mechanisms are often going to lack a sub-routine that generates an account of *how* the problem is solved, because giving such an account is not in everyday life usually part of the problem: what matters is generating a workable solution. But, if pushed, subjects in an experiment may 'surrender to demands from the experimenter (or themselves) and give false *ad hoc* rationalizations as accounts of how they arrive at judgments which are in fact obtained through direct perception. Since the processes of perception are unconscious, such rationalizations may well be based on the subjects' intellectual ideas about how judgments ought to be arrived at.' Runeson thus provides us with an evolutionarily-based cognitive explanation for the much more widely quoted (but remarkably similar) conclusions of Nisbett and Wilson (1977): 'When people attempt to report on their cognitive processes...they do not do so on the basis of any true introspection. Instead their reports are based on *a priori* implicit *theories* or *judgments* about the extent to which a particular stimulus is a *plausible* cause of a given response.'

Smart perceptual mechanisms perform quite complicated transformations, using whatever tricks they can to economise, on often quite precisely delimited types of experience. Runeson is, therefore, giving evolutionary support to exactly the type of domain-specific modular processing that we saw Fodor (1983) advocating earlier. But let us move on to look at a fascinating set of speculations about how evolution overcame a particular and important *problem* associated with modularity. In a couple of pages Dennett (1984b) sketches a theory which suggests that thinking arose as a way of coping with the fact that modules are good at being accessed from the outside, and then doing their thing, but are not (precisely *because* they are modular) so good at talking to each other. That's not what they were built for. Yet if they could pool their resources, they could generate informed hypotheses about how to deal with a greatly expanded range of unprecedented situations.

Consider, says Dennett, a community of creatures who have evolved to the point where they (a) have a language, and (b) have discovered the survival advantages (for both species and individual) of (at least sporadic) co-operation, so that (c) they sometimes 'ask for help', and sometimes get it.

> Then, one fine day, an 'unintended' short-circuit effect of this new social institution was 'noticed' by a creature. It 'asked' for help in an inappropriate circumstance, where there was no helpful audience to hear the request and respond. Except itself! When the creature heard its own request, the stimulation provoked just the sort of other-helping utterance production that the request from another would have caused. And to the creature's 'delight' it found that it had just provoked itself into answering its own question!
>
> How could the activity of asking oneself questions be any less systematically futile than the activity of paying oneself a tip for making oneself a drink? All one needs to suppose is that there is some compartmentalisation and imperfect *internal* communication between components of a creature's cognitive system, so that one component can need the output of another component but be unable to address that component directly. Suppose the only way of getting component A to do its job is to provoke it into action by a certain sort of stimulus that normally comes from the outside, from another creature. If one day one discovers that one can play the role of this other and achieve a good result by autostimulation, the practice will blaze a valuable new communicative trail between one's internal components, a trail that happens to wander out into the public space of airways and acoustics...
>
> So in this Just So Story, the creatures got into the habit of talking (aloud) to themselves. And they found that it often had good results – often enough, in fact, to reinforce the practice. They got better and better at it. In particular, they discovered an efficient shortcut: *sotto voce* talking to oneself, which later led to entirely silent talking to oneself. The silent process maintained the loop of self-stimulation, but jettisoned the peripheral vocalisation (which) had the further benefit opportunistically endorsed, of achieving a certain privacy...and privacy was especially useful when 'comprehending' members of the same species were within earshot.

Thus first talking to oneself, and, later, thought, evolved as an excellent general-purpose addressing system for improving communication between the components of a highly modularised, piecemeal experiential knowledge-base. Although it couldn't do it directly one module could ask for the help of other modules via the medium of thought. And that development would clearly have been of great survival value, enabling the creature to bootstrap its own knowledge system to a much greater extent than had previously been the case. The capacity for 'problem-solving', even for 'creativity', became available.

Just to push the story one step further, we could note, with Dennett, that:

> we wouldn't have to restrict these internal activities to *talking* to oneself silently. Why do people draw pictures and diagrams for their own eyes to look at? Why do composers bother humming or playing their music to themselves for their own benefit?...We can suppose that the creatures in our Just So Story would also be able to engage (profitably) in internal diagramming and humming. And they would be just as capable as we are of benefiting from playing an 'inner game of tennis'.

Speculation of this sort fails the experimental test outright, of course, and there doesn't seem much point in trying to write a program to simulate it. Those who apply the experimental and computational criteria strictly will have to consider Dennett's Just So Story so much hot air. Increasingly, however, with the acceptance of the evolutionary criterion and others, such theorising is being valued both as interesting in its own right, and for the guidance and perspective it gives us as we attempt to formulate more formal, explicit, falsifiable models of cognition.

The ethological criterion

There is one variant of the evolutionary viewpoint, though, that does allow the experimental and computational criteria to be retained: what we could call the ethological criterion. Having criticised the 'microworlds' strategy in AI (that is, trying to model specially created, simplified domains, like moving blocks around on a tabletop), as being destined to produce only cognitive wheels, Clark (1986) goes on to suggest what he sees as a more fruitful alternative – modelling the cognition of lower animals.

> If we accept (a) stage-wise evolutionary explanation of complexity, then we ought to be persuaded that it is possible to gain insight into the nature of a complex system by looking at the nature of its simpler forebears...The most rewarding microworlds to study, if my suspicions are correct, will be the microworlds associated with the various animal intelligences ranged in evolutionary progression along the phylogenetic tree...Thus, we could look at the biological niches which our forebears

occupied, and form an opinion as to the kinds of problems they would need to solve and the kinds of abilities they would need to have. We would then seek, as in normal AI, to find ways of modelling the competencies required...Having made sufficient progress at one level, we must then move up the phylogenetic tree and investigate ways of modifying and transforming these primitive solutions into solutions to more complex problems.

This strategy, of course, is open to the same criticism as all other forms of 'animal psychology': the application of what has been learnt to the understanding of human cognition is, in the last analysis, based on plausibility and parallel, not on logic. Nonetheless such arguments, though not deductive, are valid, and Clark's proposal opens up yet another *complementary* way of homing in on the complexities of adult mental processes.

What has been important in the last two sections has not been the 'truth' of Runeson's or Dennett's or Clark's proposals, but the fact that they exhibit a dis-ease with an approach to modelling cognition that ignores its roots, and also that they illustrate new directions that do not suffer from the same drawbacks (though they surely have their own). To quote Clark (1986) once more:

The success of the Sirius Cybernetics Corporation, Douglas Adams (1984, p. 167) tells us, is entirely due to one fact. It is that the *fundamental* design flaws of its products are completely hidden by their *superficial* design flaws. I have a similar fear about some programs in current, psychologically-motivated AI. The fear is that the superficial flaws of programs mimicking high-level cognitive feats (such as story-understand-ing, music composition etc.) merely obscure the fundamental error of trying to model such achievements without revealing them as the accidental upshot of a certain combination of much more primitive and evolutionarily useful capacities.

In other words, we did not develop higher mental processes in order to tell tales or make music. We started to recount and compose because the abilities to do so emerged as by-products of other abilities that we had already developed.

The developmental criterion

In essence the previous criterion says a good theory is one that is able to bridge the human and non-human worlds, allowing us to achieve an understanding of cognition that acknowledges and embraces our evolution-ary continuity with the rest of the animal kingdom. By the same token we can, says the developmental criterion, legitimately enquire of an adult model as to its developmental history within the life of the individual. We have already noted that a programmed knowledge-base cannot be a generally valid model of the adult human being's knowledge-base because it is merely the systematised and articulated tip of a vast iceberg of mostly tacit experience (unless you deliberately choose to model an abstract, symbolic domain, in which case the model may only be generalised to other such domains). The computer's concepts will not be 'saturated with experience', to use Vygotsky's (1962) phrase, and they will be, for that reason, accessed and used differently. But equally importantly a model of knowledge that ignores from the outset the coming-to-be of that knowledge can only add on a 'learning component' later. It is committed to a deep split between the utilisation and the acquisition of knowledge; between performance and learning. Several programs now are capable of recording modifications or additions to what they know (e.g. Anderson, 1983). But the models are bound to be 'mechanistic' rather than 'organic': lacking a massive, messy accumulation of experiential records, they cannot simulate the way scripts, plans, frames, schemas and concepts grow out of, emerge from, this rich background.

Thus the developmental perspective raises the possibility that a model of adult knowledge – what Clark (1986) called 'secondary presumptive knowledge' – that ignores the way that knowledge has come about may not only be incomplete but also fundamentally inaccurate. It invites us instead to focus on the basic capacities for development with which the child is born, and to explain how adult structures and processes come about as a result of the exposure of an organism with these capacities to the wealth and variety of experience that human beings typically encounter as they grow up. If we can take an adult ability, trace its development back to its roots in childhood, and build a model that both fits with developmental data, and is a natural outcome of such a developmental process, then the model offers a better, fuller account than one that is not able to do so. The chapter by Hitch and Halliday does this job meticulously for the concept of 'working memory' and also refers to theories that offer a similar analysis of other aspects of adult cognition.

The growth criterion

The growth criterion is the obvious complement of the developmental criterion. Where the latter looks backwards over the span of a lifetime, asking 'How has this process changed in the past, to become as it is now?', the former asks a model to say something about how it will change in the future, and in the short term. How mutable is it? How does it respond to experience or tuition? More generally, this criterion opens up an area of cognitive enquiry of its own. What learning processes and strategies do we possess? Are they given at birth, or do we acquire them? And, if so, which – and how? The old issue of 'learning to learn' that was prominent in animal psychology in the 1940s and 1950s is currently re-emerging in cognitive guise (e.g. Claxton, 1984; Nisbet and Shucksmith, 1986).

Like its developmental partner, the growth criterion suggests that you cannot start with performance and then tack on learning later. It may well be, for example, given a modular view of cognition, that the way a concept changes is a function of what the concept is. How, and under what conditions, change to a module is to be recorded may not be controlled by a general purpose 'learning strategy', but may be part and parcel of the modular package itself. And in this case a representation that does not include a model of the conditions and directions of its own mutation is seriously incomplete.

Cognition has in general been rather selective in its study of human learning, focussing on the recording of verbal events and the acquisition of symbolically well-formed concepts. As Peter Morris shows in his chapter, psychology has devoted much time to the construction of theories of 'memory' derived from the laboratory study of the retention of words, sentences or texts that bear no meaningful relationship to the current personal goals of the learner. Yet these theories seem curiously disappointing, or even inaccurate when applied to 'real-life' memories. The study of the kind of learning involved in extracting the meaning from sensible but disembedded chunks of language, reviewed by Alan Garnham, has also been intense, and perhaps the area where the development of models has been most directed by the computational criterion. Typically such models have comprised a well-defined, passive network of 'propositions' that is accessed and interrogated by an active 'procedural' component that often relies on 'production rules' (e.g. Anderson, 1976; 1983). But these types of model have appeared unsatisfactory, too, in part because they can only represent the 'meaning' of language in terms of another language. As we have seen, they lack an experiential, biological underpinning, or, if they do have one, it too has had to be programmed in a symbolic net that must of necessity have failed to capture a wealth of ill-defined detail and potentiality.

On the other hand, following the pioneering but artificial studies of concept formation by Bruner, Goodnow and Austin (1956), cognitive psychologists have increasingly concerned themselves with the kind of learning that involves the abstraction and compilation of generalities from specific experiences (e.g. Medin and Smith, 1981; Rosch and Lloyd, 1978). These generalities may concern object concepts, such as *dog* or *Mummy*, or broader routines or scenarios, such as *what happens at birthday parties* or *in restaurants*.

Up to a point, however, the application of the orthodox cognitive criteria has tended to breed models that are restricted in the kinds of learning they can address. Being relatively static and rigid representational systems, it has been much easier to see how they can be *added to*, or extended than how they might be modified, reorganised or replaced. Norman (1977) made an early attempt to flag the problem with his distinction between *accretion* (adding to), *tuning* (the gradual moulding of concepts by experience) and *restructuring*, which involved a more radical reappraisal of what had been previously known. But we have not yet got very far with modelling the important processes of 'unlearning' that must inevitably accompany much adult 'learning'. As Churchland (1984) says:

> Large-scale conceptual change – the generation of a genuinely new categorical framework that displaces the old framework entirely...is much more difficult to simulate or recreate than are the simpler types....We must learn to represent large-scale semantic systems and systematic knowledge bases in such a way that their rational evolution – and occasionally *discontinuous* evolution – is the natural outcome of their internal dynamic. This is of course the central unsolved problem of AI, cognitive psychology, epistemology, and inductive logic alike.

And casting the net even more broadly, cognition is beginning to interest itself in learning that involves the reappraisal of people's habits, attitudes and theories of self: important kinds of personal or personality change that seem to occur in, and be fostered by, conditions we call 'therapeutic'. What happens at such times of transformation, conversion or liberation from self-defeating and disabling patterns or beliefs? There are many insights into such processes in the literature of psychotherapy and humanistic psychology that are couched in, albeit informal, cognitive terms (e.g. Ellis, 1975; Kelly, 1955; Watzlawick, Weakland and Fisch, 1974). And much progress towards making these beginnings more explicit and precise is to be expected during the next decade. The challenge for cognitive psychology in this area is to increase the *rigour* without at the same time introducing the *mortis*.

The vernacular criterion

This criterion, sometimes expressed more technically as a concern with 'ecological validity', suggests that it is legitimate to ask of a cognitive theory how well it accounts for what people do, see, say or think in the course of their everyday lives. Neisser (1976) has been perhaps the most vigorous advocate for the elevation in importance of this criterion, and has been conspicuously scathing about the blatant failure of theories of memory in particular to even address vernacular questions, let alone answer them. In order to allow room for concerns with real-life performance, the experimental criterion has had to give a little ground; though, as Peter

Morris shows in his chapter, the fears that psychology would become informal in its methodology, as well as in its subject-matter, have been exaggerated. Of all the 'new' criteria, this is the one that has gained the most widespread acceptability over the last ten years.

One area of study that has emerged from the concern with everyday cognition has to do with people's own belief systems. Whereas the focus had previously been entirely on structure and process, now cognitive psychologists are beginning to be interested in the content of ordinary cognition. 'Folk psychology' has become something to be studied in its own right. So far the nature of this research has been rather diverse and inconclusive. Armed with the computational and economic criteria, Stich (1983), for example, has attempted a rather philosophical analysis of such crucial folk-psychological terms as 'feel', 'imagine', 'think' and 'believe', asking what kind of account cognitive science would begin to give of their meaning. What he concludes is that while we may build cognitive models of how people *use* these vernacular expressions, they 'ought not to play any significant role in a science aimed at explaining human cognition and behaviour'. That is, cognitive science should not and cannot be an elaborated or more sophisticated version of folk psychology. The vocabulary is incoherent, so we must start from scratch. Fodor (1987), on the other hand, in a book that refines still further his ability to teach cognitive psychologists the difference between seriousness and solemnity, reaches almost exactly the reverse conclusion.

Then there are a variety of studies that attempt to uncover what people's beliefs are in various areas of life. Very active at the moment, for example, is the investigation of children's informal, intuitive theories about the physical world (e.g. Driver, Guesne and Tiberghien, 1985; Black and Lucas, 1988). The discovery that children arrive in school science lessons with a mass of firmly embedded, largely tacit 'gut' and 'lay' theories (Claxton, 1988) about motion, heat, etc. obviously has important implications for how these topics are taught.

Perhaps of most significance for the study of cognition is the plausible suggestion (Norman, 1980) that people's belief systems actually influence their cognitive operations. We know that memory and problem-solving performance are affected by metacognitive knowledge and belief. But there may be much more specific and local influences as well. If, as has been widely discussed (see the chapter by Green in the present volume), logical inference, and even other sorts of learning, are achieved by 'setting up a mental model of a concrete analogy to the problem, using experience to guide the solution of that concrete analogy, then interpreting the result for the problem at hand' (Norman, 1980), then clearly the content of one's belief systems will have an important effect on the outcomes of one's thought processes.

The anthropological criterion

An important special case of the vernacular criterion is the concern with everyday cognition in cultures very different from our own. Valerie Curran argues most strongly in her chapter for the acceptance of the anthropological criterion. If we are seeking truly universal cognitive models, then we must examine their utility not only in accounting for the daily activities of Europeans and North Americans, but in other cultural groups as well. Laboratory-based models and experimental techniques have turned out to be rather ethnocentric, and have naively been used to show that 'they' think more primitively than 'we' do. A healthy antidote to this somewhat chauvinist approach is to take the time to observe cognition in action in these other cultures, and to allow methods of testing to be grounded in the cognitive habits that are prized and practised, which such observations will reveal. The work of Cole and his co-workers (Cole, Gay, Glick and Sharp, 1971; Cole and Scribner, 1974) has done much to reorient 'cross-cultural psychology' towards a more ethnographic viewpoint, and in the process has cast useful light on the cultural relativity of many of our taken-for-granted cognitive assumptions.

In addition, there have been parallel studies to those, referred to in the last section, of the content of people's beliefs. Heelas and Lock (1981), for instance, present examples of folk psychology collected from a range of widely differing cultures.

The CNS criterion

Perhaps in reaction to the dominant types of cognitive model selected and legitimated by the computational criterion, theorists have recently rediscovered an interest in modelling that draws inspiration from what is known about the structure and function of the human central nervous system. The CNS criterion says that a good model is one that incorporates processes and structures that are similar, or at least analogous, to those that we currently suppose to exist in the brain. In a way this is a rehabilitation of the kind of modelling that Hebb (1949) initiated so brilliantly, and which has been tacitly ignored by cognitive psychologists until very recently. Although some of the neuropsychological details are different from those assumed by Hebb (and modified by Milner, 1957), as one would expect, the types of models that are currently being developed by the 'neo-connectionists' (e.g. McClelland and Rumelhart, 1986; *Cognitive Science*, 1985, No. 1) bear a startling similarity to Hebb's 'cell assemblies', 'phase sequences' and 'conceptual nervous system'. In McClelland and Rumelhart's version, for example, cognition is represented as a patchwork of relatively autonomous modules that communicate by sending patterns of activation to each other. 'Mental states' are construed as patterns of activation lying across this modular network, and the flow of activation is determined, not by some external agency (as in most computational models) but by the current state of the system itself: specifically the pre-existing pattern of activation and priming, together with the 'weights' or activation thresholds of the links within and between modules. Learning at its most basic reflects the assumption that the activation of a link leaves behind some residue of facilitation (or in some cases inhibition), so that the same link requires less (or more) activation to 'fire' it in the future. Retrieval from the system (just as in Hebb's original model) occurs when part of a previously interlinked pattern of units (a 'record') is reactivated, and the extent of this reactivation is sufficient to recruit other parts of the same pattern – thus causing a 'process' to be 'operated' or a 'memory' to pop into our minds. Concept formation arises as recurrent aspects of a range of recorded events cause the same subset of units to be repeatedly co-active and therefore to achieve a higher degree of mutual facilitation. As McClelland and Rumelhart (1986) say, 'our distributed model leads naturally to the suggestion that semantic memory may just be the residue of the superposition of episodic traces.'

Of course there is no necessity to cast, or even couch, such parallel-processing, modular, distributed models of cognition in neural terms. But they have the benefit of (in some cases) being quite as successful as traditional computational models in terms of explanatory power, whilst sitting much more comfortably beside our physiological understanding of the brain. There is no plausible neural substrate, for example, for the distinction between declarative and procedural knowledge. Indeed the basic *modus operandi* of a neuron and a logic gate are so different that it is doubtful whether the vast collections of either that constitute brains and computers respectively are organised in anything like the same way. Logic gates emit outputs at constant high frequencies, whereas those of neurons are lower and variable. Logic gates transform binary information into more binary information, while neurons act to modulate the patterns and frequency of spike trains. And the functional characteristics of a logic gate are fixed, while neurons are decidedly plastic (Churchland, 1984).

This is not to say that CNS-like systems cannot be modelled in computer programs. Far from it. But it is to suggest that, to the extent that we allow features of *computer* design to become incorporated, wittingly or unwittingly, into the simulations we build up of *cognition*, to that extent they are likely to become neuropsychologically implausible, and (to use Dennett's image) to be wheel-like rather than lifelike.

The CNS criterion encourages a range of models from those that are *consistent* with what we know about the brain, through those (like Hebb's) that use the language of neurophysiology as *metaphors* for cognitive entities and operations, to those that endeavour to show how current theories of the cortex can also serve as theories of cognition. Marr, for example, elegantly combined the computational and the CNS criteria to produce precise simulations of low-level visual processing (see e.g. Marr, 1976, and Vicki Bruce's chapter in the present book). While in his earlier work (Marr, 1970; 1971), somewhat over-ambitious perhaps but surprisingly neglected, he developed very sophisticated models for concept formation, pattern recognition, and the storage and retrieval of memories, based purely on known properties of cortical and pyramidal neurons.

The holistic criterion

The next criterion is also beginning to take root and even bear fruit. The question which it always asks when interviewing a cognitive model is: 'How do you hook up with other aspects of the person, such as feeling and emotion, purposeful action, conscious reflection and social interaction?'

The holistic criterion judges it desirable for a model to have something to say in reply; some ideas, even if only latent, about how it fits into an integrated personal and interpersonal scheme of things. It does not demand that any model of anything has also to be a model of everything. That would obviously be absurd. What it does do is reassert the importance of a *systemic* point of view, within which cognition is seen as a servant of the organism, and therefore subject not only to evolutionary and developmental constraints, but also to ongoing, moment-to-moment control by biological, social, motivational and emotional influences.

Some progress has been made. Mandler (e.g. 1975, 1985) made some pioneering attempts to reconnect cognition with both emotion and consciousness, though in general the studies that have been produced in this area have not escaped from the debilitating concern to be both global and experimental (see Parkinson (1987) for a review). One conspicuous exception is Oatley and Johnson-Laird's (1985) very interesting 'Sketch for a cognitive theory of the emotions'. Abandoning any attempt to be experimental, or even computational, they start from an evolutionary and developmental perspective, and show how emotional states could have arisen as attempts to coordinate the response of a modular system to threats that occur intermittently to both physical survival and self-image. As in Dennett's speculations, reported above, aspects of characteristically human functioning can be seen to arise as evolutionary solutions to the problems inherent in a modular knowledge-base.

Finally it is possible to do no more than mention the progress that has been made towards building cognitive models of both normal (Marcel, 1983; Yates, 1985) and abnormal (Blackmore, 1986) states of consciousness. Perhaps the area most ripe for development at present is the rapprochement of cognition and motivation. Whilst many authors in the last decade have taken a cognitive perspective on motivation (e.g. Weiner, 1985) there are as yet few detailed models of human cognition that explicitly incorporate or highlight motivational processes or influences.

The pragmatic criterion

The final criterion is perhaps even more contentious: it reflects my own belief, which has grown over the last twelve years of working in the applied field of the psychology of education, that there is a legitimate place for models of cognition that are comprehensible by, and useful to, non-specialists. This criterion allows us to ask of a theory: 'How *useful* are you – and who to?' Teachers in particular have a strong need for models of cognition that they can readily grasp, which help them make sense of their own professional experience, and which generates practical suggestions. Traditionally they have had to rely on rather general, reach-me-down resumés of laboratory-based theories that seem to have little applicability to everyday learning situations (e.g. Child, 1986; Howe, 1984). Or alternatively they have had to turn for guidance to the appealing, but often ill-founded, popular literature of 'how to study' (Buzan, 1974) or 'lateral thinking' (de Bono, 1971). Cognitive psychology ought to be able to improve on this situation, and the attempt to couch the insights of research in accessible models, images and language is, I would argue, a worthwhile kind of 'research' in its own right. For an example of this enterprise, see Claxton (1984). The pragmatic criterion need not undermine the more scholarly, esoteric criteria that we have been discussing, but it has the right – even perhaps the obligation – to stand alongside them, asking sometimes awkward questions about the *value* of cognitive psychology to the world at large.

Conclusion

The purpose of this chapter has been to provide an overview of the way the ground-rules for the study of cognition are currently being reassessed. The future of cognitive psychology will be determined by the criteria which are accepted, and by the relative weights that are given to them. If the present trend is continued (as the psephological pundits say on election night), it looks as if the new directions in cognition will be characterised by diversity. Over the next few years we are likely to see a proliferation of models that are guided by the application of different portfolios of criteria. Researchers will be coming at the core problems of cognition from a host of different directions. And if this diversification is healthy, they will be keeping an eye on each other's progress, and we may, hopefully before too long, begin to see the emergence of a new generation of cognitive theories that satisfy many of the desirable criteria we have reviewed, and not just one or two.

Notes

1. 'Vision represents an opportunistic exploitation of a coincidence which no deductive operations on a protozoan's knowledge of the world could have anticipated. This is the coincidence of locomotor impenetrability with opaqueness, for a narrow band of electromagnetic waves' (Campbell, 1974, p. 414).
2. 'Each of us must possess a knowledge or a command of a rather substantial set of laws or general statements connecting the various mental states with 1) other mental states, with 2) external circumstances, and with 3) overt behaviours... Collectively, they constitute a *theory*, a theory that postulates a range of internal states whose causal relations are described by the theory's laws. All of us learn that framework (at mother's knee, as we learn our language), and in so doing we acquire the commonsense conception of what conscious intelligence *is*. We may call that theoretical framework "folk psychology". It embodies the accumulated wisdom of thousands of generations' attempts to understand how we humans work' (Churchland, 1984, pp. 58-9).

References

Adams, D. (1984), *So Long, and Thanks for all the Fish*. Pan: London.

Allport, D. A. (1975), 'The state of cognitive psychology' (a critical notice of W. G. Chase (ed.), *Visual Information Processing*), *Quarterly Journal of Experimental Psychology*, 27, 141-52.

Anderson, J. R. (1976), *Language, Memory and Thought*. Erlbaum: Hillsdale, New Jersey.

Anderson, J. R. (1983), *The Architecture of Cognition*. Harvard University Press: Cambridge, Mass.

Baddeley, A. D. (1982), 'Domains of recollection', *Psychological Review*, 69, 708-29.

Bierce, A. (1958), *The Devil's Dictionary*. Dover: Toronto.

Black, P. J. and Lucas, A. (eds) (1988), *Children's Informal Ideas in Science*. Routledge: London.

Blackmore, S. (1986), 'Who am I? Changing models of reality in meditation', in G. Claxton (ed.), *Beyond Therapy: The Impact of Eastern Religions on Psychological Theory and Practice*. Wisdom Publications: London.

Broadbent, D. E. (1973), *In Defence of Empirical Psychology*. Methuen: London.

Bruner, J. S., Goodnow, J. J. and Austin, G. A. (1956), *A Study of Thinking*. Wiley: New York.

Buzan, T. (1974), *Use your Head*. BBC Publications: London.

Campbell, D. (1974), 'Evolutionary epistemology', in P. A. Schilpp (ed.), *The Philosophy of Karl Popper*. Open Court: La Salle, Illinois.

Child, D. (1986), *Psychology and the Teacher*, 4th edition. Holt, Rinehart & Winston: Eastbourne.

Churchland, P. (1984), *Matter and Consciousness*. Bradford: Cambridge, Mass.

Clark, A. J. (1986), 'A biological metaphor', *Mind and Language, 1*, 45-63.

Claxton G. L. (1978), 'Special review feature: memory research', *British Journal of Psychology, 69*, 513-20.

Claxton G. L. (ed.) (1980), *Cognitive Psychology: New Directions*. RKP: London.

Claxton, G. L. (1984), *Live and Learn: An Introduction to the Psychology of Growth and Change in Everyday Life*. Harper & Row: London.

Claxton, G. L. (1988), 'Teaching and acquiring scientific knowledge', in T. Keen and M. Pope (eds), *Kelly in the Classroom: Educational Applications of Personal Construct Psychology*. Cybersystems: Montreal.

Cognitive Science (1985), 'Connectionist models and their applications', special issue, No. 1, Jan-March.

Cole, M., Gay, J., Glick, J. and Sharp, D. W. (1971), *The Cultural Context of Learning and Thinking*. Basic Books: New York.

Cole, M. and Scribner, S. (1974), *Culture and Thought: A Psychological Introduction*. Wiley: New York.

De Bono, E. (1971), *The Mechanism of Mind*. Penguin: Harmondsworth.

Dennett, D. (1984a), 'Cognitive wheels: the frame problem of AI', in C. Hookway (ed.), *Minds, Machines and Evolution*. Cambridge University Press: Cambridge.

Dennett, D. (1984b), *Elbow Room: The Varieties of Free Will Worth Wanting*. Clarendon Press: Oxford.

Driver, R., Guesne, E. and Tiberghien, A. (eds) (1985), *Children's Ideas in Science*. Open University Press: Milton Keynes.

Eich, J. (1980) 'The cue-dependent nature of state dependent retrieval', *Memory and Cognition, 8*, pp. 157-73.

Ellis, A. (1975), 'Rational-emotive psychotherapy', in D. Bannister (ed.), *Issues and Approaches in Psychological Therapies*. Wiley: London.

Eysenck, M. W. (1984), *A Handbook of Cognitive Psychology*. Erlbaum: London.

Fodor, J. A. (1983), *The Modularity of Mind*. MIT Press: Cambridge, Mass.

Fodor, J. A. (1987), *Psychosemantics: The Problem of Meaning in the Philosophy of Mind*. Bradford/BPS Books: Cambridge, Mass.

Haugeland, J. (ed.) (1981), *Mind Design*. MIT Press: Cambridge, Mass.

Hebb, D. O. (1949), *The Organization of Behaviour*. Wiley: New York.

Heelas, P. and Lock, A. (eds) (1981), *Indigenous Psychologies*. Academic: London.

Hesse, M. B. (1966), *Models and Analogies in Science*. Notre Dame Press: Notre Dame University, Indiana.

Howe, M. (1984), *A Teacher's Guide to the Psychology of Learning*. Blackwell: Oxford.

James, W. (1890), *The Principles of Psychology*. Holt: New York.

Kelly, G. A. (1955), *The Psychology of Personal Constructs*. Norton: New York.

Mandler, G. (1975), *Mind and Emotion*. Wiley: New York.

Mandler, G. (1985), *Cognitive Psychology: An Essay in Cognitive Science*. Erlbaum: Hillsdale, New Jersey.

Marcel, A. J. (1983), 'Conscious and unconscious perception: an approach to the relations between phenomenal experience and perceptual processes', *Cognitive Psychology. 15*, 238-300.

Marr, D. (1970), 'A theory of cerebral neo-cortex', *Proceedings of the Royal Society of London, Series B, 1976*, 161-234.

Marr, D. (1971, 'Simple memory: a theory for archicortex', *Philosophical Transactions of the Royal Society of London, Series B, 262*, 23-81.

Marr, D. (1976), 'Early processing of visual information', *Proceedings of the Royal Society of London, Series B, 275*, 483-524.

Marshall, J. C. (1984), 'Multiple perspectives on modularity', *Cognition, 17*, 209-42.

McClelland, J. L. and Rumelhart, D. E. (1986), *Parallel Distributed Processing*. MIT: Camb., Mass.

Medin, D. and Smith, E. E. (1981), *Categories and Concepts*. Harvard University Press: Cambridge, Mass.

Miller, G. A. and Gazzaniga, M. (1984), 'The cognitive sciences', in M. Gazzaniga (ed.), *Handbook of Cognitive Neuroscience*. Plenum Press, New York.

Milner, P. (1957), 'The cell assembly, mark II', *Psychological Reveiw*, *64*, 242-52.

Morton, J. (1985), 'Levels of modelling', paper presented at the International Workshop on Modelling Cognition, Lancaster, July.

Neisser, U. (1976), *Cognition and Reality*. W. H. Freeman: San Francisco.

Newell, A. (1973), 'You can't play Twenty Questions with Nature and win', in W. G. Chase (ed.), *Visual Information Processing*. Academic Press: New York.

Nisbet, J. and Shucksmith, J. (1986), *Learning Strategies*. Routledge & Kegan Paul: London.

Nisbett, R. E. and Wilson, T. D. (1977), 'Telling more than we can know: verbal reports on mental processes', *Psychological Review*, *84*, 231-59.

Norman, D. A. (1977), 'Notes toward a theory of complex learning', in A. M. Lesgold, J. W. Pellegrino, S. D. Fokkema and R. Glaser (eds), *Cognitive Psychology and Instruction*. Plenum Press: New York.

Norman, D. A. (1980), 'Twelve issues for cognitive science', *Cognitive Science*, *4*, 1-33. Reprinted in A. M. Aitkenhead and J. M. Slack (1985) (eds), *Issues in Cognitive Modeling*. Erlbaum: London.

Oatley, K. (1987), 'Experiments and experience: usefulness and insight in psychology', in H. Beloff and A. M. Colman (eds), *Psychology Survey, 6*. British Psychological Society: Leicester.

Oatley, K. and Johnson-Laird, P. N. (1985), 'Sketch for a cognitive theory of the emotions', *Cognitive Science Research Report*, CSRP, 045, University of Sussex: Falmer.

Parkinson, B. (1987), 'Emotion: cognitive approaches', in H. Beloff and A. M. Colman (eds), *Psychology Survey, 6*. British Psychological Society: Leicester.

Polanyi, M. (1967), *The Tacit Dimension*. Routledge & Kegan Paul: London.

Reitman, J. (1970), 'Computer simulation of an information-processing model of short-term memory', in D. A. Norman (ed.), *Models of Human Memory*. Academic Press: New York.

Reitman, W. (1970), 'What does it take to remember?', in D. A. Norman (ed.), *Models of Human Memory*. Academic Press: New York.

Rosch, E. and Lloyd, B. (eds), (1978), *Cognition and Categorization*. Erlbaum: Hillsdale, New Jersey.

Runeson S. (1977), 'On the possibility of "smart" perceptual mechanisms', *Scandinavian Journal of Psychology*, *18*, 172-9.

Shallice, T. (1984), 'More functionally isolable subsystems but fewer "modules"?' *Cognition*, *17*, 243-52.

Stich, S. (1983), *From Folk Psychology to Cognitive Science: The Case against Belief*. Bradford: Cambridge, Mass.

Vygotsky, L. S. (1962), *Thought and Language*. MIT Press: Cambridge, Mass.

Watzlawick, P., Weakland, J. and Fisch, R. (1974), *Change: Principles of Problem Formation and Problem Resolution*. Norton: New York.

Weiner, B. (1985), *Human Motivation*. Springer-Verlag: New York.

Yates, J. (1985), 'The content of awareness is a model of the world', *Psychological Review*, *92*, 249-84.

Zadeh, L. (1982), 'A note on prototype theory and fuzzy sets', *Cognition*, *12*, 291-7.

2 Perceiving

Vicki Bruce

Introduction

The modes and goals of human perception are many. Modes include seeing, hearing, touching, tasting and smelling. The goals include seeking out objects and regions of interest, avoiding dangerous situations, planning routes and recognising familiar figures in the environment. No single book could do justice to these many modes and goals, and in this short chapter, I will narrow my topic to consider only *seeing*, and, within this still over-broad area, I will concentrate primarily on the problem of how we *recognise* objects by sight.

Look at Figure 2.1. Amongst other things in this picture, you will recognise the figures of a horse and a person, though you have never seen this particular horse, or person, before and the particular pattern of light and shade in this picture is undoubtedly novel. How is it that we can recognise objects from many different instances (racehorses differ from carthorses, yet both can be recognised as horses), from a wide variety of viewpoints, in a range of lighting conditions and at different distances? Somehow you must be able to detect within this picture some essential characteristics which specify 'horse', and others which specify 'person', and it is the process of extracting appropriate characteristics which forms the subject of this chapter.

While attempting to provide a general introduction to the area of object recognition, I will, towards the end of the chapter, spend some time considering the recognition problems posed by a particular class of objects – human faces. A face must be recognised despite non-rigid transformations

This chapter was written while I was in receipt of a Social Science Research Fellowship from the Nuffield Foundation during the academic year 1985-6. I thank the Nuffield Foundation for giving me the opportunity to think about the relationship between developments in vision and the more specific area of face recognition. Glyn Humphreys and Guy Claxton both made helpful suggestions about an earlier draft of this chapter.

FIGURE 2.1 *An everyday visual scene*

which occur when expressions change, or more slowly while a face ages, as well as rigid changes produced by head turning and nodding. Later in this chapter we will consider these complications. First we will consider the simpler question of recognising objects whose shapes can be considered to be approximately rigid. The human body, for example, can be viewed as a collection of rigid parts, interlinked at joints.

Much of the work I will consider in this chapter has been conducted, not by psychologists but by a variety of workers in artificial intelligence, computer science, biology and physics. Vision is a multi- and interdisciplinary area. To develop a good robot requires the design of an artificial vision system which performs some of the same functions as the human visual system. One solution to such a problem is to try to write a program which embodies some of the design features of human vision. Even if one did not want to claim that the brain is a computer of any kind at all, computer programs are rigorous tests of certain kinds of theoretical statement, and so simulation provides an important tool for the cognitive psychologist (as will be demonstrated in other chapters of this book too).

However, many contemporary researchers see a fundamental similarity between natural and artificial brains as information-processing devices. They would argue that visual perception involves the *computation* of a series of *symbolic representations* of a visual scene, from the information initially present in the image at the retina. Earlier levels will describe features of the *image* – the 2D layout of regions, lines and so forth. Higher levels will describe features of the *scene* – the 3D arrangement of surfaces. One product of such processes would be a symbolic representation which may match a symbolic representation of similar format stored in memory, enabling object 'recognition' to occur. Recognition is only one goal of perception, and requires mediation by a certain type of representation. Other representations are needed for other purposes. For example, in order to reach out, grasp and lift a coffee mug, a detailed representation of the precise distance of the mug, its relative surface layout and its probable weight will be needed so that the task can be achieved successfully. Such a task is logically independent from knowing that the object to be grasped is a mug, as opposed to a teapot, and may rely on different kinds of representational system. One advantage of the computational approach to perception is that it makes explicit the different representations and processes which may subserve different perceptual functions.

While recognition may be but one task in perceptual processing, it is a fairly fundamental task, both in perception and in cognition generally. We recognise in all our different sensory modalities (tunes, perfumes and so forth), but also at a considerably more abstract level: we can, for example, 'recognise' the plot of *Romeo and Juliet* in the film *West Side Story*. Indeed recognising that a current event or problem fits into a known category may be seen as the fundamental act of cognition – certainly some contemporary theories stress this (e.g. Anderson, 1983). The recognition of visual objects thus exemplifies a broad category of cognitive activities, and while some of the solutions offered for visual recognition may be uniquely suited to vision, some of the problems to be overcome are common to recognition in all its many domains.

In the first section of this chapter, I will present a very broad outline of the stages involved in computing representations for recognition from retinal images, with particular emphasis on the theory of vision put forward by the late David Marr (1982). Marr stressed that theories of vision could be constructed at each of three distinct levels, that of *computational theory*, *algorithm*, and *implementation*. The computational theory describes what properties are being computed and why, and what constraints may be exploited in order to make their computation easier. Thus the computational theory of the first stages of visual processing would specify that edges should be detected in retinal images, since edges are likely pointers to structures of significance to the viewer. The algorithmic level of theory describes the nature of the computations needed to transform one representation (e.g. a retinal image) to another (e.g. a collection of edge segments). The implementation level theory describes how such an algorithm is embodied in particular hardware – for example, how cells in the retina of mammals may detect edges. In most of what follows we will concentrate on theories at the computational and algorithmic level, without worrying too much about implementation details. This will allow us to talk about computer models of perception and theories of human perception interchangeably, but, as we will see later in the chapter, thinking about the implementation of procedures in neural networks may make us think again about higher, 'computational theory' level issues.

Computing object descriptions

Finding object boundaries

Look at Figure 2.1 again. Before you can recognise the 'horse', you must have separated out the appropriate area of the image, corresponding to the horse, from other areas corresponding to different objects. In this example note that you achieve this quite successfully despite the partial occlusion of the horse's outline by that of the person. As well as separating out the relevant structures, vision does some 'filling in' of missing information.

The retinal image, the starting point for visual perception, can be considered as an array of points, each with its own particular intensity value. The structures which we see are *implicit* in this intensity array. Contours and regions must be found. Potentially important contours are the *occluding contours*, formed where one object occludes another object or the background. The occluding contour of the person in Figure 2.1 forms a readily recognised form. Other shapes can easily be recognised from such contours in silhouettes, as shown in Figure 2.2. Marr (1982) suggests that the ease with which we recognise shapes from occluding contours may reflect their important role in recognition. There are many other sources of contours in images, however. Contours may also be present due to *convex* or *concave* edges between two surfaces of a single object. For example, the two faces of a cube meet at a convex edge, while a concave edge is seen at the join between left and right pages of an open book. Other kinds of *surface contours* in an image may also be important for recognition purposes. A

FIGURE 2.2 *Shapes can easily be recognised from silhouettes like these, illustrating the importance of occluding contours for recognition purposes*

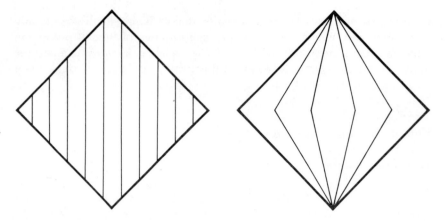

FIGURE 2.3   *Surface contours can reveal an object's shape. The occluding contours of these two shapes are similar. Surface contours suggest that the left-hand shape is flat, while the right-hand shape is not*

zebra is distinguished from a pony by its surface markings. Figure 2.3 illustrates how different kinds of surface contours may give important clues about an object's shape.

How can we find these contours in an image? One computational approach is to locate all the places in the image where there are intensity changes, and then connect these places together to form larger edge segments. Edge-finding algorithms (e.g. Marr and Hildreth, 1980) apply mathematical operators to an intensity array in order to reveal discontinuities in intensity. The result of applying the procedures is a representation of all the little bits and pieces of edges in the image – a representation which Marr (1976) called the *raw primal sketch*. To get from the raw primal sketch to a level at which larger sections of occluding and surface contours are revealed requires a number of additional procedures. At the 2D level, the little bits and pieces of edge may be grouped together into larger structures by application of rules which link parts on the basis of proximity, similarity and so forth (see Marr, 1976). Potentially significant structures can be revealed by such processes – in the 2D representation called the *full primal sketch*.

Edge detection followed by the joining together of edges into larger contours is only one possible approach to image segmentation. Other computer scientists have taken the converse approach – that of *region growing* (see Ballard and Brown, 1982), in which progressively larger 'patches' in the image are associated together through similarity and proximity. Occluding and surface contours are then found by plotting the boundaries of these patches. However, the edge detection procedures favoured by Marr and his colleagues are more compatible with what is known of the functions of cells early in the mammalian visual system.

Contours in the primal sketch are not the only source of information about significant boundaries in the scene. The analysis of stereoscopic information and motion also aid in the segmentation of the scene, and the reader is referred to Marr (1982) for details of his own and his colleagues' approach to these aspects of visual processing.

Representations for recognition

At this point we should draw a distinction between pattern recognition and object recognition. Pattern recognition involves detecting 2D structures in 2D images – recognising circles and squares, letters and numbers, and is initially easier to consider than 3D shape recognition.

Pattern recognition

Most introductory texts begin their section on recognition by discussing *template matching* as one possible technique for recognition. For each pattern that is known, a template of it is stored, and new patterns are compared with all the templates held in memory to see which gives the best fit. Template matching can be accomplished by computing the correlation between a template function and an image, at a series of possible locations in the image.

Template matching is a bit like trying to fit a key into a lock. If the key is too misshapen it will not fit, and may fit another lock instead. Practical recognition systems can work through template matching only if the shapes of the characters to be recognised can be constrained to remain constant, as in the numbers on the bottom of bank cheques. The system which recognises these figures does not have to deal with variations of size, orientation or shape. However, even if we restrict ourselves to considering the simple task of recognising letters, it is clear that it would be difficult to construct the 'templates' for human recognition. The shapes of letters that we recognise may vary tremendously. How would a system of templates distinguish the Ps from the Qs in Figure 2.4?

FIGURE 2.4   *How do you tell the p's from the q's?*

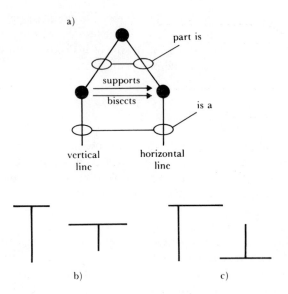

FIGURE 2.5   *a) A structural description for the letter T. b) Shapes which are consistent with this description and c) Shapes which are not (Adapted from Bruce and Green, 1985)*

During the 1960s, *feature detection* theories of pattern recognition became popular, with the discovery by Hubel and Wiesel (1959, 1968) of what were thought to be 'feature detectors' in the visual cortex of cats and monkeys. These cells responded maximally when the anaesthetised animal was presented with a bar or an edge at a particular orientation. It became commonplace to suppose that letters or numbers might be represented as lists of critical features such as horizontal and vertical lines, right angles and so forth. A popular theory of this kind was an adaptation of Selfridge's (1959) Pandemonium model (e.g. see Lindsay and Norman, 1972), in which feature detectors signalled to a set of 'cognitive demons', one for each character to be recognised. The cognitive demon would 'shout', in proportion to the number of its feature tests satisfied, to a decision demon which selected the cognitive demon with the loudest shout to represent the letter actually presented.

The Pandemonium system was an interesting example of a system in which a large number of local computations (feature detectors) combined to produce a decision about a global configuration. Through training (Selfridge, 1959; Doyle, 1960) the weights on different feature tests could be adjusted to produce maximal discrimination between a set of patterns to be learned. Such a system is an example of the kind of parallel device which is currently enjoying a revival (see page 58). However, a Pandemonium system which makes use only of simple, local feature tests for structures such as lines and curves has certain shortcomings (Minsky and Papert,

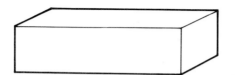

FIGURE 2.6 *Two different views of a block. Different 2D features are seen at each viewpoint*

1969), since a set of purely local computations does not capture important aspects of *configuration*.

To recognise even shapes as simple as letters reliably requires some representation of the configuration of features present, and not just a 'list' of such features. An adequate representation must describe the *structure* of a pattern. *Structural descriptions* are symbolic representations which make explicit the relationships between the parts of the image, as well as specifying the parts themselves. Thus a structural description for a letter T would describe the two parts (horizontal and vertical line) but also that one part *supports* and *bisects* the other (see Figure 2.5). In the next section, we turn to consider structural descriptions of 3D objects, in terms of the relationships between their constituent parts – surfaces and volumes.

From patterns to shapes

When we turn to consider 3D shape recognition, we must confront the additional problem that features (lines, angles) and their relationships will vary according to viewpoint, even if the structure viewed is quite simple (see Figure 2.6). We must relate the image features to an intermediate representation of the object's shape. Information about 3D shape may be obtained from the analysis of shading, depth and motion, but a good deal of information is obtained from considering only contours. To determine an object's shape from the contours present in a 2D image of it requires that we have some set of rules for translating from image features (e.g. regions) to scene features (e.g. surfaces).

Examples of the kinds of rule which might be useful in relating 2D image features to 3D scene features are found in the work of Guzman (1968), Clowes (1971), Waltz (1975) and others who tackled the problem of segmenting pictures of groups of simple block structures (see Figure 2.7). Their goal was to write procedures which would correctly label regions such as *a, b* and *c* (in our example in Figure 2.7) as belonging together as one object, and *d, e* and *f* as belonging together as a separate one.

Guzman originally showed how the detection of different patterns of lines meeting at vertices could be used to guide hypotheses about the connections which existed between regions in the picture, and hence surfaces in the scene. For example, a 'fork' (see Figure 2.7) suggested that all three regions enclosed by the lines of the fork belonged together, while a 'T' suggested

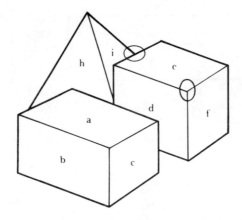

FIGURE 2.7 *A picture of overlapping blocks. Regions a, b and c; d, e and f; h and i; belong together as distinct objects. Examples of TEE and FORK vertices are circled. What other vertex types are there in this picture?*

that the three regions arose from distinct objects. Huffman (1971) and Clowes (1971) showed how Guzman's rules worked, by showing the relationship between patterns of lines at vertices, and the nature of the *edges* in the scene depicted by these lines. Edges in scenes of the kind shown in Figure 2.7 can be convex, concave or occluding. Only certain combinations of edge types can coexist at certain types of vertex. Figure 2.8 shows the possible combinations at an arrow junction. Research of this type thus illustrates how the nature of the contour junctions present in an image constrains the possible local surface arrangements in the imaged scene.

Mackworth (1973), in his work on scene segmentation, introduced a different, and powerful technique, which allows us to describe the orientations of the surfaces of such solids relative to the viewer. The orientation of a surface can be described by the *direction* pointed by its 'surface normal'. If the surface is a plane (as in the face of a cube), the surface normal is just a line perpendicular to this plane. If the surface is curved, then we must describe the surface normal as a line perpendicular to a plane tangential to the surface at a point whose orientation we wish to

FIGURE 2.8 *The three possible labellings for lines at an ARROW vertex. Occluding (>), convex (+) and concave (−) edges are marked*

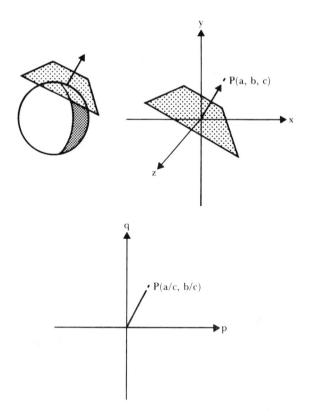

FIGURE 2.9   *Gradient space representation for surface orientation. We wish to represent the orientation of the surface at different points. First consider drawing a line perpendicular to a plane which touches the surface at one such point. This surface normal can be represented as a vector in 3 dimensions (coordinates a,b,c). Since only the direction of the vector is important, this can be rewritten with coordinates a/c, b/c, 1, which results in the 2D vector shown at the bottom of the figure (Adapted from Marr, 1982)*

represent (see top left panel of Figure 2.9). These directions of the surface normals can be expressed as vectors with three dimensions – two describing the direction in which the surface normal points and one describing its length. Since we are not interested in the length of a surface normal, we may assign this an arbitrary value of unity, and plot the direction vectors in a 2D rather than a 3D coordinate system (see Figure 2.9). This 2D *gradient space* representation provides one way to describe the shape of an object in terms of the orientation of points on its surface relative to the viewer.

Kanade (1981) and his colleagues have made use of the gradient space representation in the computation of surface descriptions of objects more complex than the simple block structures used by Guzman and others. This is achieved by *approximating* the surface of an object by a set of planar surfaces. These approximations to objects (e.g. see Figure 2.10) resemble

FIGURE 2.10   *An Origami horse*

the structures which result from Origami, the Japanese craft of paper-folding. Kanade suggests further rules that can be used to relate picture features to scene features – among them the use of skewed symmetry in the image to suggest true symmetry of the surface, and the use of parallel lines in the image to suggest parallel edges of the surface.

Some of the heuristics studied by Kanade may be generally useful in the computation of shape descriptions, but nevertheless the approximations of the Origami world seem highly artificial, particularly when applied to natural shapes, such as those attained by growth. Following Binford (1971), Marr (1977, 1982) argues that many such shapes may be approximated, not by a set of planar *surfaces*, but by the *volumes* of shapes he terms *generalised cones*. Generalised cones are the shapes which result from sweeping a cross-section of constant shape, but variable size, along an axis (which may itself curve). The vase shape shown in Figure 2.2 is one example. All kinds of objects such as bananas, sausages and limbs can be described as generalised cones, or approximations to them. Marr (1977) suggests that we interpret the shapes of silhouettes as if we assume that such figures were produced by generalised cones. The axis of a generalised cone (which, as we will see, may play an important role in recognition) can be derived from its occluding contours in an image. The axes of the generalised cone components in an image thus provide a rather different way to describe the shape of an object.

The above discussion seems some way divorced from our goal of accounting for how objects are recognised, but in fact such considerations are essential, since our aim is to suggest ways in which descriptions derived from images can be matched to those stored in memory. It is no use devising an elaborate scheme which could be used to represent shapes in memory, if there is no way of accessing such representations from images,

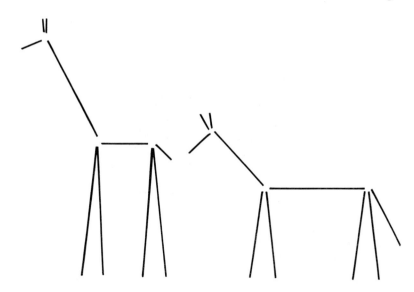

FIGURE 2.11   *Stick figures capture the overall spatial organisation of shapes whose component parts have natural axes. It is easy to tell the giraffe from the horse*

before knowing what shape is present. In many artificial intelligence and computer science applications, this problem is partially alleviated by having the interpretative processes guided from 'above' by quite specific hypotheses about what shape or shapes there might be present. While there is considerable evidence, which I later review, for facilitation of recognition by appropriate context, there are also many circumstances in human vision where we perceive the unexpected or the novel. Perception must be able to operate in the absence of specific prior information, and one of the strengths of Marr's approach to perception is that he shows how much can be achieved with the help of very general rules about the world, rather than specific hypotheses about objects within it.

To return to our goal of accounting for object recognition, we need to match the derived shape of an object with some stored representation of that shape. In terms of the representations we have been discussing so far, we would need to have stored a different representation for each different viewpoint, since the representations for shape that we have discussed are all *viewer-centred*. Some theories of object recognition suggest that each known object is represented via an interlinked set of descriptions of different views. Minsky's (1977) frame system theory is one example.

However, a more parsimonious representation for recognition would be one in which *object-centred* descriptions are established, stored and compared. If object-centred representations are used, then we need store

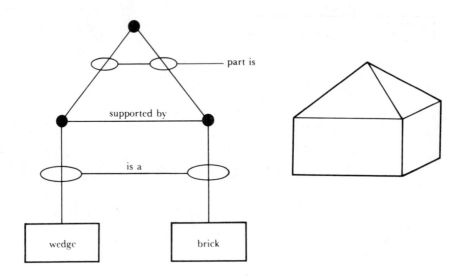

FIGURE 2.12   *A toy 'house', and a structural description which captures its overall spatial representation (Adapted from Winston, 1973, 1975)*

only one representation for each object category which is known, since the representations will not depend on viewpoint. Marr (1982) and Nishihara (1983; Marr and Nishihara, 1978) have argued that object-centred representations are a more satisfactory basis for recognition purposes.

A second issue is whether representations for recognition should be *surface-based* or *volumetric*. Gradient-space representations describe surfaces, while the axis of a generalised cone describes the length and inclination of the solid volume occupied by the cone. Marr and Nishihara argue that volumetric primitives are better able to capture the relationship between different parts of an overall structure comprised of several generalised cones (Figure 2.11).

A third issue to be considered is that of the *sensitivity* of a given shape description to capture forms at different scales. Ideally, a representational format must be sufficiently flexible to capture global structure as well as local detail. Such sensitivity can be obtained if shapes are represented hierarchically, with descriptions of the fine details of component parts (e.g. a human hand) nested beneath more global descriptions of how the components are linked together (e.g. a human body).

One example of a simple hierarchial system for the recognition of simple block structures, like arches, houses, etc. (see Figure 2.12) is that employed by Winston (1973, 1975) in his study of concept learning. At the highest level of description, the overall structure is described in terms of the relationship between component parts, which are simple shapes such as

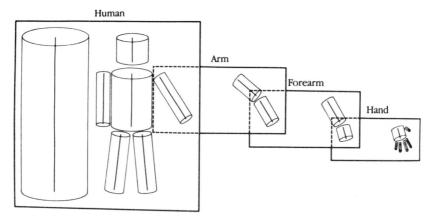

FIGURE 2.13 *A hierarchical stick-figure representation for a human figure. Each box contains a stick describing the orientation of the overall shape at the left, and a set of sticks describing the orientations of component parts to the right. Each component can be described independently in the same way; so there are boxes for arm, forearm and hand, as well as for human. Boxes for leg, foot etc are not shown here (Reproduced, with permission, from Marr and Nishihara, 1978)*

wedges and bricks. Thus the top level description of a house would show that there are two parts, a wedge (the roof) and a brick (the main body of the house), and that the former is supported by the latter. At a lower level of description, the details of 'wedge' and 'brick' shapes are themselves specified in terms of the appropriate arrangements of surfaces.

Winston's system becomes particularly interesting where he shows how certain details in the structural description may be left optional, while others become obligatory features of the learned concept. Thus the nature of the supported structure in an arch is irrelevant to the structural 'definition' of an arch. The structure could be a brick or a wedge. However, other aspects of an arch structure are crucial. The supporting structures *must not touch* each other, for example.

Winston's program was one which *learned* to recognise certain object categories by being shown examples of legitimate members of the category along with 'near misses'. Space does not permit us to explore the development of pattern and object recognition abilities in this chapter, but merely to note that this is an essential consideration, and does indeed form a central component of some pattern recognition models (e.g. Pandemonium and WISARD, which we consider later).

Marr and Nishihara's theory of object recognition

Marr and Nishihara (1978) described a possible system for the recognition of certain kinds of shapes – ones composed of generalised cones – in which the representations for recognition are object-centred, hierarchically

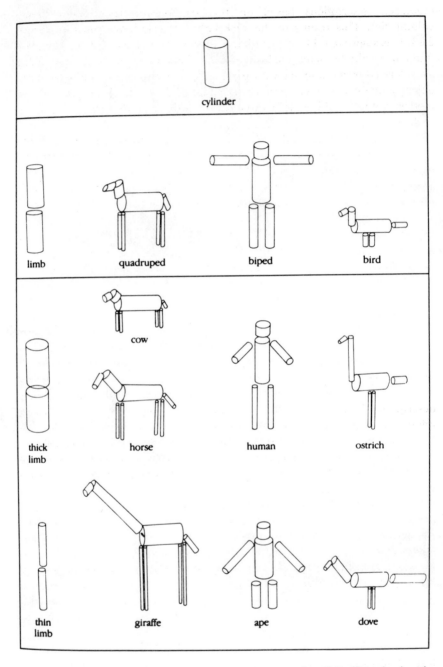

FIGURE 2.14   *A catalogue of 3D models, organised in terms of specificity (Reproduced, with permission, from Marr and Nishihara, 1978)*

organised descriptions based on the *axes* of the cones (and hence volumetric). This results in the stick figure descriptions shown in Figure 2.13. It is suggested that recognition of a general category such as 'horse' or 'human' might be achieved by matching the configuration of component axes derived from an image with the appropriate entry in a catalogue of 3D object models stored in memory (see Figure 2.14). Each of these object models will itself address a hierarchical set of descriptions at different levels of detail.

I will illustrate Marr and Nishihara's theory by returning to our example of a 'horse' and considering how we might obtain the axis-based description needed to access the catalogue. The first stage would be to find all the edge segments in the image, and group these up into larger structures. Such processes should reveal the occluding contour of the horse (see Figure 2.15). We now need to find the 'components' of this shape. Hoffman and Richards (1984) provide some convincing demonstrations of the importance of concavities in the segmentation of complex shapes into their component parts. Marr (1982) describes a program by Vatan which achieves this segmentation for the image of a toy donkey (cf. a horse) by finding concavities in the occluding contour and sectioning the image at particularly salient concave points (Figure 2.15). We can therefore divide the occluding contour up into a set of smaller parts, and represent each by its axis (to describe its length and extent) along with a variable width to denote the thickness of the part. This then gives us a stick-figure representation of a horse from this viewpoint. A further stage of processing will be needed to convert this representation into an object-centred description, in which each of the horse's legs, for example, is described relative to its trunk, rather than relative to us. Information from the analysis of depth, shading, motion, may all play a role in producing the final description which may be used to access the appropriate place in the stored object catalogue. Only when the match to the catalogue is made do we know that this is a 'horse'.

Marr and Nishihara's point about the necessity of hierarchical shape descriptions is an important one. There are two ways in which the representations they describe are organised hierarchically. First, their *catalogue* of 3D models (Figure 2.14) is organised hierarchically in terms of the specificity of the categorisation achieved. A fairly crude description will distinguish a biped from a quadruped, but more accuracy is needed to distinguish a human from an ape, and yet more to tell a man from a woman (all this, of course, assumes that we have only something like a silhouette to go on...). We should not be surprised, perhaps, that our imaginations may play tricks with impoverished images, as when sailors saw mermaids instead of sea elephants.

Under more normal viewing conditions, there seems to be a level of specificity which is preferred, and which Rosch (e.g. Rosch, Mervis, Gray,

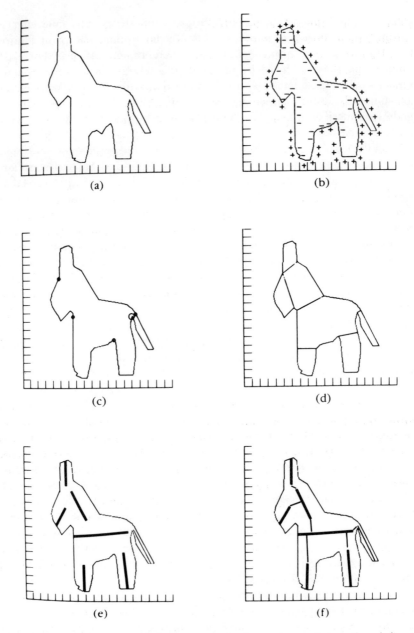

FIGURE 2.15   *Deriving a stick-figure representation from an image. a) shows the occluding contour of an image of a toy donkey; b) convex (+) and concave (−) sections are labelled, and strong segmentation points identified (such as that circled in c)); d) the shape is divided into segments and e) the axis of each component segment derived; f) Nose and ear axes are related to the neck axis, and leg axes related to the trunk axis, by the thin lines shown (Reproduced, with permission, from Marr and Nishihara, 1978)*

Johnson and Boyes-Braem, 1976) has termed the 'basic level' of categorisation. Presented with a picture of a horse, we tend spontaneously to categorise it as a 'horse' rather than as an 'animal' or a 'racehorse'. A table is described as a 'table' rather than as 'furniture' or as a 'gateleg table'. Rosch's basic level seems to correspond to the most general category which can be established through vision alone. Members of superordinate categories such as 'animals' or 'furniture' do not share much in common in terms of their shape – they are semantic rather than perceptual categories.

Marr and Nishihara's shape descriptions are also organised hierarchically in terms of the nested set of descriptions stored for each object category (cf. Figure 2.13, human – arm – hand). 'Stick'-figure representations can be used at each of these different levels, from the global human figure to the local details of the hand. The details of the configuration of a horse's head will be held in a description nested beneath the description for the whole of a horse's body. This means that a horse might be recognised simultaneously at many different levels of scale. It may be that some of the details needed to make subordinate category decisions, to distinguish between different breeds of dog or horse, will require a finer scale of analysis than that needed to make basic level categorisations. Later in this chapter we will consider evidence that points to the priority of global configuration over local detail.

Recognising faces

Our discussion of Marr and Nishihara's theory has described, in outline form, one possible representational format which could allow us to recognise certain kinds of objects from occluding contours in the retinal image. The primitives in this scheme represent the *volumes* of shapes, using axes of different dimensions. Now while an axis-based description may be used to describe certain kinds of shapes, there is evidence that not all shapes are encoded in a way consistent with the establishment of an axis-based structural description (e.g. see Humphreys and Quinlan, in press), and when we turn to a different recognition problem – that of recognising human faces – we find that this representational format appears inadequate for some of the uses we want of the information contained within faces (Bruce and Young, 1986).

Face recognition provides an interesting and challenging problem, since the task of distinguishing faces of friends from those of strangers is one which we can (almost) all perform effortlessly, (see Ruth Campbell's chapter in this volume for descriptions of breakdowns in face recognition following brain injury), yet the detailed information which distinguishes one face from another may defy description, and people are poor at reconstructing even well-known faces using tools such as Photo-fit (see Davies, Ellis and Shepherd, 1981, for a review). While face recognition is a

FIGURE 2.16   *You can easily see which of these faces looks puzzled, and which looks surprised. Despite the different views, however, you can also tell that the faces belong to the same person*

commonplace activity, it is also bound up with other ongoing activities. We must know that a face belongs to a friend in order to smile and greet the person concerned. We must be able to see whether they are smiling at us, or whether they look displeased, tired or worried. While engaging in conversation, movements of the lips help disambiguate speech (Dodd and Campbell, 1987, see also Campbell, this volume), and eyebrow flashes can signal emphasis (Ekman, 1979). Faces do a lot, and we do a lot with the information they provide. So face perception provides a good example of the interlinking of different modes and goals of perception.

The human face thus poses multiple recognition problems, and here we will consider just three:

(1)   We can recognise a face as a particular category of *object* (as opposed to a house, a horse or an elephant, say).
(2)   We can recognise an *expression* from a face, irrespective of whose face it is. We can easily decide which of the faces in Figure 2.16 looks puzzled and which looks surprised.
(3)   We can recognise a known individual's face irrespective of its expression, or angle, or, to some extent, age. We can easily tell that both the faces in Figure 2.16 are of the same person, despite the differences between their expressions.

The kinds of structural descriptions we have considered up till now might

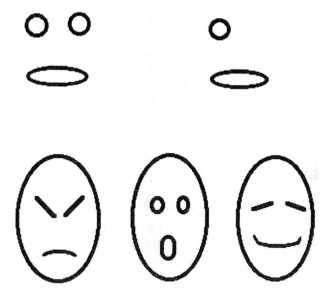

FIGURE 2.17 *Schematic faces can reveal how minimal is the information needed to perceive a pattern as a 'face'. Expressions can also be perceived from schematic faces such as these*

allow us to distinguish a face from another object category, or to tell one expression from another, but I will argue that we need a different kind of description to allow us to distinguish one individual identity from another from the face alone.

Recognition of a 'face'

The category 'face' is a highly salient one which can be depicted with minimal information (Figure 2.17), and to which infants are responsive soon after birth (e.g. Fantz, 1966; Goren, Sarty and Wu, 1975).

As Figure 2.17 shows, almost any kind of arrangement can be seen as a 'face' provided that there are two, similar small 'parts', arranged fairly symmetrically above a third, usually elongated 'part'. If these conditions are violated, we do not see faces in these very simple, schematic forms. We need much more in the way of detailed feature information, or a head-shaped outline to provide more information about overall configuration, before we will see a face without these 'key' attributes. It would not be too difficult to devise a structural model for a face in which such key attributes were made obligatory. Such a structural model might appear rather like those used by Winston for toy block structures. The structural description for the internal features of a face might comprise, at minimum, three parts. One of the parts would be some kind of 'slit', the other two parts might be *similar* to one another in shape, lie *above* the slit, but *beside* each other, in an arrangement that was roughly *symmetrical* about the central axis of the pattern.

Perception of expression

The recognition of expressions can also easily be achieved from simple schematic faces (McKelvie, 1973; see Figure 2.17). Again, it would not be too difficult to imagine a catalogue of facial postures (cf. Marr and Nishihara's catalogue of animal stick-figures), in which the shape of the eyes, the orientations of the axes of the eyebrows and the orientation of the axis of the mouth were represented in different combinations to yield different categories of 'anger', 'surprise', 'happiness', etc. Schematic such as these illustrate that powerful perceptual effects can be obtained from the most impoverished data, suggesting (cf. Marr's discussion of the salience of stick-figures and silhouettes) that such schematic forms somehow capture the essential 'primitives' of the representations used for seeing faces and expressions.

The kinds of structural descriptions considered as candidates for defining faces and their expressions show that some kind of axis-based representation might play a role in face perception. The structural descriptions would need to be related to the overall axis of elongation of the face, rather than to the vertical, to allow us to cope with slight departures from the vertical. To cope with the changes produced by rotation in depth of the face (head turning) will require that the description be related to the axis of the head itself, rather than of the 2D image of the head. Thus the necessity of an object-based description is underlined by our perception even of relatively simple properties of faces.

Recognising individuals

The important point here is that individual identity cannot similarly be captured with a few pencil strokes. Cartoonists who produce 'likenesses' of, say, Margaret Thatcher, with a few lines are supported both by the context in which their cartoon appears (political news), by the punchline, and by the conventions which arise in the depiction of such characters. (I am not suggesting that all caricatures require the assistance of context and convention for their interpretation – merely that extremely minimal cartoons probably do.) In general, we require a more detailed image to tell a person's identity from their face. What kind of description allows us to do this?

We don't usually recognise people from the backs of their heads, and we also experience more difficulty with profiles than with full-face or three-quarter views. Upside-down faces pose disproportionate recognition problems, compared with other objects (Yin, 1969; Valentine and Bruce, 1986). These observations suggest that representations for recognition may be based upon the particular view or views of the face that we usually see. Most work on face perception has emphasised the full-face view.

There is considerable evidence that both the nature of facial features, and their configural relationships with one another, are important in specifying facial identity (Matthews, 1978; Sergent, 1984). However, much of the research on facial processing, and the development of systems such as Photofit as aids to facial recall, seems to assume, implicitly, that a face can be treated conceptually as a fairly arbitrary 2D pattern of features. Yet real human faces are structured by growth in 3 dimensions, and there are important underlying constraints on facial form (Enlow, 1982). A new direction to research into face perception might be given by considering representations for recognition based on 3D, rather than 2D structure.

However, volumetric representations of the kind used by Marr and Nishihara are unlikely to be suitable for distinguishing between faces, which all share a similar 3D structure (though see Pentland, 1986, for an attempt to decompose head structures into their component volumes). Some kind of *surface-based representation* would appear to be more adequate, in which the shape of the head and the form of the features was made explicit. The problem with the human face is that it does not consist of a nice discrete set of surfaces. The face surface varies smoothly almost everywhere, and is thus more reminiscent of objects for which generalised cone descriptions proved useful.

Nevertheless, a surface-based representation can be applied to a face, if its surface is split up into a number of more-or-less planar facets – for example by scattering polygons onto the surface (Figure 2.18). This kind of surface-based representation has proved useful in the applied context of translating cross-sectional medical scan images into a surface model of the head from which the images were obtained (Baker, Hogg and Lloyd, 1984). Such a representation has also found application in the work of computer animation artists who wish to create moving images of faces (Parke, 1982). While not suggesting that the human visual system itself decomposes faces into facets like this, it seems likely that consideration of surface-based representations for faces may yield new insights into the mechanisms of face perception and recognition (Bruce, 1988, for more detail).

Our discussion of face recognition indicates some potential limitations of the Marr and Nishihara theory of object recognition, but this in no way constitutes a refutation of their theory: it is quite possible that certain kinds of representational scheme will prove more suitable for making certain kinds of perceptual classification. Indeed any 'unique' aspects of face perception and recognition (see Hay and Young, 1982) could lie in the

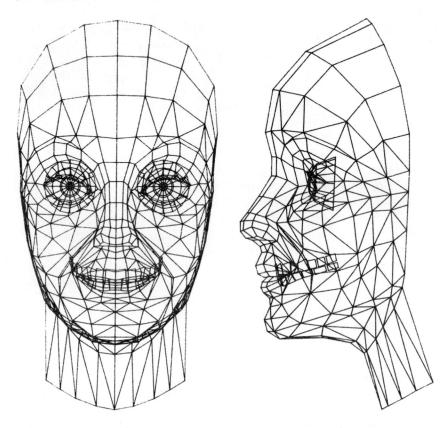

FIGURE 2.18   *Front and side views of a face represented by a large number of polygonal facets (Reproduced, with permission, from Parke, 1982, copyright © 1982 IEEE)*

'unique' nature of the representational format needed to achieve subtle discriminations between one person's face and another's. Such considerations could also allow us to explain why face recognition and object recognition may be disrupted independently following certain kinds of brain damage (see Ruth Campbell, this volume, for more about such deficits).

Context effects in recognition

So far, I have discussed object recognition as though it occurred in a perceptual and conceptual vacuum – in isolation from other acts of recognition occurring simultaneously or prior to the one in question. In recent years there have been numerous experimental demonstrations of the powerful effects upon recognition of the surrounding or immediately preceding context.

```
S         S
S         S
SSSSSSS
S         S
S         S
```

FIGURE 2.19   *A large letter H made up of small letter S's (adapted from Navon, 1977)*

Biederman (1972, 1981) has shown how recognition of an object within a scene is impaired if the scene depicted is incoherent. Subjects are impaired at recognising which of a small set of objects appears in a particular part of the scene when other areas of the scene are jumbled up, compared with when they remain intact, and this effect occurs even when subjects have advance warning of the possible set of objects and the location of the target in the scene. Homa, Haver and Schwartz (1976) demonstrated a similar phenomenon in the recognition of facial features from schematic faces. Subjects were more accurate at choosing the particular feature which had appeared (e.g. the correct nose from a set of different noses) if the feature appeared in a normally organised face than if it appeared in a jumbled face. These experiments seem to demonstrate that the recognition of the overall configuration of 'parts' of a scene can facilitate the recognition of the individual objects or parts of objects themselves.

In a rather different kind of experiment, Navon (1977) has also shown that priority in processing is given to global structure rather than local details. In his experiments, subjects were shown large letter shapes made up of smaller letters (see Figure 2.19). They were asked to make decisions about either the large letter (e.g. is it an H?) or the smaller letters (are they Ss?). Navon found that the nature of the large letter could interfere with decisions about the small ones, but that the small letters had no effect on decisions made to the large ones. This suggests that shape descriptions may be first constructed and recognised at the level of the overall shape, and that scrutiny of smaller components is a slower process. (These observations, however, probably only apply where the global shapes occupy a relatively small area of the field of view (e.g. Kincha and Wolf, 1979).)

The nature of the scenes viewed immediately prior to the current one can also affect recognition. Palmer (1975) asked subjects to identify briefly presented line drawings of objects (e.g. a loaf of bread) which were preceded by drawings of scenes which were appropriate (e.g. a kitchen) or inappropriate (a bedroom) for the objects which were to be identified. Appropriate contexts led to more accurate identification, and inappropriate contexts to less accurate identification, compared with a condition in which context was absent. Bruce and Valentine (1986) have demonstrated facilitation in the recognition of familiar faces through appropriate prior context. Subjects were faster to decide that a face (e.g. Princess Diana) was familiar if it was preceded by the face of a close associate (e.g. Prince Charles), than if preceded by an unfamiliar or an unrelated face (e.g. Stan Laurel).

Several authors have discussed effects of prior context in terms of the priming of 'recognition units' for objects or for faces, which play the role of lexical units or 'logogens' (Morton, 1969) in theories of word recognition. (For example, see Palmer (1975), Seymour (1979), for object recognition, and Hay and Young (1982) and Bruce and Young (1986) for face recognition.) In the terms of this chapter, a 'recognition unit' may be considered to be the collection of structural descriptions which specify a particular category of object, or an individual's face. Context effects of these kinds are most easily explained by assuming that activity within semantic memory (the system which knows the 'meanings' of objects, for example that a loaf of bread is edible) leads to the 'priming' or mobilisation of representations for items that are particularly likely.

Thus far in this chapter we have taken for granted the prevailing 'computational' metaphor for visual perception, and given an account of different recognition processes in terms of the construction and access of explicit symbolic descriptions. In the remaining two sections, I turn to two rather different perspectives which are likely to influence the development of computational theories over the next few years.

Patterns of change: the Gibsonian influence

While the account I have been offering of the perception of objects and faces reflects the mainstream of thought in psychology and artificial intelligence, there is a movement within perceptual psychology which rejects any appeal to explicit symbolic representations as *mediating* perceptual activity. The theory of 'direct information pickup' (Gibson, 1950, 1966, 1979) emphasises the rich and densely structured light rays in the optic array which surrounds the perceiver, and the changes in structure which result from movement in the world. Object identities, according to this view, are specified by *invariant* properties of spatially and temporally extended patterns of light. When a face is viewed, so the claim would go, something remains invariant despite all the transformations of pose, expression and so forth that we have already noted. The perceiver simply 'detects' these invariants, through a process vaguely described by Gibson as 'resonance'.

The notion that invariant properties underlie our perception of constant object categories is, of course, central to many traditional theories of object recognition. Where the Gibsonians differ is in the nature of the invariants which they propose, which may take the form of higher-order ratios and gradients of surface texture, and patterns of change over time. Their major departure, however, lies in their claim that such invariants do not require 'computation'.

One example of the kind of 'invariant' which might play a role in person perception is seen in the work of Pittenger, Shaw, Mark and Todd (e.g. Pittenger and Shaw, 1975; Mark and Todd, 1985). They have shown that the changes in skull structure which result from growth can be simulated by a global transformation on an underlying, cardioidal (heart-shaped) function which describes the shape of the skull profile. Individual identity is preserved at the level of the details of the underlying cardioidal shape, while age level is specified by the transformational status of the shape. This kind of work may prove useful for understanding other aspects of facial structure, and Mark and Todd's (1983) extension of the work to 3D modelling is particularly interesting. Can we describe changes of expression in terms of transformations on an underlying structure?

The Gibsonian or ecological school has attracted a wide following in recent years (e.g. Michaels and Carello, 1981; Shaw and Bransford, 1977; Turvey, 1977). While most psychologists reject the 'direct perception' claim, it is possible to find some reconciliation between the Gibsonian and the computational perspectives by considering that certain kinds of computation may occur in a 'fully compiled' manner, uninfluenced by more cognitive factors (e.g. Fodor and Pylyshyn, 1981; Bruce and Green, 1985). Whatever view one takes on the 'direct perception' debate, the Gibsonian emphasis placed on animals and people behaving in complex environments has been an important influence on recent developments in perception, and computational theorists are now investing much more effort in the analysis of movement, and optical flow in particular (Ullman, 1979; Clocksin, 1980; Longuet-Higgins and Prazdny, 1980; Hildreth, 1984; Buxton and Buxton, 1983). In Chapter 3 of the present volume, Nigel Harvey describes how important information for the control of gross postural adjustments may be contained within optical flow patterns, though he also takes issue with the extreme Gibsonian position.

That patterns of movement can lead to the recognition of familiar categories is shown in the famous demonstrations of Johansson (1973). Point-light displays formed by illuminating the joints of darkly-clad actors can immediately be seen as human figures, *provided* the actors are shown walking, dancing or moving in some other way. When stationary, the displays are uninterpretable. An important direction in the immediate future will be to investigate further the role that movement may play in the recognition of objects.

Patterns of activity: the new connectionism

In the first part of this chapter I emphasised an approach to object recognition which trades elaborate (and hence costly) computation, for a parsimonious memory store of object descriptions. Marr and Nishihara's (1978) scheme emphasised the computation of a single, object-centred, nested set of descriptions for each category of object known. However, principles of parsimony may not be too relevant to the human brain which seems to have sufficient storage capacity and redundancy to encode multiple instances of each known object.

In recent years, the availability of cheap computer memory and techniques for storing and retrieving information in parallel, have led to two distinguishable, though interrelated developments in the computational camp.

(1)   A resurgence of interest in the modelling of intelligent activities with *networks* of simple, neuron-like units, which operate in parallel.
(2)   An interest in the properties of representations and memories which can be attained by *distributed* patterns of activities in neural networks.

I will conclude this chapter by giving examples of such 'connectionist' approaches, which seem to represent the direction that much future theory will take (see, for example, Feldman, 1985).

Aleksander, Stonham and Wilkie (e.g. Aleksander, 1983; Stonham, 1986) have developed a general object recognition system (named WISARD, an acronym for the Wilkie, Stonham and Aleksander's Recognition Device), which functions by virtue of massive dedication of memory to the storage of the responses to the patterns on which it is trained.

WISARD works on principles similar to those of an early program of Bledsoe and Browning (1959), and I will base my description on this earlier program, before returning to details of WISARD itself. A letter is represented as an array of picture elements, each of which will register 0 or 1 depending on whether it contains a pattern element or not. Let us suppose that the array is of 64 (8×8) pixels. We now select *at random* sets of n such pixels, so that all pixels are sampled eventually. If n is 2, we will sample pairs of pixels, and will need 32 pairs to sample the entire image.

Two such pairs are shown in Figure 2.20. There are four possible results of sampling each pair. Both elements could be light (0,0), both dark (1,1), or one light and one dark (0,1, or 1,0). Each pair is associated with a set of four addresses in computer memory, corresponding to each of these four possible states, and one or other address will be accessed depending on the state recorded in the pair.

When a particular pattern (such as the T shown in Figure 2.20) is shown

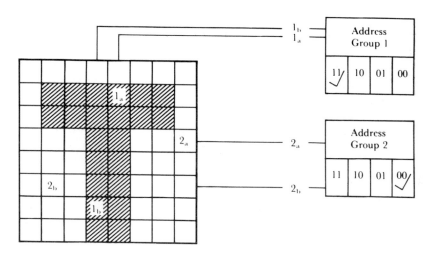

FIGURE 2.20 *Illustrating the operation of a pattern recognition system of the type introduced by Bledsoe and Browning (1959). The letter T is displayed on a matrix of 64 pixels. 32 pairs of pixels, chosen at random, will sample the whole matrix. Only two such pairs are shown here. Each pair has an associated set of four addresses, corresponding to its four possible states*

on the array, one of four possible addresses will be accessed for each of the 32 pairs. If a different example of a letter T is shown, a slightly different set of addresses will be contacted, but some states will *never* occur if the pattern is a T, and others will almost *always* occur. A different letter (an S, say) will lead to a different pattern of addresses contacted from the same set of 32 pixel pairs. We can conceive of the memory in this system being organised as a set of 32 units, each with 4 states, with one such set for *each* of the letters which the system must learn to distinguish. Following training with several examples of each letter to be learned, the system performs well at classifying unknown patterns. This is achieved by comparing the pattern of activity resulting from an unknown letter with the stored patterns which result from all the training instances of each known letter, and choosing the letter which gives the greatest overlap between these two response patterns.

A system such as this will become more and more powerful as the array size is increased (and hence the number of 'n-tuples' sampled), and as n itself is increased. The WISARD system is like that described above, but the image is represented in a much larger array ($512 \times 512 = 2^{18}$ pixels). WISARD deals with real images, which have variations in grey level, though the array can be represented as a set of 0's and 1's by application of a threshold device – anything darker than a certain amount gets a 1, anything lighter gets a 0. The number of n-tuples (sets of n pixels) that must be sampled is clearly huge for a 512×512 array. If n = 8, 2^{15} octuples are needed to sample the whole image. Each octuple can give rise to 2^8

different states. So a memory of $2^{15} \times 2^8$ bits is needed for each of the patterns which WISARD must learn.

The interesting aspect of WISARD is that, by virtue of its brute force (through massive memory) but ignorance (of any explicit representation of the structure of the world), it can achieve remarkably accurate recognition of any kinds of objects on which it is trained. Take its performance on faces (Stonham, 1986). It can be trained to recognise any one of 16 different individuals, by storing the responses to the sets of n-tuple samples derived from about 200 different images of each of them. Following training it will accurately recognise new instances of each of the 16 people, *provided* these instances don't depart too much from the range of different views on which it was trained. Alternatively, it may be trained to recognise a 'smile', despite differences in the faces shown smiling. For those familiar with the laborious performance of most serial computers on vision tasks, the most striking aspect of WISARD is the way in which its discriminations are achieved in real time!

The performance of WISARD illustrates that a large, uneconomical memory system can do object recognition quite well in the absence of an explicit symbolic representation of the structure of the object. The system obviously has interesting practical application, since it can be trained to make virtually any discriminations needed in a particular domain, without needing to have stored explicit models of the objects to be encountered in that domain. Its main limitation is its inability to extrapolate to views of objects outside the range it was trained with. While we do not extrapolate perfectly to novel views, we have a flexibility which WISARD clearly lacks.

WISARD illustrates how much can be achieved by virtue of a large memory and parallel access, but does not depart too much from the traditional conception of memory as highly localised. Each category that WISARD learns is given its own portion of memory space. A more radical theme, and one of more interest to psychologists, is the related work on *distributed* memory networks (e.g. see Hinton and Anderson, 1981; McClelland and Rumelhart, 1985). Several authors have now demonstrated that successive instances of the same or different categories can be encoded as patterns of activity over the same set of neurones. (In WISARD, successive instances of the same category are stored in a distributed manner, but each different category has its own memory network devoted to it.) McClelland and Rumelhart, for example, show how *in principle*, a network exposed to instances of 'Fido' and 'Rover' could extract a general concept of 'dog', as well as retaining the ability to identify each individual dog, and to remember recent instances of each. Sensitivity to the similarity between a current exemplar and a recently encountered instance is shown by such a network – a sensitivity which is not predicted by traditional 'recognition unit' models of pattern classification. Such distributed memory networks show properties of generalisation, and can accommodate new instances – often behaving in the manner predicted by a model which stored an *explicit* representation of the 'prototype' or average of each learned category. However, like WISARD, the systems at present have limited powers to extrapolate. The further limitations of such networks at present lie in the lack of any interface with lower levels of visual feature extraction. Arbitrary (McClelland and Rumelhart, 1985a) or implausible (Kohonen, Lehtio and Oja, 1981) assumptions are made about the visual properties which drive the networks – and this seriously limits the status of these systems as models for *vision*.

Nevertheless, the new connectionism seems exciting for several reasons. First, neural networks potentially provide a computational metaphor for the human brain which meshes closely with what is known of brain structure and function. Experimentation with highly parallel systems may well suggest new solutions to old problems in perception. This suggestion, is, however, controversial, since it is not clear what is the theoretical status of such highly parallel, 'connectionist' accounts, compared with the more familiar, serial, 'symbolic' computational accounts. Mayhew and Frisby (1984) and Broadbent (1985) have objected that the connectionist theories are theories set at the *implementation* level, rather than at the *computational* level of theory at which so much of Marr's work was aimed. Whatever the resolution of this point, which some connectionists contest) e.g. Rumelhart and McClelland, 1985), it is the case that implementation level considerations may bring back into play certain procedures which were thought to be inefficient or uneconomic when implemented in a different way. For example, the suggestion that concept learning might proceed through the storage of large numbers of separate instances has been labelled 'unparsimonious' by Marr (and others). If it can be shown that all instances can be encoded over the same network of units, such arguments lose their force.

Even more controversially, the new connectionism may provide a means of reconciliation between Gibsonian 'direct perception' camp, and the information-processing tradition in perception. Gibsonians have never denied the *physiological* mediation of perception, but have taken issue with an information-processing approach in which representations of the world 'outside' are constructed 'inside' the head. Neural networks replace explicit symbolic computation with complex patterns of neural activity. The connectionists seek biologically plausible algorithms to solve the computational problems posed by nature, and I anticipate considerable progress as a result of these efforts.

Further reading

A lively, well-illustrated and thorough introduction to the computational approach to vision is provided by Frisby (1979). Marr (1982) is essential reading for the more advanced student in this area. Michaels and Carello (1981) give a good introduction to the ecological approach to perception. Bruce and Green (1985) provide an overview of both these traditions in visual perception. Hinton and Anderson (1981) and McClelland and Rumelhart (1986) provide introductions to parallel models of the connectionist kind. However, only some of the articles in these books are specifically concerned with vision, and both collections are aimed at a research audience.

References

Aleksander, I. (1983), 'Memory networks for practical vision systems', in O. J. Braddick and A. C. Sleigh (eds), *Physical and Biological Processing of Images*. Springer-Verlag: Berlin.

Anderson, J. R. (1983), *The Architecture of Cognition*. Harvard University Press: Cambridge, Mass.

Baker, K. D., Hogg, D. C. and Lloyd, R. O. (1984), 'Interpreting medical images by computer', Report by Charles Hunnisett Research Group, Univ. of Sussex.

Ballard, D. H. and Brown, C. M. (1982), *Computer Vision*. Prentice-Hall: Englewood Cliffs, New Jersey.

Biederman, I. (1972), 'Perceiving real-world scenes', *Science*, 177, 77-80.

Biederman, I. (1981), 'On the semantics of a glance at a scene', in M. Kubovy and J. R. Pomerantz (eds), *Perceptual Organization*. Erlbaum: Hillsdale, NJ.

Binford, T. O. (1971), 'Visual perception by computer', paper presented at IEEE Conference on Systems and Control, Miami.

Bledsoe, W. W. and Browning, I. (1959), 'Pattern recognition and reading by machine', *Proceedings of the Eastern Joint Computer Conference*, 225-32. (Reprinted in L. Uhr (Ed.) (1966), *Pattern Recognition*. Wiley: New York.)

Broadbent, D. E. (1985), 'A question of levels: comment on McClelland and Rumelhart', *Journal of Experimental Psychology: General*, 114, 189–92.

Bruce, V. (1988), *Recognising Faces*. Erlbaum: London.

Bruce, V. and Green, P. R. (1985), *Visual Perception: Physiology, Psychology and Ecology*. Erlbaum: London.

Bruce, V. and Valentine, T. (1986), 'Semantic priming of familiar faces', *Quarterly Journal of Experimental Psychology*, *38A*, 125-50.

Bruce, V. and Young, A. (1986), 'Understanding face recognition', *British Journal of Psychology*, 77, 305-27.

Buxton, B. F. and Buxton, H. (1983), 'Monocular depth perception from optical flow by space-time signal processing', *Proceedings of the Royal Society of London, Series B*, *218*, 27-47.

Clocksin. W. F. (1980), 'Perception of surface slant and edge labels from optical flow: a computational approach', *Perception*, 9, 253-71.

Clowes, M. B. (1971), 'On seeing things', *Artificial Intelligence*, 2, 79-112.

Davies, G., Ellis, H. and Shepherd, J. (1981), *Perceiving and Remembering Faces*. Academic Press: London.

Dodd, B. and Campbell, R. (eds) (1987), *Hearing by Eye: The Cognitive Psychology of Lipreading*. Erlbaum: London.

Doyle, W. (1960), 'Recognition of sloppy, hand-printed characters', *Proceedings of the Western Joint Computer Conference*: San Francisco, California.

Ekman, P. (1979), 'About brows: emotional and conversational signals', in M. von Cranach, K. Foppa, W. Lepenies and D. Ploog (eds), *Human Ethology*. Cambridge University Press: Cambridge.

Enlow, D. H. (1982), *Handbook of Facial Growth*. W. B. Saunders: Philadelphia.

Fantz, R. L. (1966), 'Pattern discrimination and selective attention as determinants of perceptual development from birth', in A. Kidd and J. L. Rivoire (eds), *Perceptual Development in Children*. International Universities Press: New York.

Feldman, J. A. (1985), 'Four frames suffice: A provisional model of vision and space', *The Behavioural and Brain Sciences*, *8*, 265-89.

Fodor, J. A. and Pylyshyn, Z. W. (1981), 'How direct is visual perception? Some reflections on Gibson's "Ecological Approach"', *Cognition*, *9*, 139-96.

Frisby, J. P. (1979), *Seeing: Mind, Brain and Illusion*. Oxford University Press.

Gibson, J. J. (1950), *The Perception of the Visual World*. Houghton Mifflin: Boston.

Gibson, J. J. (1966), *The Senses Considered as Perceptual Systems*. Houghton Mifflin: Boston.

Gibson, J. J. (1979), *The Ecological Approach to Visual Perception*. Houghton Mifflin: Boston.

Goren, C. C., Sarty, M. and Wu, R. W. K. (1975), 'Visual following and pattern discrimination of face-like stimuli by new-born infants', *Paediatrics*, *56*, 544-9.

Guzman, A. (1968), 'Decomposition of a visual scene into three-dimensional bodies', *AFIPS Proceedings of the Fall Joint Computer Conference*, *33*, 291-304.

Hay, D. C. and Young, A. W. (1982), 'The human face', in A. W. Ellis (ed.), *Normality and Pathology in Cognitive Functions*. Academic Press: London.

Hildreth, E. (1984), 'The computation of the velocity field', *Proceedings of the Royal Society of London, Series B*, *221*, 189-220.

Hinton, G. and Anderson, J. A. (1981), *Parallel Models of Associative Memory*, Erlbaum: Hillsdale, NJ.

Hoffman, D. and Richards, W. A. (1984), 'Parts of recognition', *Cognition, 18*, 65-96.

Homa, D., Haver, B. and Schwartz, T. (1976), 'Perceptibility of schematic face stimuli: evidence for a perceptual Gestalt', *Memory and Cognition*, *4*, 176-85.

Hubel, D. H. and Wiesel, T. N. (1959), 'Receptive fields of single neurons in the cat's striate cortex', *Journal of Physiology, 148*, 574-91.

Hubel, D. H. and Wiesel, T. N. (1968), 'Receptive fields and functional architecture of monkey striate cortex', *Journal of Physiology, 195*, 215-43.

Huffman, D. A. (1971), 'Impossible objects as nonsense sentences', in B. Meltzer and D. Michie (eds), *Machine Intelligence 6*. Edinburgh UP.

Humphreys, G. W. and Quinlan, P. T. (in press), 'Normal and pathological processes in visual object constancy', in G. W. Humphreys and M. J. Riddoch (eds), *Visual Object Processing: A Cognitive Neuropsychological Approach*. Erlbaum: London.

Johansson, G. (1973), 'Visual perception of biological motion and a model for its analysis', *Perception and Psychophysics*, *14*, 201-11.

Kanade, T. (1981), 'Recovery of the three-dimensional shape of an object from a single view', *Artificial Intelligence*, *17*, 409-60.

Kinchla, R. A. and Wolf, J. M. (1979), 'The order of visual processing: "Top-down", "bottom-up" or "middle-out"', *Perception and Psychophysics*, *25*, 225-31.

Kohonen, T., Lehtio, P. and Oja, E. (1981), 'Storage and processing of information in distributed associative memory systems', in G. Hinton and J. A. Anderson (eds), *Parallel Models of Associative Memory*. Erlbaum: Hillsdale, NJ.

Lindsay, P. N. and Norman, D. A. (1972), *Human Information Processing*. Academic Press: New York.

Longuet-Higgins, H. C. and Prazdny, K. (1980), 'The interpretation of moving retinal images', *Proceedings of the Royal Society of London, Series B, 208*, 385-97.

McClelland, J. L. and Rumelhart, D. E. (1985), 'Distributed memory and the representation of general and specific information', *Journal of Experimental Psychology: General, 114*, 159-88.

McClelland, J. L. and Rumelhart, D. E. (1986), *Parallel Distributed Processing: Explorations in the Microstructure of Cognition, Vols 1 & 2*. Bradford Bks: Cambridge: Mass.

Mackworth, A. K. (1973), 'Interpreting pictures of polyhedral objects', *Artificial Intelligence, 4*, 121-37.

McKelvie, S. J. (1973), 'The meaningfulness and meaning of schematic faces', *Perception and Psychophysics, 14*, 343-8.

Mark, L. S. and Todd, J. T. (1983), 'The perception of growth in three dimensions', *Perception and Psychophysics, 33*, 193-6.

Mark, L. S. and Todd, J. T. (1985), 'Describing perceptual information about human growth in terms of geometric invariants', *Perception and Psychophysics, 37*, 249-56.

Marr, D. (1976), 'Early processing of visual information', *Philosophical Transactions of the Royal Society of London, Series B, 275*, 483-524.

Marr, D. (1977), 'Analysis of occluding contour', *Proceedings of the Royal Society of London, Series B, 197*, 441-75.

Marr, D. (1982), *Vision*. Freeman: San Francisco.

Marr, D. and Hildreth, E. (1980), 'Theory of edge detection', *Proceedings of the Royal Society of London, Series B, 207*, 187-217.

Marr, D. and Nishihara, H. K. (1978), 'Representation and recognition of the spatial organisation of three-dimensional shapes', *Proceedings of the Royal Society of London, Series B, 200*, 269-94.

Matthews, M. L. (1978), 'Discrimination of Identikit constructions of faces: evidence for a dual processing strategy', *Perception and Psychophysics, 23*, 153-61.

Mayhew, J. and Frisby, J. (1984), 'Computer vision', in T. O'Shea and M. Eisenstadt (eds), *Artificial Intelligence: Tools, Techniques and Applications*. Harper and Row: New York.

Michaels, C. F. and Carello, C. (1981), *Direct Perception*. Prentice-Hall: Englewood Cliffs, New Jersey.

Minsky, M. (1977), 'Frame-system theory', in P. N. Johnson-Laird and P. C. Wason (eds), *Thinking: Readings in Cognitive Science*. Cambridge University Press.

Minsky, M. and Papert, S. (1969), *Perceptrons*, MIT Press: Cambridge, Mass.

Morton, J. (1969), 'The interaction of information in word recognition', *Psychological Review, 76*, 165-78.

Navon, D. (1977), 'Forest before trees: the precedence of global features in visual perception', *Cognitive Psychology, 9*, 353-83.

Nishihara, H. K. (1983), 'Recognition of shape in visible surfaces', in O. J. Braddick and A. C. Sleigh (eds), *Physical and Biological Processing of Images*. Springer-Verlag: Berlin.

Palmer, S. E. (1975), 'The effects of contextual scenes on the identification of objects', *Memory and Cognition, 3*, 519-26.

Parke, F. I. (1982), 'Parameterised models for facial animation', *IEEE: Computer Graphics & Applications, 2*, Nov., 61-8.

Pentland, A. P. (1986), 'Perceptual organisation and the representation of natural form', *Artificial Intelligence*, *28*, 293-331

Pittenger, J. B. and Shaw, R. E. (1975), 'Aging faces as visual elastic events: implications for a theory of non-rigid shape perception', *Journal of Experimental Psychology: Human Perception and Performance*, *1*, 374-82.

Rosch, *et al.* (1976), 'Basic objects in natural categories', *Cognitive Psychology*, *8*, 382-439.

Rumelhart, D. E. and McClelland, J. L. (1985), 'Levels indeed! A response to Broadbent', *J. Experimental Psychology: General*, *114*, 193-7.

Selfridge, O. G. (1959), 'Pandemonium: a paradigm for learning', in *The Mechanisation of Thought Processes*. HMSO: London.

Sergent, J. (1984), 'An investigation into component and configural processes underlying face perception', *British Journal of Psychology*, *75*, 221-42.

Seymour, P. H. K. (1979), *Human Visual Cognition*. Collier-Macmillan: London.

Shaw, R. E. and Bransford, J. (1977), *Perceiving, Acting and Knowing: Toward an Ecological Psychology*. Erlbaum: Hillsdale, NJ.

Stonham, T. J. (1986), 'Practical face recognition and verification with WISARD', in H. Ellis, M. Jeeves, F. Newcombe and A. Young (eds), *Aspects of Face Processing*. Martinus Nijhoff: Dordrecht.

Turvey, M. T. (1977), 'Contrasting orientations to the processing of visual information', *Psychological Review*, *84*, 67-89.

Ullman, S. (1979), *The Interpretation of Visual Motion*. MIT Press: Cambridge, Mass.

Valentine, T. and Bruce, V. (1986), 'The effect of race, inversion and encoding activity upon face recognition', *Acta Psychologica*, *61*, 259-73.

Waltz, D. L. (1975), 'Generating semantic descriptions from scenes with shadows', in P. H. Winston (ed.), *The Psychology of Computer Vision*. McGraw-Hill: New York.

Winston, P. H. (1973), 'Learning to identify toy block structures', in R. L. Solso (ed.), *Contemporary Issues in Cognitive Psychology; The Loyola Symposium*. Hemisphere: Washington.

Winston, P. H. (1975), 'Learning structural descriptions from examples,' in P. H. Winston (ed.), *The Psychology of Computer Vision*. McGraw-Hill: New York.

Yin, R. K. (1969), 'Looking at upside-down faces', *Journal of Experimental Psychology*, *81*, 141-5.

3 The psychology of action: current controversies

Nigel Harvey

Since the review by Harvey and Greer (1980), the cognitive psychology of motor control has matured considerably. Then, it was a reasonable ambition to provide shallow coverage of the whole area in the space of a chapter. Now, it is not. Then, there were no books to provide any better coverage. Now, there are (Holding, 1981; Kelso, 1982; Schmidt, 1982a; Smyth and Wing, 1984). Thus my approach here will be different from the one adopted in the earlier review. I shall limit myself to discussing five issues that are currently centre stage. These are (1) Is control of action a cognitive process? (2) Is motor learning like statistical regression? (3) How is anticipation involved in movement production? (4) Are muscles like springs? (5) Is knowledge of results necessary for learning?

First, however, I shall provide a brief outline of the conceptual framework within which work on these issues has taken place. It was originally developed by the Soviet scientist, Bernstein (1967). Most of his innovative work was done prior to 1960 but it is only within the last twenty years that its importance has been recognised in the West (Hughes and Stelmach, in press; Whiting, 1984). Many of the important developments in cognitive psychology (Miller, Galanter and Pribram, 1960) echo Bernstein's earlier ideas. His work even foreshadows some of the more recent computational approaches in psychology (e.g. Marr, 1982).

Bernstein felt that the vast number of muscles that have to be controlled in movement poses the brain with a computational problem. Although it now appears that the problem is not as severe as he had thought (Hinton, 1984), most psychologists working in the area still favour his solution to it. His contention was that this solution is achieved by use of mechanisms that control muscles as global units. These mechanisms impose certain biochemical or neural constraints on the muscles prior to the delivery of commands for explicit movement. He argued that the global unit encodes,

I should like to thank A. R. Jonckheere for helpful criticism of an earlier draft of this chapter.

as a manipulable whole, the complete time course of a particular type of movement (e.g. walking, scratching). In other words, it stores a function that specifies the dynamic characteristics of a whole class of movements. Movement variants within a particular class area are specified or tuned by altering certain parameters in the function.

Bernstein argued that control is hierarchical (cf. Miller et al., 1960). The function generator is imposed on a low level of the system where it has some degree of independence. The higher level then has to do no more than sanction operation of the lower one and insert new parameters into the function whenever new tunings become necessary. For example, walking is controlled by spinal function generators. Its speed is altered when the brain inserts new parameters into these function generators. The function generators are responsible for the pattern in walking that remains the same despite changes in speed. Tuning of the function generators depends on required outcome of the movement, on feedback received during it and on internalised models that allow prediction of changes in the environment and in the performer's relationship to it.

Is the control of action a cognitive process?

Bernstein's ideas have provoked all sorts of questions. For instance, how are parameters selected so as to ensure that function generators are appropriately tuned to the environment? Ecological psychologists (e.g. Fitch, Tuller and Turvey, 1982; Shaw, Turvey and Mace, 1982; Reed, 1982), influenced by the work of Gibson (1979), have argued that perceptual systems have evolved in a way that ensures that these parameters are provided with a minimum of analysis. There are no cognitive representations that act as internal mediators between the output of a perceptual system and the input of an action system. 'Cognitive theories, with their Pandora's boxes of intervening variables, can no longer be accepted' (Reed, 1982, p. 125). Instead, we must think of sensory systems, such as vision, tuning function generators directly – 'the subparts of the perception and action systems are thought of as pieces of a jigsaw puzzle that are made to fit each other' (Fitch et al., 1982, p. 274).

Consider, for example, an observer who is approaching an object with constant velocity. Rate of magnification of the object's optical texture gives a measure of the time that remains before the observer will physically contact it. Studies by Lee and his colleagues have shown that observers behave in a manner that suggests that they use this measure to control their action. The tasks they have examined include control of braking by drivers of motor cars (Lee, 1976), control of gait by long-jumpers (Lee, Lishman and Thomson, 1982), and control of wing folding by gannets as they dive into the sea (Lee and Reddish, 1981). The body sway observed in subjects when the walls of a room are moved over a stable floor can be interpreted as inappropriate use of this same information in postural control (Lee and Lishman, 1974). The notion that action is directly controlled by a parameter that has been directly extracted from the environment does appear to be the most parsimonious account of the findings in these particular studies and in others like them (e.g. Dietz and Noth, 1978; Todd, 1981). However, it is a large step from acceptance of this limited proposition to endorsement of the general view that action is always controlled in this non-cognitive manner. Nevertheless, some of the more extreme neo-Gibsonians would have us take this step (Reed, 1982; Turvey and Kugler, 1984). The basis for their argument is that cognitive psychology is inherently dualist (i.e. our minds cause our bodies to move), whereas a true scientific account of behaviour must be consistent with realism (i.e. only matter exists and so it must cause our bodies to move), and Gibsonian ecological psychology is the only such account. This view that all cognitive psychologists are dualists and that ecological psychologists are the only realists appears to be rather unreasonable. Let us examine one presentation of it in detail.

Descartes argued that an act of understanding enables us to extract knowledge of the world from awareness of our own body/brain states. In other words:

(1) perception is mediated by internal representations and
(2) we are conscious of these internal representations.

Turvey and Kugler (1984) refer to psychologists accepting these two assumptions as accepting the Cartesian program. They say that a scientific account of perception consistent with realism 'has been thwarted in our view, by the almost universal acceptance of the Cartesian program' (p. 379). It is indeed true that cognitive psychologists usually accept the first of the above assumptions. However, most of them totally ignore the second one. After Broadbent (1958), reference to conscious awareness became virtually excluded from psychology. Those few stalwarts who have mentioned it (Dixon, 1971, 1981) have not done so in the automatic acceptance of the second assumption of the Cartesian program. Instead, they have asked how, if at all, the reported contents of consciousness relate to the internal representations used in information processing. One does not have to be a dualist to attempt an answer to this question. One certainly does not have to be a dualist to develop theories in which internal representations abound but in which there is no reference to conscious awareness (e.g. Norman and Rumelhart, 1975; Rumelhart and McClelland, 1986). So Turvey and Kugler (1984) are wrong to argue that the only alternative to accepting both the above assumptions (i.e. the Cartesian program) is rejection of them both (i.e. the Gibsonian program). The third alternative (the cognitive psychology program) is to accept only the first assumption.

It is important to recognise that explanations of performance in terms of direct perception may be more parsimonious than those that employ cognitive mediators. However, some authors see risks attendant on a purely ecological approach. 'To deny the existence of internal structures entirely would be a serious mistake: it would eliminate any hope of linking the theory of perception with the rest of cognitive psychology' (Neisser, 1985, p. 106). For Newell and Barclay (1982) 'there seems a potential for the Gibsonian position...to focus principally on the environment and stimulus characteristics at the expense of the organism. There are heuristic merits in providing the strong position to one's theoretical viewpoint, but the direct perception position in doing this could undermine its adherence, at least in the way in which it is interpreted, to the organism-environment interaction' (pp. 185–6). Perhaps more important than either of these concerns is the fact that many types of performance are just not easily amenable to an ecological interpretation. A flexible strategy recognises the strengths of both the ecological and cognitive approaches and applies each of them as appropriate. The crucial questions become: In what types of task is performance amenable to an ecological explanation? What is it about a task that enables the tuning of action to be direct rather than mediated?

The ecological approach appears to be particularly useful for interpreting phenomena where (a) subjects have little choice over their actions and (b) the interval between the eliciting stimulus array and the resulting action is negligible. The visually induced body sway studied by Lee and Lishman (1974) is an example of a phenomenon where these two conditions hold. Consider now a situation in which just the second condition holds. When you are playing a game of squash, you have to do more than just hit the ball. You have to decide the position in the court to which you would like to return it and how you would like to do so. Different courses of action have different costs and benefits associated with them. A particular shot may be difficult for your partner to return but, if she succeeds in doing so, you may be badly placed for the next shot. Different possible courses of action also have different levels of risk associated with them. The potential pay-off from a successful lob shot may be high but the probability of executing it well may be low relative to that of a smash shot. While a Gibsonian account of how it is possible to swing a racquet to hit a moving ball is clearly viable (cf. Lee, Young, Reddish, Lough and Clayton, 1983), a similar account of *the manner* in which the ball is hit would be more difficult to formulate. A cognitive psychologist would argue that to be a good player, a person must have internal models of the opponent's strategy and of how balls behave in court when hit in different ways. Some would argue that these models are used to extract subjective expected values associated with different types of shot and that the highest valued alternative determines the parameters inserted into whatever function generators subserve squash playing (cf. Alain, Lalonde and Sarrazin, 1983; Alain, Sarrazin and Lacombe, 1985).

Now consider a case in which there is some interval between eliciting stimulus and resulting action. A singer is to perform a new song. She must learn the score (the stimulus array) off by heart as she will not have the opportunity to sightread it during the performance (resulting action). Here action cannot be directly controlled by a parameter that has been directly extracted from the environment. An internal representation (memory for the score) must act as a mediator. It is this internal representation that specifies the parameters that tune the function generators subserving singing performance (Harvey, 1985).

Finally, it is important to question whether those performances held to exemplify direct control of action are truly free of mediation. A driver may start to apply car brakes when rate of dilation of a retinal image reaches some critical point. This critical point must be represented somehow in the system. Furthermore, the critical point will depend on how far in front of the object the driver wishes to stop or alternatively, if he wants to crash into the object, it will depend on how strong a collision he desires. So, there must be an internalised rule relating the rate of dilation parameter to desired outcome. Furthermore, this rule will depend on certain initial conditions, especially the braking power of a vehicle. In other words, there must be some internally represented cognitive rule or schema that enables the critical action-triggering value of the perceptual parameter to be specified when it is given the desired outcome and the initial conditions. In other words, the critical value (P_c) of the perceptual parameter (P) is some function of the required outcome (O) and the relevant initial conditions (I_1, I_2,...I_N). Thus:

$$P_c = f(O, I_1, I_2,...I_N).$$

Just how do subjects learn what this function is? Salzman and Kelso (1983) argue that critical parameter values are just discovered. However, it is legitimate to ask how they are discovered – and, indeed, I shall be doing so in the next section.

Ecological psychologists do not merely suggest that action is triggered by perception but argue that it is directly controlled by a perceived feature of the stimulus. For this to occur, a motor parameter, M, in the function generator controlling the movement must take on the value that the perceptual parameter, P, has at the time action is triggered – i.e. P_c. (The parameter, M, may, for instance, specify the relative stiffness of the agonist and antagonist muscles involved in the ankle extension movement that subserves car braking.) Thus, we have what is known as a production system (Allport, 1980; Newell, 1973) or condition-action rule.

When $P = P_c$, make $M = P_c$

Substituting the 'action' part into the perceptual schema given above

When $P = P_c$, make $M = f(O, I_1, I_2,...I_N)$

The action part of this rule has now become what is known as a motor schema (Schmidt, 1975, 1976). The production system specifies that, when certain perceptual conditions are met, the function generator subserving the movement should be re-tuned by inserting into it the new parameter value given by the motor schema.

The ecological approach should not be seen as diametrically opposed to the cognitive approach. As the above demonstrates, ecological theories implicitly include components (such as motor schemata) that are often regarded as cognitive in nature.

Is motor learning like regression?

We have seen that schemata are required for specifying either the motor parameter, M, or else the critical perceptual parameter, P_c, that becomes equivalent to it. How are these schemata acquired? Schmidt (1975, 1976, 1982a, b) has suggested that they are extracted from information obtained on each occasion on which use is made of a particular function generator (or generalised motor program, as he terms it).

Consider a hypothetical example. Someone is playing golf. A generalised motor program is responsible for the execution of golf swings. A muscle parameter M inserted into this program specifies, say, the forces to be developed by certain muscles involved in the swing. The movement outcome, O, obtained when the program is executed, is the distance that the ball goes. This will depend on certain initial conditions, I, such as the weight of the club. Whenever the program is executed the values of M, O and I that are associated on that occasion are stored. A set of associated values can be shown graphically. Figure 3.1 shows associated values of M and O from a number of swings with the same weight of club (i.e. I is constant). A regression line has been put through these points. Schmidt (1982a) has suggested that a regression line in a graphical representation such as Figure 3.1 can be taken to represent a schema. We should 'consider the rule as analogous to a regression line' (Shapiro and Schmidt, 1982, p. 117). In other words, the *outcome* of a regression procedure should be taken as analogous to the outcome of schema abstraction. In what follows, I want to go one step further and consider the usefulness of statistical regression *procedures* as computational models of the *procedure* used by subjects to extract schemata. I suggest that this identification has already been made implicitly by many of those who have researched into the predictions of schema theory. By making it explicit, the importance of some of their results may become clearer.

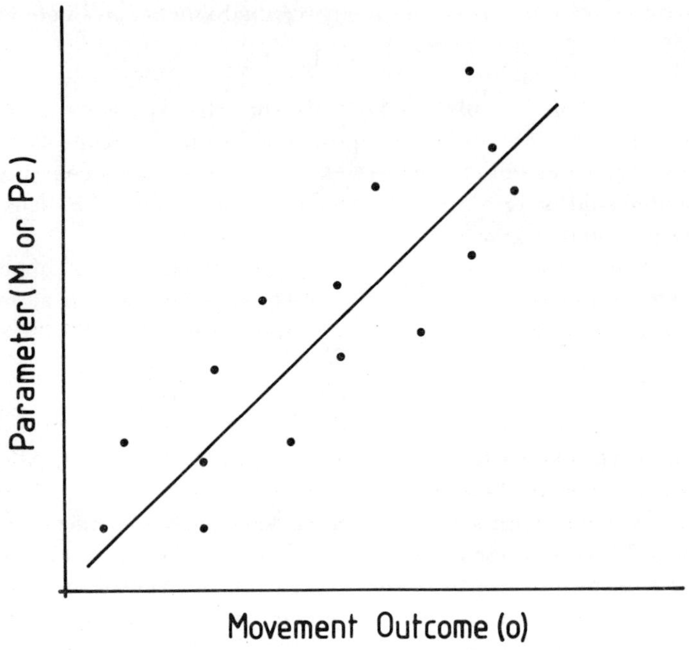

FIGURE 3.1   *The hypothetical relationship between movement outcomes and the parameters giving rise to them*

There are many features of Schmidt's (1975) theory other than the suggestion that schemata are analogous to regression lines. These range from adoption of a general Bernsteinian framework to a specification of the particular muscle variable that corresponds to the motor parameter, M. Others have discussed these aspects of the theory (Frohlich and Elliot, 1984; Rossum, 1980). I shall be concerned with them in so far as they have some bearing on the proposal that motor learning is like regression.

The most widely researched prediction from schema theory concerns variability of practice. Schmidt has only explained this prediction in relation to diagrams such as Figure 3.1. 'When the range of movement outcomes and parameters is small, all of the "data points" are clustered together in the centre of the diagram, and less certainty will exist about the placement of the line. So when a new movement is required, greater error will occur in estimating the parameters' (1982b, p. 599). Shapiro and Schmidt (1982) reviewed evidence for this prediction. They concluded that 'taken together, the results of these studies provide, at best, minimal support for the variability prediction for recall memory for adult subjects' but that 'children's motor skills are apparently more easily affected by variability of practice than are those of adults' (pp. 120-1). They argued that this was because adults may have already developed schemata for the relatively simple tasks employed in the experiments. But what is it, then, that is learned by adults in experimental motor learning situations? They suggest that subjects discover 'the size of the value that has to be added to the parameters in order to make the program "work" in this particular situation' (p. 142). This value is situation-specific in that it reflects aspects of the situation that are not explicitly included in the schema rule as initial conditions. It must be derived for each environment in which the schema is used. For instance, our golfer may not explicitly encode state of the grass as an initial condition and so takes some time to adapt to it when playing a new course. Thus, in adult motor learning, schemata are rarely acquired or even refined. New circumstances are taken into account by modifying the output from schemata rather than by modifying the schemata themselves. This interpretation by Shapiro and Schmidt (1982) of the weaker evidence in favour of the variability of practice prediction in adults than in children is not the only one possible within schema theory. It is worth examining the assumptions underlying the prediction in a little more detail.

The variability of practice prediction appears to be based on what is known about the effect of restricting the range of a variable on the strength of the relation between that variable and another (e.g. Guilford and Fruchter, 1973). The exact form of the expression is not important for our purposes. What is important is to recognise that its validity depends on a crucial assumption. The regression line fitted to the restricted data must be an adequate estimate of the regression line fitted to the whole sample. Suppose that this assumption is indeed met in the case of children – as shown in Figure 3.2a. Consequently, the correlation is indeed higher in the unrestricted sample (r = .76) than in the restricted one (r = .52). Adults, however, can achieve a broader range of outcome than children. Because of this, curvilinear components may appear in the relationship between motor parameter and movement outcome when their unrestricted range is considered (Figure 3.2b). This would mean that different regression lines would fit the unrestricted and restricted samples. Furthermore, because the restriction eliminates the curvilinear components in the relationship, the correlation may be at least as good in the restricted sample (r = .71) as in the unrestricted one (r = .76).

Commentators (e.g. Johnson, 1984) have occasionally viewed variability of practice as an assumption of schema theory. It is not. It is a prediction based on a particular version of the theory. As Figure 3.2b demonstrates, it does not follow when the relationship between muscle parameters and movement outcomes is more complex (e.g. in the sense of containing higher order polynomial components) in the high variability condition than in the low variability one. When this is the case, subjects in the high variability condition could do one of two things. They could fit a rule of the same level of complexity as the low variability subjects but, in consequence, achieve a

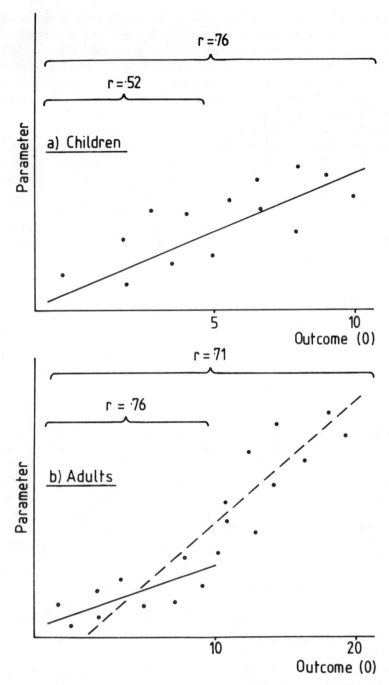

FIGURE 3.2   *Graphical representation using hypothetical data of an explanation for why variability of practice affects transfer in children (a) but not adults (b)*

worse fit (Figure 3.2b). Their transfer to a new version of the task would therefore suffer. Alternatively, the rule they fit could be more complex (i.e. containing higher order polynomials) than the one fitted by the low variability group. However, because fitting more complex rules requires more data points to achieve the same degree of fit, their rule will not be as well specified at the end of the training session. Transfer to a new version of the task will again suffer.

Must the variability of practice prediction be expected to hold when the actual (as opposed to fitted) relation between motor parameters and movement outcomes has the same general form for both high and low variability subjects? Not necessarily. For a number of reasons, errors in the registered values of the dependent variable (i.e. motor parameters) and its predictors (i.e. movement outcomes, initial conditions) could be higher in the high variability group. For example, this group has to switch attention between a larger number of movement outcomes and motor parameters than the low variability group. This may reduce the accuracy with which they are stored prior to inclusion in the schema. Error in both dependent and predictor variables reduces the strength of the relationship that can be established between them (Linn and Wertz, 1982) and so this would reduce transfer performance of the high variability group relative to that of the low variability one. Is there any circumstantial evidence that schemata are extracted from noisy values and that noise is greater in high variability conditions? Yes, there is. A secondary effect of error in a predictor variable is to lower the value of the coefficient associated with that variable in the regression equation (Linn and Wertz, 1982). This results in an underestimate in the amount of change in the dependent variable that accompanies a unit change in the predictor. Given that the schema has zero intercept, this should produce negative constant errors (i.e. undershooting). Constant error is not always reported but, when it is, it is undershooting that is typically found (e.g. Gersen and Thomas, 1977). Furthermore, this effect is numerically larger in high than in low variability groups (McCracken and Stelmach, 1977).

How is a schema derived from a set of discrete associations between muscle parameter and movement outcome values? When a subject first attempts a task 'he pairs the response specifications and the actual outcome on that particular trial. After a number of such attempts, there begins to form a relationship between the two variables, and this relationship (the recall schema) is updated on each successive trial. After a great deal of experience the schema becomes well established' (Schmidt, 1976, p. 47). Thus Schmidt suggests that the first attempts at a new type of performance function largely as a means of collecting data. After a number of movements have been made, a preliminary schema is abstracted from these data *en bloc*. Data from later trials serve to tune and strengthen this rule.

A number of questions arise from this account. How many trials have to contribute data before the subject begins to abstract a preliminary schema from them? Presumably these data have to be held in some memory store. Perhaps subjects first abstract the preliminary schema when the data show signs of exceeding the capacity of this store. Is there evidence of a discontinuity in an individual subject's performance after the point corresponding to preliminary schema extraction? One might be expected because memory capacity has been released and there is now a principled though approximate basis on which to respond. How does a single data point late in practice update the preliminary schema? Is the means by which it does so fundamentally different from the way in which the set of initial data points contribute to original formation of the preliminary schema?

As an alternative to what Schmidt (1976) proposes, we should consider whether subjects abstract schemata recursively. This would mean that

(1)　A preliminary schema is formed after the very first trial.
(2)　Memory load is minimised.
(3)　There is no difference between schema formation and updating.

Furthermore, this interpretation allows schema theory to be expressed in the signal processing terms that are increasingly common in other areas of cognitive psychology.

Usually, the least squares estimate of the coefficient, b, in the simple regression of Y on X is obtained from a block of data via the following expression:

$$b = \frac{N \Sigma XY - \Sigma X \Sigma Y}{N \Sigma X^2 - (\Sigma x)^2}$$

However, instead of waiting until the complete block of data has been collected, b can be estimated as each new data point is acquired. Suppose it is the kth trial. The coefficient estimated on the basis of the previous trial was b_{k-1}. A new data point (X_k, Y_k) is now obtained. This is used to transform the old coefficient into a new one, b_k, according to the expression

$$b_k = b_{k-1} + P_k X_k (Y_k - X_k b_{k-1}), \text{ where}$$

$$P_k = P_{k-1} - P^2_{k-1} X^2_k / (1 + P_{k-1} X^2_k)$$

Initial values used for b and P on the very first trial can be arbitrary as long as P is large. In signal processing terms, the above recursive expression for b_k is a discrete-time low-pass filtering algorithm. Figure 3.3 shows a block diagram representation of it, where Z^{-1} is the 'backward shift' operator. The parameter, P_k, is the gain of the filter and, as the above expression for it shows, it is a strictly decreasing function of time. This means that mismatches between actual and predicted values of the signal, Y, have a decreasing effect on bk as time passes. As Schmidt (1982b) says 'Clearly, if

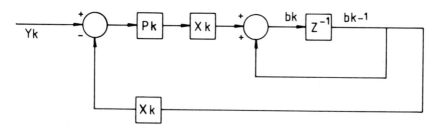

FIGURE 3.3 *Block diagram showing the recursive regression algorithm as a low-pass filter system (For further explanation, see text)*

there are 10,000 "data points" and one more is added, the relation is not adjusted very much; but if there are a few data points when the level of practice is low, the relation could be adjusted substantially' (p. 228).

Subjects may or may not use least squares estimation procedures to abstract schemata. The point to be made here is that use of a recursive algorithm to carry out whatever type of estimation they do employ imposes less memory load on the subject than an *en bloc* method. In the above example, the recursive technique only requires retention of the current coefficient and the parameter P. The *en bloc* technique required retention of all previous data points. Furthermore, no discontinuities in performance at the point of schema abstraction are to be expected with the recursive technique because there is no distinction between the way the rule is formulated and the way it is updated.

The above discussion serves to emphasise that the extraction of rules from data does itself require rules. It makes sense to ask whether these schema extraction algorithms are innate or learnt and, if the latter, how they are acquired. Their operation may be expected to be revealed by the presence of certain types of invariance in data obtained from widely differing motor learning experiments.

How is anticipation involved in movement production?

Schema theory was originally developed to account for the learning and performance of single discrete movements. Use of schemata allows specification of a set of motor parameters to be used simultaneously for production of a discrete movement at a particular time. If another discrete movement within the same class is to be made at a later time, then the same set of schemata have to be used again. What happens when the movements are not separate and discrete but are, instead, sequentially dependent? And what happens when this sequence of movements must be related to a succession of changes in the environment? In other words, can schema theory be modified to cope with tracking tasks, such as driving motor cars or using sewing machines? In many tracking tasks, movements that will be required in the future are often predictable to some degree.

In a seminal paper, Poulton (1957a) identified three types of prediction that may be required in skilled movements. First, when reaching for a stationary target, it is necessary to predict the size and nature of the muscular contractions required. He termed this 'effector anticipation'. Schmidt's (1975) schema theory requires no modification to account for it. Second, when reaching for a moving target whose future track is displayed ahead, it is necessary to predict the duration of one's own response movement in addition to the size and nature of the required muscular contractions. Poulton (1957a) termed this additional requirement 'receptor anticipation.' Schema theory can account for it without modification as long as the relevant kinematic features (e.g. target velocity) are included in the schema as predictor variables – in much the same way that club weight was in my golf playing schema example. Poulton (1957a) termed the third type of prediction 'perceptual anticipation'. It can be employed in addition to the previous two types of anticipation to improve performance in tasks in which the track of a moving target is governed by known constants or statistical properties. Perceptual anticipation involves forecasting the future of a track on the basis of its past. Schema theory needs some modification to account for it.

Changes in motor parameters, M, must be related to changes in required outcome, O. Changes in required outcome could be specified as a time series relating current required outcome, O_t, to previous ones, O_{t-1}, O_{t-2}... For instance,

$$O_t = f(O_{t-1}, O_{t-2}...)$$

This would allow prediction of O_t given O_{t-1}, O_{t-2}...etc. Then, as long as changes in the environmental conditions throughout the movement are irrelevant, the following schema could be developed to specify movement parameters at time t.

$$M_t = f(O_t, I_o)$$

where I_o represents initial conditions at the start of the movement.

If changes in environmental conditions are important but cannot be predicted, it may be possible to improve specification of motor parameter values by including a component in the schema that corresponds to the environmental conditions most recently perceived. Suppose that when a movement has to be made at time t, details of the environmental conditions present at time $t-1$ are the most recent that are available. Then

$$M_t = f(O_t, I_{t-1})$$

Of course, when familiar with a task, a subject may be able to predict the environmental conditions that will be present when the movement is made. In other words, experience will have enabled the subject to extract a rule:

$$I_t = f(I_{t-1}, I_{t-2} ...)$$

This could be used to predict the environmental conditions at time t and these could then be inserted into the schema as follows:

$$M_t = f(O_t, I_t)$$

If I_t depends on more prior values of I than just I_{t-1}, this schema will provide better specification of muscle parameters than the previous one.

The time series of environmental conditions outlined above could be extracted recursively in a manner similar to that previously outlined for recall schema. After a series has produced a forecast for I_t, the true value of I_t will be registered and, no doubt, there will be some error of prediction. This true value of I_t could be used both to correct ongoing movement and to update the coefficients in the series and so reduce future errors of prediction (cf. Pew, 1974). Neisser (1976, 1985) refers to these rules for predicting environmental conditions as schemata. This is fair enough. They are indeed rules – though rules for anticipating perceptual events rather than rules for movement production (Schmidt, 1975). The similarity in terminology is useful. It serves to emphasise that the same type of statistical estimation procedures can be used to model the procedures used for extracting perceptual (Neisser, 1976) and motor schemata (Schmidt, 1975).

Empirical and theoretical work on anticipation seems to have been somewhat out of synchrony over the last fifty years. This may have been because the issue is best studied within the context of tracking tasks. These tasks were well studied during the twenty years following World War Two but the investigations were largely governed by applied rather than theoretical considerations. As Holding (1981) pointed out, 'the real impetus for skills research came from wartime demands for high-speed and high-precision performance. Tracking skill, which requires the accurate following of a target or course...is involved in critical tasks like flying, driving or aiming. Thus, although many studies of single movements were made, the tracking task became a major skills exemplar' (p. 2). However, this applied approach did not produce much in way of theory. As late as 1968, Schmidt (1968, p. 643) was justly able to conclude his review of research on anticipation with the comment that the 'general lack of interesting theoretical ideas is certainly one reason for the relative lack of interest in the area'. Because of this, and because tracking tasks are relatively complex to investigate, experimenters shifted their attention during the late 1960s and the 1970s to simpler paradigms that allowed them to test assumptions underlying information processing models of motor skill that were being developed at that time. Thus, as Holding (1981, p. 2) points out, 'discrete movement tasks...have supplanted the tracking task as the preferred experimental setting'. However, there is an irony in this. Just as the shift in experimental paradigm was taking place, Bernstein (1967) and Anokhin (1969) were developing interesting theoretical ideas emphasising the importance of incorporating anticipation into our model of the world and of using forecasts in motor control. Although their ideas were appreciated by one or two Westerners still working on tracking (notably Pew, 1974), it was not until very recently that their work in this area was recognised to be a major theoretical contribution. In fact, Requin, Semjen and Bonnet (1984, p. 488) 'consider Bernstein's most important contribution to reside in his emphasis – that has, in our opinion, been underestimated and that we find premonitory – to set out the invariant frame of reference of the organisation of action within an elaborated model of the future which reduces uncertainty and takes into account the variability of the context as well as the potential multiplicity of strategies of action.'

So how can tracking tasks be used to examine the phenomenon that Poulton (1957a) termed perceptual anticipation? I shall outline three approaches. The first involves what I call the continuation paradigm. Tracking movements after the target or course has disappeared from view are examined. For instance, Gottsdanker (1952a, b; 1955) showed that subjects who had been following linear or smoothly curved paths were able to continue tracking the target accurately for at least two seconds after their vision of it has been obscured. Poulton (1957b, c) found that people could track sine waves for five seconds after they had been removed from view but that performance became impaired much sooner with less predictable tracks.

A second way of examining anticipation involves comparing pursuit tracking and compensatory tracking. In the former task, subjects see both the target and their response cursor. In the latter, they only see their performance error (i.e. the difference between target and response cursor) and they are instructed to keep this error at zero. Poulton (1952a) found that the lag between target and the response (and, hence, tracking error) was greater in compensatory than in pursuit tracking. He argued that this difference arises because subjects are able to anticipate the target track in pursuit tasks. Pew, Duffendack and Fensch (1967) developed this paradigm. They required subjects to follow sine waves and found that the difference between pursuit and compensatory tracking was negligible at low signal frequencies (e.g. 0.1Hz). On the basis of this they suggested that at low frequencies performance does not involve anticipation but is based on error correction mechanisms alone.

The third means of examining anticipation is much more direct. It involves a step-tracking paradigm in which signals jump from one position to another at discrete points in time. Subjects are instructed to use the time interval between jumps to anticipate the position of the next signal by moving their response cursor to where they think that signal will be. The degree to which they succeed in doing this can be measured directly. During the signal's appearance they can correct any errors in their anticipation. Poulton (1952b) appears to have been the first to use this type of technique but it was employed more extensively in a series of studies by Noble, Trumbo and their colleagues (e.g. Trumbo, Noble, Cross and Ulrich, 1965).

Early work on anticipation using these three paradigms was oriented towards practical issues. How good are people at anticipating? Can they learn to anticipate tracks that have some uncertainty or randomness built into them? In other words, can they extract statistical properties of the input from their experience with it? How long does such learning take? In fact, these issues are of some interest to those currently concerned with examining and developing Bernstein's ideas on anticipation. The difference is that nowadays we are interested in the underlying processing ability to anticipate. If people can anticipate uncertain tracks, how do they do it?

Poulton (1957c) argued from his own work that subjects are able to extract statistical properties of the input from their experience of it in step-tracking tasks, use these properties to predict required movements and thereby reduce their performance error. However, Trumbo et al. (1965) found that although subjects could anticipate steps in fully determined tracks made up of a fixed repeating sequence of 12 signal positions, anticipation of partially determined tracks (in which only alternate signals in a sequence of 12 were repeated and the rest were random) was very poor. In fact, subjects were no better at predicting signal positions in a track partially determined in this way than at anticipating totally random signal positions.

I suspect that this result may have occurred not because subjects were poor at predicting *per se* but because they had to support a much greater load in working memory for successful prediction in the alternating random-fixed position condition than in the totally fixed track condition. For instance, given that the fixed sequence of signal positions 11, 4, 1, 10, 4, 7, 1, 15, 2 has been stored in long-term memory and that the current stimulus is 1, it is only necessary to remember that the previous signal was 7 in order to predict that the next one will be 15. But given the alternating fixed-random sequence 11, R, 1, R, 4, R, 1, R, 2 has been stored in long-term memory and that the current stimulus is 1 as before, it is necessary to remember that the previous signal but one was four in order to predict that the next but one will be two. Thus, both past signals and predictions have to be remembered for longer than they do when the sequence is fixed and both memory traces may be subject to interference from intervening signals and movements.

In Harvey's (1988) experiment, no fixed sequences had to be stored in long-term memory and the working memory load necessary for successful prediction was kept low. Signals moved between windows displayed horizontally on a screen. The position of a given signal depended only on its two immediate predecessors. For the purposes of generating the signal sequence, the central window was designated zero, those increasingly to the left were increasingly negative and those increasingly to the right were increasingly positive. The position of the next signal (x_t) depended on the previous two (x_{t-1}, x_{t-2}) according to the equation

$$x_t = .707\, x_{t-1} - .5\, x_{t-2} + e$$

where e was a normally distributed random error with mean of zero and standard deviation of 2.6. Signals lasted for one second and there was a one second interval between them. Subjects were instructed to move a cursor during this interval to the position at which they thought the next signal would appear. Over the session their anticipation of the next signal became increasingly successful. Was this because they had learned the statistical properties of the signal sequence? Possibly. Halfway through and at the end of the experiment, subjects had been asked to feed in signal positions such that their simulated signal sequence would be as similar as possible to the ones they had been tracking. The equations describing these simulated sequences tended to have the same general form as the one used to generate the tracks. Furthermore, the equations describing the sequences simulated at the end of the experiment were more similar to the track-generating algorithm than the equations describing those simulated half-way through. But this, in itself, does not indicate that the statistical properties extracted by the subjects were time domain parameters of the sort employed by the experimenter to generate the tracks (and used above to extend schema theory to account for performance in this type of task). The tracks produced by the algorithm were non-deterministically periodic. Subjects could have been using frequency domain parameters for their simulations. As a matter of fact, there have been a number of recent suggestions that both movements (Gallistel, 1980; Pribram, Sharafat and Beekman, 1984) and temporal changes in the environment (Kruse, Stadler, Vogt and Wehner, 1983) are represented in the brain in frequency analysed form. Both Pew (1974) and Stadler and Wehner (1985) feel that anticipation in tracking tasks is based on frequency-domain analyses. However, their views await experimental test.

Are muscles like springs?

When muscles are controlled by function generators, what sort of physical system results? Following Asatryan and Feldman (1965), many authors (e.g. Cooke, 1980; Nichols and Houk, 1976; Sakitt, 1980) have suggested that it can be regarded as a mass-spring system. The position of a limb is governed by the relative stiffness of agonist and antagonist muscles. If stiffness of an extensor muscle decreases relative to that of a flexor, then joint angle will decrease. This mass-spring model predicts that a limb will reach its target position from any starting position without the use of feedback and despite external perturbations during the movement. Experiments in which simple movements have been examined in deafferented animals have confirmed that this is the case (Bizzi, Polit and Morasso, 1976; Polit and Bizzi, 1979). Testing the prediction in humans is not as easy because they cannot be experimentally deafferented. However, Kelso (1977) found that finger movements were not significantly impaired when a wrist block was used to induce ischaemia and thereby remove feedback.

Three brief comments should be made. First, support for the mass-spring model depended (in the above studies) on failure to reject the null hypothesis. Given that the statistical power of the experiments was low, this support was easy to obtain (Corcos, Agarwal and Gottlieb, 1985). (Of course, there are those (e.g. Meehl, 1967) who argue that identifying the theory of interest with the null rather than with the alternative hypothesis is the hallmark of a mature science – see Oakes (1986) for a discussion of the issue.) Second, ischaemic blocks are commonly used as a means of experimentally inducing pain. An increase in pain may affect assessment of whether feedback has been eliminated while simultaneously counteracting the effects of any reduction in feedback that does occur (Greer and Harvey, 1987). Third, the mass-spring model may not describe the characteristics of movements more complex than those examined in the studies cited above (Viviani and Cenzato, 1985).

In fact there are many different muscle characteristics that the nervous system could alter in order to ensure that movements are made as required. Stein (1982) assessed evidence concerning control of muscle force, length, velocity, stiffness and viscosity and argued that it was insufficient to allow the conclusion that any one of these was solely responsible for movement. Although Schmidt originally thought that schemata specify how the forces generated by muscles change over time (Shapiro and Schmidt, 1982), there is no necessary link between schema theory and this impulse timing model. Schemata could just as well specify the parameters (e.g. stiffness, viscosity) of a mass-spring system. However, Shapiro and Schmidt (1982) considered that the mass-spring model provides problems for schema theory because it suggests that initial conditions do not have to be inserted into schemata to obtain motor parameters – only the required outcome does. In fact, it only demonstrates that initial position does not have to be inserted into the schema. Initial conditions other than initial position may have to be. This is particularly clear in tasks in which isometric muscle contraction affects movement outcome (Harvey and Greer, 1982). For example, skiers use their legs as shock absorbers. In the same way that toughness of vehicle suspension should increase with the load carried and with the unevenness of the terrain, so should the absolute stiffness in both the agonist and antagonist muscles of skiers' legs. In other words, schemata may use required outcome to specify the relative stiffness of agonist and antagonist muscles and use environmental condition (e.g. unevenness of terrain, load carried) to ensure that this relative stiffness is expressed at the appropriate absolute level.

Is knowledge of results necessary for learning?

The relation between response outcome and knowledge of results (KR) in schema theory is unclear. Response outcome could be 'what happened in the environment...this information usually *comes from* knowledge of results or feedback' (Schmidt, 1982b, p. 226) or that 'response outcome *is* the actual outcome or knowledge of results (KR)' (Shapiro and Schmidt, 1982, p. 116, italics mine). In any case, 'the individual stores the outcome of the movement in the environment in terms of KR' (Schmidt, 1982a, p. 594) and so this outcome is potentially a verbalisation (Schmidt, 1975). In other words, subjects' internal representations of KR and outcome are not separate. What happens when KR is not explicitly given? An error labelling schema formed from prior associations between actual KR and sensory feedback is employed. It enables sensory feedback to be used to obtain an estimate of the KR that would have been given. This implicit KR is then taken to represent movement outcome. Thus:

sensory feedback → estimated KR = estimated outcome

In this way, Schmidt's model allows learning to occur in the absence of KR once the relation between KR and sensory feedback has been established. There is good evidence that learning can occur in these circumstances (e.g. Zelaznik, Shapiro and Newell, 1978).

Now consider a singer who is learning the laryngeal manoeuvres necessary for precise control of the pitch and quality of the voice (Harvey, 1985). The outcome of a movement is a particular configuration of the larynx. However, the singer cannot verbalise what this configuration is and neither can her trainer. Of course, direct but largely non-conscious information about it is available to the singer via laryngeal proprioceptors. Exhalation through this laryngeal configuration produces vocal characteristics heard by the singer. Knowledge of results will tell her the extent to which these correspond to those her trainer specifies as correct. Thus, in this example, outcome is not verbalisable and its relation to KR is mediated by sensory feedback. Thus:

KR → estimated sensory error → estimated outcome

There is no reason to suppose that this relationship between KR and response outcome is restricted to singing. It could, for instance, apply to limb movement. It implies that learning should be possible in the absence of KR even when a relation between KR and sensory feedback has not been previously established. However, there must be some sensory feedback that reflects movement outcome. In their review of this issue, Salmoni, Schmidt and Walter (1984) suggest that the data are consistent with this notion. Learning can occur in tasks when KR is not present and never has been present as long as 'some other form of feedback intrinsic to the task has provided sufficient information for learning' (p. 361). Of course, there is no need for subjects to be consciously aware of this feedback. Harvey, Garwood and Palencia's (1987) subjects improved their singing performance in the absence of KR and in the absence of any ability to monitor consciously errors in their own performance.

Summary

One of the common intellectual threads running through much of cognitive psychology is the notion that behaviour depends on learning, using and modifying rules. At its most general, schema theory comprises the view that (1) motor learning is like a regression procedure for extracting a rule from data and (2) motor control involves a procedure similar to the use of a regression rule for prediction. Thus schema theory embodies the cognitive approach to motor control. To persuade you that this theoretical orientation will become ever more important, I would like to draw out four general points from what I have said.

(1) Ecological psychologists have argued that their approach is non-cognitive – and so it may be for the limited set of situations that they have studied. However, if they are to develop their ideas to account for more complex, flexible behaviours, then they will have to make use of schema notions to explain how individuals specify the critical values of perceptual parameters. Either a cognitive ecological psychology must develop or else ecological psychologists must maintain restrictions on the topics they study.

(2) Up to now, most tests of schema theory have actually been tests of the implicit and explicit assumptions of a specific version of the theory proposed by Schmidt (1975). Some of these tests may have failed because a different version of schema theory is correct. Other specific versions of the theory need to be formulated and investigated experimentally. The theory has great scope. It is easy to extend it to account for tracking behaviour and for the role of anticipation in movement. However, if these extensions are to be useful and testable, they must be computational models and couched in the signal processing terms that are becoming increasingly prevalent in othr areas of cognitive psychology (for example, see Bruce, this volume).

(3) Muscles may well behave like springs. However, this does not affect

the viability of schema theory. Schemata may specify the relative stiffness of agonist and antagonist muscles. If such parameters are specified, certain types of initial conditions may still have to be included in schemata to ensure that required outcomes are attained.

(4)   In at least some tasks, learning appears to take place without knowledge of results ever being given. There are various ways in which schema theory could account for this type of finding but which is the most appropriate remains unclear at present.

References

Alain, C., Lalonde, C. and Sarrazin, C. (1983), 'Decision-making and information processing in squash competition', in H. Reider, K. Bos, H. Meckling and K. Reischle (eds), *Motorik und Beuregungsforschung (Motor Learning and Movement Behaviour)*. Verlag Karl Hofman: Schorndorf.

Alain, C., Sarrazin, C. and Lacombe, D. (1985), 'The use of subjective expected values in decision-making in sport', in *Sport and the Elite Performer*. Human Kinetics Publishers: Champaign, Illinois.

Allport, D. A. (1980), 'Patterns and actions: cognitive mechanisms are content-specific', in G. Claxton (ed.), *Cognitive Psychology: New Directions*. Routledge & Kegan Paul: London.

Anokhin, P. K. (1969), 'Cybernetics and the integrative activity of the brain', in M. Cole and I. Maltzman (eds), *A Handbook of Contemporary Soviet Psychology*. Basic Books: New York.

Asatryan, D. G. and Feldman, A. G. (1965), 'Biophysics of complex systems and mathematical models. Functional tuning of nervous system with control of movement or maintenance of steady posture. I. Mechanographic analysis of the work of the joint on execution of a postural task', *Biophysics, 10*, 925-35.

Bernstein, N. A. (1967). *The Coordination and Regulation of Movement*. Pergamon Press: London.

Bizzi, E., Polit, A. and Morasso, P. (1976), 'Mechanisms underlying achievement of final head position', *Journal of Neurophysiology, 39*, 435-44.

Broadbent, D. E. (1958), *Perception and Communication*. Pergamon Press: London.

Cooke, J. D. (1980). 'The organization of simple, skilled movements', in G. E. Stelmach and J. Requin (eds), *Tutorials in Motor Behaviour*. North-Holland: Amsterdam.

Corcos, D. M., Agarwal, G. C. and Gottlieb, G. L. (1985), 'A note on accepting the null hypothesis: problems with respect to the mass-spring and pulse-step models of movement control', *Journal of Motor Behavior, 17*, 481-7.

Dietz, V. and Noth, J. L. (1978), Preinnervation and stretch responses of triceps bracchii in man falling with and without visual control', *Brain Research, 142*, 576-9.

Dixon, N. F. (1971), *Subliminal Perception: The Nature of the Controversy*. McGraw Hill: London.

Dixon, N. F. (1981), *Preconscious processing*. Wiley: New York.

Fitch, H. L., Tuller, B. and Turvey, M. T. (1982), 'The Bernstein perspective: III. Tuning of coordinative structures with special reference to perception', in J. A. S. Kelso (ed.), *Human Motor Behaviour: An Introduction*. Erlbaum: Hillsdale, New Jersey.

Frohlich, D. M. and Elliot, J. M. (1984), 'The schemata representation of effector function underlying perceptual-motor skill', *Journal of Motor Behavior, 16*, 40-60.

Gallistel, C. R. (1980), *The Organization of Action: A New Synthesis.* Erlbaum: Hillsdale, New Jersey.

Gersen, R. F. and Thomas, J. R. (1977), 'Schema theory and practice variability within a neo-Piagetian framework', *Journal of Motor Behavior, 9,* 127-34.

Gibson, J. J. (1979), *The Ecological Approach to Visual Perception.* Houghton-Mifflin: Boston.

Gottsdanker, R. M. (1952a), 'The accuracy of prediction motion', *Journal of Experimental Psychology, 43,* 36-46.

Gottsdanker, R. M. (1952b), 'Prediction motion with and without vision', *American Journal of Psychology, 65,* 533-43.

Gottsdanker, R. M. (1955), 'A further study of prediction motion', *American Journal of Psychology, 68,* 432-7.

Greer, K. and Harvey, N. (1987), 'Pain induced by nerve compression blocks affects voluntary movements and assessment of peripheral nerve ischaemia', *Human Movement Science, 6,* 17-36.

Guilford, J. P. and Fruchter, B. (1973), *Fundamental Statistics in Psychology and Education.* McGraw Hill: New York.

Harvey, N. (1985), 'Vocal control in singing: a cognitive approach', in P. Howell, I. Cross and R. West (eds), *Music Structure and Cognition.* Academic Press: London.

Harvey, N. (1988), 'Are models of the future used to anticipate targets in tracking tasks?', in A. Colley and J. Beech (eds), *Cognition and Action in Skilled Behaviour.* North-Holland, Amsterdam.

Harvey, N., Garwood, J. and Palencia, M. (1987), 'Vocal matching of pitch intervals: learning and transfer effects', *Psychology of Music, 15,* 90-106.

Harvey, N. and Greer, K. (1980), 'Action: mechanisms of motor control', in G. Claxton (ed.), *Cognitive Psychology: New Directions.* Routledge & Kegan Paul: London.

Harvey, N. and Greer, K. (1982), 'Force and stiffness: further considerations', *The Behavioral and Brain Sciences, 5,* 547-8.

Hinton, G. (1984), 'Parallel computations for controlling an arm', *Journal of Motor Behavior, 16,* 171-94.

Holding, D. H. (ed.), (1981), *Human Skills.* Wiley: New York.

Hughes, B. G. and Stelmach, G. E. (In press), 'On Bernstein as a contributor to cognitive theories of motor behavior', *Journal of Movement Science.*

Johnson, P. (1984), 'The acquisition of skill', in M. M. Smyth and A. M. Wing (eds), *The Psychology of Movement.* Academic Press: London.

Kelso, J. A. S. (1977), 'Motor control mechanisms underlying human movement reproduction', *Journal of Experimental Psychology: Human Perception and Performance, 3,* 529-43.

Kelso, J. A. S. (ed.), (1982), *Human Motor Behavior: An Introduction.* Erlbaum: Hillsdale, New Jersey.

Kruse, P., Stadler, M., Vogt, S. and Wehner, T. (1983), 'Raum-Zeitliche Integration wahrgenormmener Bewegung durch Frequenzanalyse', *Gestalt Theory, 5,* 83-113.

Lee, D. N. (1976), 'A theory of visual control of braking based on information about time-to-collision', *Perception, 5,* 437-59.

Lee, D. N. and Lishman, J. R. (1974), 'Visual proprioceptive control of stance', *Journal of Human Movement Studies, 1,* 87-95.

Lee, D. N., Lishman, J. R. and Thomson, J. A. (1982), 'Regulation of gait in long-jumping', *Journal of Experimental Psychology: Human Perception and Performance, 8,* 448-59.

Lee, D. N. and Reddish, P. E. (1981), 'Plummeting gannets: a paradigm of ecological optics', *Nature, 293,* 293-4.

Lee, D. N., Young, D. S., Reddish, P. E., Lough, S. and Clayton, T. M. H. (1983), 'Visual timing in hitting and accelerating ball', *Quarterly Journal of Experimental Psychology, 35A*, 333-46.

Linn, R. L. and Wertz, C. E. (1982), 'Measurement error in regression', in G. Kernen (ed.), *Statistical and Methodological Issues in Psychology and Social Sciences Research*. Erlbaum: Hillsdale, New Jersey.

Marr, D. (1982), *Vision*. W. H. Freeman: San Francisco.

McCracken, H. D. and Stelmach, G. E. (1977), 'A test of the schema theory of discrete motor learning', *Journal of Motor Behavior, 9*, 193-201.

Meehl, P. E. (1967), 'Theory-testing in psychology and physics: a methodological approach', *Philosophy of Science, 34*, 103-15.

Miller, G. A., Galanter, E. and Pribram, K. H. (1960), *Plans and the Structure of Behaviour*. Holt, Rinehart & Winston: New York.

Neisser, U. (1976), *Cognition and Reality: Principles and Implications of Cognitive Psychology*. W. H. Freeman: San Francisco.

Neisser, U. (1985), 'The role of invariant structures in the control of movement', in M. Frese and J. Sabini (eds), *Goal Directed Behavior: The Concept of Action in Psychology*. Erlbaum: Hillsdale, New Jersey.

Newell, A. (1973), 'Production systems: models of control structures', in W. G. Chase (ed.), *Visual Information Processing*. Academic Press: New York.

Newell, K. M. (1974), 'Knowledge of results and motor learning', *Journal of Motor Behavior, 6*, 235-44.

Newell, K. M. and Barclay, C. R. (1982), 'Developing knowledge about action', in J. A. S. Kelso and J. E. Clark (eds), *The Development of Movement Control and Co-ordination*. Wiley: New York.

Newell, K. M. and Shapiro, D. C. (1976), 'Variability of practice and transfer of training: some evidence towards a schema view of motor learning', *Journal of Motor Behavior, 8*, 233-43.

Nichols, T. R. and Houk, J. C. (1976), 'The improvement of linearity and the regulation of stiffness that results from the actions of the stretch reflex', *Journal of Neurophysiology, 39*, 119-42.

Norman, D. A. and Rumelhart, D. E. (eds) (1975), *Explorations in Cognition*. W. H. Freeman: San Francisco.

Oakes, M. (1986), *Statistical Inference: A Commentary for the Social and Behavioural Sciences*. Wiley: New York.

Pew, R. W. (1974), 'Human perceptual-motor performance', in B. H. Kantowitz (ed.), *Human Information Processing: Tutorials in Performance and Cognition*. Erlbaum: Hillsdale, New Jersey.

Pew, R. W., Duffendack, J. C. and Fensch, L. K. (1967), 'Sine-wave tracking revisited', *IEEE Transactions on Human Factors in Electronics, 8*, 130-4.

Polit, A. and Bizzi, E. (1979), 'Characteristics of motor programs underlying arm movements', *Journal of Neurophysiology, 42*, 183-94.

Poulton, E. C. (1952a), 'Perceptual anticipation in tracking with two-pointer and one-pointer displays', *British Journal of Psychology, 43*, 222-9.

Poulton, E. C. (1952b), 'The basis of perceptual anticipation in tracking', *British Journal of Psychology, 43*, 295-302.

Poulton, E. C. (1957a), 'On prediction in skilled movements', *Psychological Bulletin, 54*, 467-78.

Poulton, E. C. (1957b), 'On the stimulus and response in pursuit tracking', *Journal of Experimental Psychology, 53*, 189-94.

Poulton, E. C. (1957c), 'Learning the statistical properties of the input in pursuit tracking', *Journal of Experimental Psychology, 54*, 28-32.

Pribram, K. H., Sharafat, A. and Beekman, G. J. (1984), 'Frequency encoding in motor systems', in H. T. A. Whiting (ed.), *Human Motor Actions: Bernstein Reassessed*. North-Holland: Amsterdam.

Reed, E. S. (1982), 'An outline of a theory of action systems', *Journal of Motor Behavior*, *14*, 98-134.

Requin, J., Semjen, A and Bonnet, M. (1984), 'Bernstein's purposeful brain', in H. T. A. Whiting (ed.), *Human Motor Actions: Bernstein Reassessed*. North-Holland: Amsterdam.

Rossum, J. H. A. van. (1980), 'The schema notion in motor learning theory: some persistent problems in research', *Journal of Human Movement Studies*, *6*, 269-79.

Rumelhart, D., McClelland, J. L. and the PDP Research Group (1986), *Parallel Distributed Processing: Explorations in the Microstructure of Cognition*. MIT Press: Cambridge, Massachusetts.

Sakitt, B. (1980), 'A spring model and equivalent neural network for arm posture control', *Biological Cybernetics*, *37*, 227-34.

Salmoni, A. W., Schmidt, R. A. and Walter, C. B. (1984), 'Knowledge of results and motor learning: a review and a critical reappraisal', *Psychological Bulletin*, *95*, 335-86.

Salzman, E. L. and Kelso, J. A. S. (1983), 'Toward a dynamic account of motor memory and control', in R. A. Magill (ed.), *Memory and Control of Action*. North-Holland: Amsterdam.

Schmidt, R. A. (1968), 'Anticipation and timing in human performance', *Psychological Bulletin*, *70*, 631-46.

Schmidt, R. A. (1975), 'A schema theory of discrete motor skill learning', *Psychological Review*, *82*, 225-66.

Schmidt, R. A. (1976), 'The schema as a solution to some persistent problems in motor learning theory', in G. E. Stelmach (ed.), *Motor Control: Issues and Trends*. Academic Press: New York.

Schmidt, R. A. (1982a), *'Motor Control and Learning: A Behavioral Emphasis*. Human Kinetics: Champaign, Illinois.

Schmidt, R. A. (1982b), 'The schema concept', in J. A. S. Kelso (ed.), *Human Motor Behavior: An Introduction*. Erlbaum: Hillsdale, New Jersey.

Shapiro, D. C. and Schmidt, R. A. (1982), 'The schema theory: recent evidence and developmental implications', in J. A. S. Kelso and J. E. Clark (eds), *The Development of Movement Control and Co-ordination*. Wiley: New York.

Shaw, R. E., Turvey, M. T. and Mace, W. (1982), 'Ecological psychology: the consequences of a commitment to realism', in W. Weimer and D. Palermo (eds), *Cognition and the Symbolic Processes (II)*. Erlbaum: Hillsdale, New Jersey.

Smyth, M. M. and Wing, A. M. (eds) (1984), *The Psychology of Human Movement*. Academic Press: London.

Stadler, M. and Wehner, T. (1985), 'Anticipation as a basic principle in goal directed action', in M. Frese and J. Sabini (eds), *Goal Directed Behavior: The Concept of Action in Psychology*. Erlbaum: Hillsdale, New Jersey.

Stein, R. B. (1982), 'What muscle variable(s) does the nervous system control in limb movements?' *The Behavioral and Brain Sciences*, *4*, 535-77.

Todd, J. T. (1981), 'Visual information about moving objects', *Journal of Experimental Psychology: Human Perception and Performance*, *7*, 795-810.

Trumbo, D., Noble, M., Cross, K. and Ulrich, L. (1965), 'Task predictability in the organising, acquisition and retention of tracking skill', *Journal of Experimental Psychology*, *70*, 252-63.

Turvey, M. T. and Kugler, P. N. (1984), 'An ecological approach to perception and action', in H. T. A. Whiting (ed.), *Human Motor Actions: Bernstein Reassessed*. North-Holland: Amsterdam.

Viviani, P. and Cenzato. M. (1985), 'Segmentation and coupling in complex movements', *Journal of Experimental Psychology: Human Perception and Performance, 11*, 828-45.

Whiting, H. T. A. (1984), *Human Motor Actions: Bernstein Reassessed*. North-Holland: Amsterdam.

Zelaznik, H. N., Shapiro, D. C. and Newell, K. M. (1978), 'On the structure of motor recognition memory', *Journal of Motor Behavior, 10*, 313-23.

4 Memory research: past mistakes and future prospects

Peter Morris

'It is a capital mistake to theorise before you have all the evidence. It biases the judgement.' Sherlock Holmes in *A Study in Scarlet* (Conan Doyle, 1887).

One major feature of the study of memory throughout much of the past hundred years is that it has proceeded from strong theoretical assumptions that were initially developed upon a very small base of empirical evidence. These theoretical assumptions have then largely driven the subsequent research on memory. The result has been that we have concentrated upon very specialised aspects of memory which may have little relevance to the way memory is used in everyday life. Two examples of this theory-driven research are (1) the assumption that memorising is essentially the developing of new associations, and (2) the short-term and long-term memory distinction. In both cases the theories were developed long before any systematic effort had been made to survey just when and how we use our memories. The associationist account of memory comes with a pedigree stretching back at least to Aristotle, but based always on the speculations of philosophers. I do not want to assert that either of these theoretical examples is wholly misguided, although both can be denied without requiring too much reinterpretation or ignoring of the available evidence. What I do want to point out is that the acceptance of these theoretical positions then determined the framework for many years of experimental research which in retrospect seems blinkered in the questions that it did and did not consider. Once the associationist view was adopted it seemed sensible to introduce the methods that became the stock-in-trade of the verbal learning psychologist who presented lists of unrelated words or nonsense syllables with the object of studying how varying the repetitions, the similarity of the items and so on would influence the learning of new associations. In the study of short- and long-term memory the search was on for the capacity and type of coding in short-term memory, the way information was lost, and so on. To many non-psychologists these seemed strange questions to be dominating the focus of research, but they were the obvious ones to those working in the area, and each new result stimulated a further set of questions within the accepted framework (see Baddeley, 1976, for a good review of both areas of research).

Currently few people studying memory would find much to draw upon from the research on the learning of new associations or that distinguishing between short- and long-term memory, even though both probably captured kernels of truth within their own assumptions. Why? The answer is that more and more people stopped asking questions within the old frameworks and began wondering just what our memories are for. When do we use them? Why do we have them? In this chapter I want to illustrate how the new directions in the study of memory can be seen as filling the gaps and replacing the inadequacies of more traditional approaches to the study of memory.

This re-framing of research by asking about the functions of our memories is well illustrated by Baddeley's research, where he has remoulded the study of short-term memory by asking what role short-term remembering may play, and then elaborating the concept of working memory (e.g. Baddeley, 1983). However, perhaps the best statement of the importance of these questions was made by Neisser (1978) in the opening paper at the first Practical Aspects of Memory Conference. He asked 'What do we use the past *for*?' He was able to produce a list of several different ways in which we use our memories based upon an examination of his own experience. He pointed out, first, that everyone uses the past to define themselves. Secondly, that one frequently recalls past experiences in search of some sort of self-improvement. Then, on other occasions, personal memories achieve a kind of public importance when, for example, legal testimony is required. Another feature of memory is that we learn many things secondhand through friends, acquaintances and literature. Neisser pointed out that memory is involved in many activities in daily life. We make plans and have to carry them out, we put things down and need to recall where we left them, we are given directions and must follow them to reach our destination, and we meet people and need to pick up the relationship where we left off. In the next section of the chapter I want to enlarge upon the ways in which the associationist, list-learning tradition that arose from the work of Ebbinghaus ignored these important aspects of memory, and how, in recent years, first steps have been taken to rectify this omission. The result has been to make the study of memory vastly more interesting and challenging. Here, however, I want to point out that the limitations imposed by the rigid theoretical positions of the earlier part of the century became obvious only when people began to ask what really happens when we remember things. Neisser's question – What do we use the past for? – directs our attention towards the data that the theories need to explain.

Psychology, in general, is an unusual science in that the leap towards strong theoretical positions and intense study of specialised topics often takes place before very many relevant facts have been discovered. Of course, the idea that all scientific data gathering is theory-driven has been popular in the philosophy of science. In practice, however, the creation of a good theory requires a good supply of facts which will help both to stimulate the theorist's thinking and delimit the range of possibilities she or he has at their command. Most of the important theoretical developments in the natural sciences have followed the acquisition over many years of empirical facts to be explained by the resulting theory. Two famous examples are the way in which Tycho Brahe's observations of planetary movements were necessary for Kepler's calculation of the elliptical movement of the planets, and secondly how Darwin's painstaking collection of evidence led to the development of the theory of evolution. In most sciences it has been fairly clear what the problem is, and what its range and limitations are before useful theories have been developed. In psychology we have often sneered at the collection of empirical generalisations about the way that people behave and it is still common for journals to reject papers that describe interesting empirical observations about memory on the grounds that they make insufficient theoretical contributions. This low regard for the data for which the theories must be explanations has, I believe, seriously hampered the development of psychology. In the study of memory we seem to be breaking through that disregard for facts which are, in the last analysis, what the subject is about. We are beginning to look at the world of everyday life to see what it is that we have to explain.

We will probably find that before we can produce good, usable theories of the way memory functions in its many roles we will have to develop at least a sketch of a 'natural history' of memory phenomena. Without that we will not be able to choose between competing theories nor develop theories which are truly appropriate. Nor will we concentrate upon what will be really useful in our understanding of the way memory functions.

The fact that we are only now beginning to sketch in the borders of such a natural history is the result of the importance throughout most of this century of the Ebbinghaus tradition.

The Ebbinghaus tradition

It is just over 100 years since Ebbinghaus (1885) published one of the most influential books in experimental psychology. Ebbinghaus' book is fascinating because it reveals the author's interest in a wide range of memory phenomena. It reports, for example, his studies of his own memorising of verses from Don Juan. It would, therefore, be quite wrong to blame Ebbinghaus for all that followed in the tradition which grew out of his initial work. In the years subsequent to the publication of Ebbinghaus' classic there were many important preliminary investigations of real world remembering. For example, Colegrove (1899), collected detailed recollections after 33 years of the situations in which people heard of Lincoln's assassination. Cattell (1895) studied memory for the weather and Stern (1904) was laying the groundwork for research on eyewitness testimony. However, the assumptions underlying Ebbinghaus' main work were ones which fitted so well with those of the behaviourists when the latter came to dominate psychology during the early and middle years of the twentieth century, that the study of memory was for many years based upon the learning of lists of nonsense syllables or unrelated words in laboratory conditions. I want to review the ways in which many of the assumptions of this research have turned out to be misleading, and to see how in recent years there has been a rapid return to those topics which interested Colegrove, Cattell and Stern.

Ebbinghaus' research was based on a strong theoretical position. He followed many philosophers in assuming that learning builds up through the establishment of new associations. Given this assumption, it seemed obvious that the right procedure was to study completely new associations so that the misleading effects of earlier learned associations would not distort the research findings. This philosophy was incorporated into the mainstream study of memory, or 'verbal learning' as it was more respectably called during the behaviourist era. The traditional verbal learning experiment of the 1950s involved the learning of lists of nonsense syllables paired with adjectives. The testing involved presenting for (usually) two seconds the initial nonsense syllable and requiring the subject within those two seconds to report the adjective with which it had been paired. Learning was tedious, slow and easily forgotten. (See, for example, Postman and Keppel, 1969, for examples of some of the best research in this tradition).

Let us look at the factors which such research eliminates or controls and then consider its assumptions and its implications. The use of nonsense syllables and adjectives that have no meaningful relationships within the lists means that prior knowledge and experience is minimised or, if possible, eliminated. Subjects have no interest in what is to be learnt, but this is not regarded by the experimenter as important since in this way possible variations through interest are being controlled. The activity at the time of learning is limited both by the time for which the individual items are presented and by the nature of the material itself. Any memorising strategies which the subjects might attempt to adopt are equally minimised both by the brief presentation and, often, by instructions to the subjects to avoid them. In any case, the material appears so unrealistic that suitable ways of memorising it do not spring to mind. The learning and retrieval conditions and the material to be memorised are standardised and very similar in most of these experiments. Finally, notice how the cues available for retrieval are normally limited to the items with which the word or nonsense syllable was paired and to the conditions (i.e. the same memory drum, the same room), in which the original memorising had taken place.

All this restriction on the conditions of learning was imposed for a very sensible reason. It was not that the experimenters believed that the variables which they controlled were unimportant but rather that they recognised that to understand and experimentally investigate memory processes they needed to control extraneous variables and carefully manipulate the ones which were believed to be important. Nevertheless, the question occurred to most experimental subjects, and even to some experimenters, of whether this devotion to experimental control meant the losing of the metaphorical baby with the extraneous bath of water.

One key assumption of the verbal learning tradition was that there are basic memory processes which were being sampled in the experiments and which could then be identified under more natural conditions. It was unusual for individual differences in memorising performance to be considered. This probably reflected the belief that there were basic memory processes which everyone possessed and which were being carefully unravelled in the controlled experimentation. Unfortunately, as we shall see later in the chapter, both these assumptions of basic memory processes and the unimportance of individual differences were misguided.

Finally we should note implications that follow from the way that the experiments were conducted. They are that memorising is often intentional, and that there are easily discriminable stages of learning and retrieval. So the memory experiments were based upon a clearcut difference between the learning and the retrieval stage.

Criticisms of the Ebbinghaus tradition

The new directions in memory research that have been developing in recent years depend upon reversing most of the Ebbinghaus tradition. One might almost call the new approach the 'Suahgnibbe view', if only it were easier to pronounce!

First, consider the implication that memorising is intentional and involves separate and discrete learning and retrieval stages. The misleading nature of such an implication becomes clear immediately when we ask the question – what do we use our memories for? (Cf. Neisser, 1978, 1982.) Without our knowledge of the past we would not be able to make sense of our present experience nor could we predict what was likely to happen in the future to guide our actions. Once we recognise that our memories are for making sense of the present and for predicting the future it becomes obvious that for them to be of any use they must be continuously encoding new information about our current experience and retrieving any potentially useful information about what has happened to us in the past. Thus, our memories are a continuously exploited resource and the system of memory functioning that we must have evolved will be one which continuously enters new information and is always interrogating what is already stored for suitable, usable past information. When, for example, you are reading this book you are continuously drawing from your memory the meaning of the words, conventions about the way they will be put together and you are interpreting the whole experience through higher order structures which give you a framework for understanding what you read (see, for example, Garnham's chapter in the present volume; Schank, 1982, and Smyth, Morris, Ellis and Levy, 1987). All this depends upon what you can retrieve from memory. Without your memory you could tell no difference between what you read here and an output from some random letter generator. Also, you will be able to remember details of what you have just read as a spin-off from the process of making sense of the page in front of you. Of course, it still makes sense to consider separately the entering of information into memory and its retrieval from store. However, what is obvious is that those entries into memory which come about through our deliberate attempts to memorise are a very tiny fraction of the actual entries that we will have in memory. Similarly the number of times we retrieve deliberately from memory are tiny compared to those which happen automatically as part of servicing the comprehension processes of the cognitive system. One incidental consequence of this is that there is no fear of overloading memory through deliberate memorisation, perhaps for exams, because the amount that is encoded on these occasions is trivial compared to what is coded automatically with or without our intentions to learn. Another implication of the role of memory in comprehension is that the form in which information is stored must be appropriate to the way comprehension occurs, and be rapidly retrievable. The units of memory (if there are such things) will normally be small packages of information. When we recall longer sequences (tell stories, jokes, give evidence) it will be a matter of stringing together these memory packages, with all the opportunities for errors that this implies, together with the need to mould the whole into a coherent account (e.g. Bartlett, 1932; Neisser, 1981). (For further discussion of the role of memory in cognition, see Smyth et al., 1987.)

There are many specific memory skills

One of the major assumptions of the Ebbinghaus tradition was that the type of memory being studied by the verbal learning, paired associate experiment was sufficiently typical of normal memory processes to mean that the results could be generalised to most other situations. Unfortunately, however, while it may be true that there are certain generalisations which it is reasonable to make about most memory processes, the evidence suggests that there is so much variability in the type of material, the types of processes, the strategies and the processing skills upon which people can draw when they tackle memorising in different situations that the way in which information is entered into memory will often be very different from one situation to another. This makes drawing generalisations about memory very difficult. In other words, the processes that underlie memorising people's faces may be quite different to those used when remembering stories and these again may be different to those for conversations, for intentions to do things, for the geography of the world around us, and so on. Even learning two types of list may involve different sorts of memory processes.

The evidence for the frequent independence of memory abilities between different tasks comes from the study of individual differences. As I pointed out earlier, the investigation of individual differences in memorising was regarded as largely unnecessary for most of the early and middle years of the twentieth century. However, in more recent years it has become more respectable to examine and compare the performance of individuals on different tasks. If the same individuals when tested on a number of tasks turn out to have quite different abilities upon those tasks then it becomes difficult to believe that there is a general memory principle underlying their performance. So, for example, if someone who is good at memorising faces turns out to be no better than average at recalling the plots of stories that they have read and are worse than most people at remembering to do things then, as in other psychometric studies, we should begin to consider these as separate abilities rather than as reflecting one underlying process.

Perhaps the strongest evidence that memory skills are frequently independent came from a large study by Underwood, Boruch and Malmi (1978). They tested 200 students on 31 different laboratory memory tasks. They took special care to make the memory performance measures as reliable as possible since poor reliability is a common feature of many memory tests (see P. Morris, 1984). When Underwood and colleagues factor-analysed their subjects' performance they found that separate factors emerged for free recall, paired associate learning, memory span, verbal discrimination, spelling ability and vocabulary. These factors seemed virtually independent of each other. Therefore, even for the common laboratory tests it appears that different underlying skills are involved and that there is not some general memory ability which is high in some people and low in others.

Further support for this view that memory skills are task specific comes from several other experiments where people have compared performance on list learning with the memory abilities of people doing more realistic learning tasks. Morris, Tweedy and Gruneberg (1985) found insignificant correlations of .26 and .32 respectively between the amount that subjects could free recall from a list of common words and either the performance of the same individuals on a quiz about football knowledge or their recall of new football scores which they had just heard. Morris and Morris (1985) reported correlations of less than .3 between the narrative free recall by eyewitnesses and the accuracy with which they answered subsequent questions. In both cases one might have expected that those subjects with a good general memory would perform well in all tasks. However, clearly special features about the encoding and retrieval conditions had differential effects upon the individuals in the different tasks.

These small and usually insignificant correlations between the performance of the same subjects in different memory tasks is well illustrated by an unpublished study of mine with Penny Walters. In this experiment 25 students were tested in a variety of different memory tasks. They were initially selected for having been present at an inter-college pool competition within the university. They were tested upon their recall of a particular pool match which they had witnessed, including the appearance of the competitors. Subsequently, they took part in several further tests. The first of these was a measure of their memory span, combining their recall performance both for lists of digits and for lists of letters. Secondly, they were shown a set of common advertisements and were required to recall which ones they had seen after a brief delay. Thirdly, they were presented with a set of photographs of faces and had to identify these faces when mixed with an equal number of distractors. Finally, they were tested on their recall of Bartlett's 'War of the Ghosts' story. While the split half reliability of these tests was reasonably high (.66-.85) there were very few significant intercorrelations between performance upon the five different tests. In fact, only that between memory span and recall of the advertisements reach significance with a correlation of .57. All other correlations range between .06 and .24. In other words, how well someone does on one memory task is no predictor of how well they will do on another unless that task is highly similar to the first one.

The independence of the many memory skills has also been suggested by the work of other researchers (e.g. Battig, 1979; Coughlan and Hollows, 1986; and Wilkins and Baddeley, 1978). In general, therefore, when individual differences are studied, it becomes clear not only that they are important but that the assumption that list learning provides a reasonable sample of a basic memory ability is extremely doubtful. Future research on memory will need to take the generality of its findings into account, and some thought will need to be given to ways of identifying the tasks and situations to which a particular memory skill generalises.

The baby and the bathwater

Finally, in our examination of the limitations of the Ebbinghaus tradition let us look at the factors which they chose to control or eliminate. As I described earlier the list-learning paradigm was designed to control or eliminate prior knowledge and experience, interest, variations in the activities at learning, subject strategies, differences in learning and retrieval conditions, the range of material memorised and the types of retrieval cues. Experimental control is essential in research but so is the retention of the thing to be studied. The question arises whether anything of normal memory is left when these variables are controlled in the way they were in laboratory list-learning experiments. Rather than answer the question immediately I want to turn to sketching what I would see as the important factors that influence memory in the world. We will then be able to turn these back to the list-learning experimental conditions and observe whether the list-learning experiment provided a reasonable sample of real world memorising.

Any sketch of the processes that determine memory must begin with the external world. That world contains a wide variety of potential inputs to the human cognitive system. We see events, we listen to conversations, we read books, we watch television and so on. The external world imposes tasks upon us that we have to fulfil. A university lecturer, for example, has to prepare lectures, mark course work assignments and examinations, plan research, guide seminars, supervise practicals and so on. Each task places special demands upon our cognitive system as it attempts to make sense of what is happening and direct our future actions.

In coping with this external world and its current task demands there is continuous internal cognitive activity. Our cognitive systems are always busily processing the input in order to comprehend it, to select a special message from other background information, to identify what is new and how it links with what is old, to devise the ways in which what is happening fits or does not fit our plans, to carry out the specific tasks that the world demands or we wish to impose upon the world and to calculate the implications in general of what we are experiencing. In the process of all this there is a personal context of moods and emotions created by our success and failure.

To achieve the successful processing of the world we draw upon internal resources. We have vast stored knowledge of the meanings of words, of regularities about the world, and of high-level schemas which specify what is likely to happen. We have memories of episodes from the past and we possess control programmes to help direct our processing. These internal resources are what we generally classify as memory and it is these that are in continuous use. They are continuously probed and supply potentially useful information to aid the internal activities of the cognitive system. At the same time, new information as a result of the ongoing processing is stored away in memory alongside previously acquired knowledge. There is, I believe, nothing controversial about that sketch of the processes surrounding memory. Most of them have been the topics of research in recent years (see Smyth et al., 1987, for a review).

If we compare the aspects of the traditional list-learning experiment with this survey of the processes determining memory we quickly see that the list-learning experiment contains almost none of the important factors that determine memory. As a sample of tasks within the world, list-learning is extremely rare. Most of our normal memory functions are irrelevant to list-learning experiments and our normal psychological processes are baffled by the abnormal input. In part they are baffled because the internal resources we possess have almost nothing to say about the material being processed. Perhaps, if meaningful words are used, then word meanings can be abstracted from memory. However, these meanings will normally be of little use except as an adjunct of some special-purpose mnemonic strategy such as imaging or making up stories (see, for example, Morris, 1979). The word lists activate no other useful stored knowledge, nothing to do with the schemas that frame our lives, episodes from our lives, no regularities about the world at all (cf. Schank, 1982). It is not, therefore, surprising that this list-learning tradition has told us little about the way that our memories normally work. If you do not put into the experiment what you might wish to study there is no hope of getting out from the result much useable information.

Exploring the low road

In the preface to his book *Memory Observed* (1982) Neisser commented that psychology has followed two routes in the study of memory. Travellers on the high road have hoped to find basic mental mechanisms that can be demonstrated in well controlled experiments. Those on the low road want to understand the specific manifestations of memory in ordinary human experience. Neisser describes *Memory Observed* as 'a kind of guide book to the lower road'. It is certainly a fascinating guide book and highly recommended reading. As we have seen, attempts to study what Neisser calls the high road have led to experimental paradigms which have left out what we would now regard as the important aspects of memory. What happens if we start down the low road and ask what are the main landmarks of memory in everyday life?

In the last few years, as people have begun to study the range of ways that we use memory in everyday life, there have developed many new and interesting research themes. There have been several interesting examples of how, in real life, what we remember is not a simple function of the number of times we experience the stimulus: not, that is, a simple matter of associations building up through frequency. So, for example, an intensive publicity campaign to advertise changes in radio frequencies led to almost no learning by the general public (Bekerian and Baddeley, 1980). People have very poor memories of the details on the coins that they use every day (Nickerson and Adams, 1979). Recently, when I asked 100 students to identify the correct representation of the face of a British 10p coin, 48 of them chose an alternative in which the Queen's head faced in the wrong direction! On the other hand, one experience of a salient event in one's life can lead to memories of many apparently irrelevant details about the situation one was in. Such vivid and detailed memories, sometimes known as flashbulb memories, have re-emerged as a topic for research following the pioneering work of Colegrove (1899) (see, e.g., Neisser, 1982).

One popular topic has been autobiographical memory (Rubin, 1986). Techniques originally used a hundred years ago by Sir Francis Galton, of asking for specific personal memories triggered by cue words, are being applied not only to explore the memories of normal individuals, but also those of the clinically depressed or demented. The study of eyewitness testimony has become a major theme in its own right and, in the process, has restored the study of memory for events which was originally begun by Stern (1904) (e.g. Wells and Loftus, 1984). The context and emotional states under which learning and recall take place have turned out to be major determinants of what people can recall (e.g. Malpass and Devine, 1981; Bower, 1983). There has been fascinating research on the representations that we possess of our geographical surroundings. Distortions in our 'mental maps' seem common, and can perhaps be understood in terms of the activities through which we build up our knowledge (see, e.g., Bartram and Smith, 1984). The permanence and plasticity of our memories have been important research topics. Bahrick (1984a, 1984b) has shown that in some circumstances our memories seem to be resistant to decay or interference for periods of 25 years or more. On the other hand, Loftus and her associates (e.g. Loftus and Loftus, 1980) have illustrated how easy it is to substitute misleading information during subsequent questioning so that the recall of the original information is virtually impossible except under very special conditions (e.g. Bekerian and Bowers, 1983; Bowers and Bekerian, 1984). Hunter (1985) has reviewed research upon what he calls lengthy verbatim recall. He has shown that the common belief that accurate memory is encouraged in non-literate societies and decays when a written language allows records to be kept and the memory to be supplemented is, in fact, a myth. The reality is that in non-literate societies where there is no record against which to compare memory performance the verbatim accuracy of recall is not what is valued. Recall is for another purpose, for example, the singing of technically sophisticated sagas for the enjoyment of an expert audience or the justification of the present ruler by the construction of an appropriate genealogy.

One major research topic has been the study of remembering to do things. When people are questioned about the memory problems that they have, or the methods that they use to overcome memory lapses (e.g. Harris, 1980; Reason and Mycielska, 1982), it is problems in remembering planned intentions that feature most prominently. Diary studies by Reason and his associates (e.g. Reason, 1984; Reason and Lucas, 1984; Reason and Mycielska, 1982) have helped to locate when such errors occur. The development of models of the processes underlying human slips and lapses has considerable implications for public safety, since many industrial accidents and public transport disasters appear to stem from human errors in the remembering and control of actions (e.g. Reason and Embrey, 1985). Harris (1984) has reviewed the experimental research on remembering to do things which often reflects great ingenuity and inventiveness by the experimenters.

One of the methods initially adopted in the study of everyday memory was the memory questionnaire, asking subjects to indicate their level of memory ability on a wide range of possible areas. Subjects rated how well they remembered people's faces, whether they frequently forgot where they had placed things and so on. The major finding of this research was that while people are consistent in their beliefs about their own memory abilities these beliefs did not seem to match up to the actual performance of subjects in objective attempts to assess their abilities. Herrmann (1984) reviews the poor performance of the memory questionnaires as predictors of actual performance. Elsewhere, (Morris, 1984) I have tried to indicate the many reasons why such questionnaire performance is poor. This lack of general awareness of the strengths and limitations of our own memories makes even more important the careful experimental investigation of everyday memory phenomena.

Finally, in this sketch of some of the recent topics in everday memory, the importance of the prior knowledge of subjects on the particular type of material to be remembered has been shown to have massive implications for the amount of new information on that topic that they can pick up in one exposure. One example of the influence of prior knowledge on the acquisition of new information is a study by a former post-graduate student of mine (Morris, 1983). Valerie Morris looked at the memory subjects had for details from a video film made up of clips showing part of a football match, a gardening programme, a snooker game and a pop music programme. Her subjects had previously completed a questionnaire on their knowledge of these topics. She found that the ability to recall new information acquired from the film was very well predicted by the subject's performance on this prior knowledge questionnaire. This was so even though the questions on the film were designed not to be guessable by knowledgeable subjects. She found, for example, that the knowledge about football questionnaire correlated .74 with the recall of the questions about the football part of the film.

In a series of experiments I have been interested in the acquisition of new football scores by individuals from a range of knowledge about the soccer world. In our first study (Morris, Gruneberg, Sykes and Merrick, 1981), we showed that there was a correlation greater than .8 between people's general knowledge about soccer and the number of new scores they could correctly recall after hearing the Saturday afternoon results just once. This was so despite the fact that experts are very poor at predicting the likely scores in advance. In a second study (Morris, Tweedy and Gruneberg, 1985) we replicated the finding that general knowledge about football correlates above .8 with the number of new scores correctly remembered. One important finding in this experiment was that simulated scores which were designed to be as realistic as possible, but which the subjects knew were in fact constructed by the experimenters, were recalled far differently from the real scores. For those subjects who had least knowledge about football, real and simulated scores were equally well recalled, but as football knowledge increased then the superiority of the recall of real scores steadily grew. While recall of the real scores was unrelated to the recall of a list of words there was a high correlation between the recall of the simulated scores and the free recall word list. The implication was that the attempt to simulate the football score condition failed and that two different skills were involved in the experiment. One involved knowledge of football, the other an ability to free recall lists of words and numbers. I will return to this point in a later section.

The importance of prior knowledge in the memorising of new information would not, perhaps, surprise a devotee of the old verbal learning tradition. In list-learning experiments what was known as 'learning to learn' took place where, as subjects were tested on a series of similar lists, they improved their performance for several of the lists. On the other hand, a central tenet of most of the list-learning research was the importance of interference from similar material. Underwood (1957), for example, demonstrated that the more similar lists a person had learned the quicker that information was lost. This was ascribed to problems with similar information in memory interfering with the items to be remembered. It is important to show that the memorising of new information by experts is not simply improved initially but lost rapidly as would be expected from interference theorists. I was able to show this in a recent experiment carried out with Leslie Edkins. In this experiment subjects with high and low knowledge of soccer studied a list of football scores allegedly coming from the same week ten years earlier. This was chosen to avoid the problems using simulated scores mentioned above. That is, we hoped to 'switch in' the knowledge and interest of the soccer 'experts'. In fact, the fixtures were real but the scores were fictitious and immediately after the presentation of the lists the subjects were informed of this fact. The purpose of this design was to avoid the experts spending more time in the intervening period before test discussing and thinking about the scores. After either twenty minutes or three days recall of the lists was tested. After both time intervals recall was better for the more knowledgeable subjects and there was no sign of an interaction over time. Both groups showed similar declines in the amount recalled. There was therefore no evidence that the better acquisition of information by the knowledgeable subjects was counter-balanced by any more rapid forgetting. Interference theory clearly does not apply to meaningful, interesting material that clicks nicely into a rich, well-developed schema.

Theoretical issues in the nature of the memory representation

The study of memory in everyday life raises many theoretical questions, among the most important of which is the way in which memories are encoded so that they can be retrieved later at an appropriate time. The traditional view that memory is based upon associations has been extended and formalised by cognitive scientists who have developed network models of memory representations that can be simulated on computers. Best developed of these network models is Anderson's ACT theory (e.g. Anderson, 1976, 1983, 1984). Network models, such as ACT, assume that when a new item of information is acquired it is attached appropriately to already existing information so that an interconnected knowledge base is developed which can be explored by activation spreading through the network when information is required. In Anderson's model the information is stored as productions, that is, as condition-action rules which allow for a particular action to take place if the conditions specified by the rule are fulfilled.

Anderson's production system distinguishes between two sorts of memory; declarative memory and procedural memory. Declarative memory is memory for facts while procedural memory involves specifications of what to do. This distinction between what Ryle (1949) called knowing that and knowing how (e.g. that something is a bicycle versus how to ride it) is a widely accepted distinction between the types of information stored in memory. It is worth, however, noting that computer simulations of such knowledge involve similar representations of the production rules them-selves: differences occur mainly in the acquisition of the rules and in their execution. Beyond the procedural/declarative distinction there has been more discussion around the possible distinction between episodic and semantic memories. Episodic memories are those for particular personal events while semantic memories store factual knowledge unconnected to the original events which led to the acquisition of the information. Tulving (1983, 1984) has argued that while episodic and semantic memories are interrelated they are sufficiently distinct to justify incorporating separate episodic and semantic memories into models of memory. Prototypical examples of episodic and semantic memories certainly appear very different and can be imagined as serving different functions. An easily accessible semantic memory seems essential for, for example, language comprehension. The reason for the evolution of our ability to remember with considerable detail, often via mental images and re-experienced emotions, events that happened to us in the past is less obvious. Such memories may help in the planning and decision-making that comes with the complex potential for different actions available to human beings. Episodic memory may be a late addition in the evolution of the human species. However, it has been by no means obvious to theorists of memory that the episodic/semantic distinction requires incorporating into their models. Anderson, for example, does not specifically distinguish between the types of memory in his models but it is assumed that differences in the associative network and the types and richness of the associations involved distinguish between memories normally classified as episodic or semantic. Episodic entries retain information about the time and place of their occurrence while semantic information is obtained from nodes in the network where many past experiences have accumulated a large number of associations which specify the meaning of the concepts involved.

In addition to episodic and semantic memory it may be necessary to propose a prospective memory where intentions to act are stored. How our actions are planned and ordered is still relatively poorly understood. However, control systems clearly exist and must be serviced by memory resources. Considerable work needs to be done in unravelling the sort of information that would be required to efficiently serve the many functions of memory. If the cognitive system is composed of many separate but interacting modules (e.g. Fodor, 1983) the form in which the information is stored for use by these modules may differ considerably. For example, the form in which information is stored and used for face recognition may differ considerably from the way it is used for language comprehension and be different again from that used in planning our actions.

Much work remains to be done on the development of and interrelationship between the several types of memory that have been postulated. Do semantic memories develop from the reorganisation of a set of episodic memories or are the processes independent? How are schema developed and what is their relationship to the semantic networks?

The problem in the design and use of any information storage system with a very large capacity such as the human memory is to encode information when it is acquired in such a way that it can be retrieved on the appropriate occasion in the future and to ensure that similar but unwanted information is not also retrieved to confuse or block processing. At some point in the future detailed theories of the process of retrieval must be developed because, while retrieval is the fundamental function of memory, few models of memory have discussed it in sufficient detail to provide a model that could adequately simulate the impressive performance of the human memory system.

Issues arising from the study of everyday memory

Few people will doubt that the study of memory has become much more interesting in recent years. However, the Ebbinghaus tradition had much good sense behind it. How does one develop an adequate theory of memory without experimental control to identify the important variables? It would, I think, be quite wrong to draw as a lesson from the fate of the Ebbinghaus tradition that laboratory research on memory is misguided. On the contrary, I would suggest that we should make every effort possible to obtain similar degrees of control for the aspects of memory that we study. The problem with the Ebbinghaus tradition was not that memory was studied in the laboratory but that the particular choice of elements to control meant that the type of memorising that took place in the experiments was unrealistic and brought with it none of the features of the real world. As I suggested at the beginning I think that we need a sketch map, a natural history, of when and how memory is used to help us identify important topics. Having done so, however, we need as much experimental control as possible. While modern developments in statistical techniques and in computing have meant that analyses such as multiple regression which were technically beyond the means of many psychologists up to the 1960s are now possible even for undergraduate projects, it still remains necessary whenever possible to undertake experimental control. What we need, therefore, is to bring into the laboratory the very aspects of memory which we wish to study. We need, also, to check that we have got them there once we have brought them in! The Morris et al. (1985) study using simulated football scores is a salutary reminder that although one may simulate the real world so that it appears identical in the laboratory we may, if we fail to capture the essential elements, end up studying the wrong thing. We need to continually check that we do really have the important memory skills activated in our laboratory tasks. One means to do this is to use the technique employed in the Morris et al. (1985) study. If in one's research one employs a real-world task and a laboratory task that is meant to capture the real world's components, and if the same individuals take part in the experiment then one may check by looking at the individual differences in the two experiments whether the same skill appears to be captured. If one finds that there is little or no correlation in the performance of the subjects in the real-world task and the simulation then it is time to think again about the quality of the simulation. In retrospect, it is surprising how few attempts have been made to check the validity of many psychological experiments developed in the laboratory.

One result of the recognition that what we remember depends very much upon the particular task we are undertaking will be, I think, that memory will be studied much more as a component in particular cognitive processing. Memory is, after all, a resource, a vital helper but not the central character in the cognitive world. It is the act of comprehension and the control of our actions that are central. Ironically, the study of memory may be held up for a while since many of the areas of psychology such as perception, decision-making and planned actions are all still frequently studied in artificial situations which may, as in the case of memory, bear little resemblance to the processing that takes place in everyday life.

Finally, it would be wrong to end a chapter which has been so critical of much early memory research by not pointing out that many useful concepts may be salvaged from the earlier work. We will need many new theories, but, as Baddeley and Wilkins (1984) have pointed out, many of the theoretical concepts from the earlier research may well be relevant to what we now recognise to be more appropriate topics for research on memory. However, which of the theoretical concepts are appropriate and which are not must be tested under the experimental paradigms based upon the use of memory in everyday life.

My conclusion, then, refers back to my initial quotation from Sherlock Holmes. It is a capital mistake to theorise before you have all the evidence, or at least enough evidence, to be sure that your theories are taking you in the right direction. For too long we were unwilling to ask fundamental questions, such as What is our memory for? Things have changed and many new research themes have been the result. However, there remains the danger that each of these themes will develop a life of its own and drift away from the development of general knowledge about memory. We still have a great deal to learn about how we can structure our knowledge of memory and how we can at the same time capture the fundamental memory processes and experimentally control misleading variables. Nevertheless, psychologists are now starting to make statements about memory which people outside the subject recognise as important and valuable for them. For example, there is collaboration between psychologists and the police and psychologists are advising the nuclear industry on ways of improving the memory of its operators. In the prevailing atmosphere where scientists are being asked to justify the expenditure on their research it is fortunate that we are at last, if belatedly, starting to generate findings which have an obvious interest and potential benefit to others than academic psychologists. In the study of memory there are many new directions opening up.

References

Anderson, J. R. (1976), *Language, Memory and Thought*. Erlbaum: Hillsdale, NJ.

Anderson, J. R. (1983), *The Architecture of Cognition*. Harvard University Press: Cambridge, Mass.

Anderson, J. R. (1984), 'Spreading activation', in J. R. Anderson and S. M. Kosslyn (eds) *Tutorials in Learning and Memory*. W. H. Freeman: San Francisco.

Baddeley, A. D. (1976). *The Psychology of Memory*. Basic Books: New York.

Baddeley, A. D. (1983), 'Working memory', *Philosophical Transactions of the Royal Soiciety, Series B, 302*, 311-24.

Baddeley, A. D. (1983), *Your Memory: A User's Guide*. Penguin, Harmondsworth.

Baddeley, A. D. and Wilkins, A. (1984), 'Taking memory out of the laboratory', in J. E. Harris and P. E. Morris (eds), *Everyday Memory. Actions and Absentmindedness*. Academic Press: New York.

Bahrick, H. P. (1984a), 'Memory for people', in J. E. Harris and P. E. Morris (eds), *Everyday Memory, Actions and Absentmindedness*. Academic Press: New York.

Bahrick, H. P. (1984b), 'Semantic memory content in permastore: fifty years of memory for Spanish learned at school', *Journal of Experimental Psychology: General, 113*, 1-29.

Bartlett, F. C. (1932), *Remembering: A Study in Experimental and Social Psychology*. Cambridge University Press: Cambridge.

Bartram, D. and Smith, P. (1984), 'Everyday memory for everyday places', in J. E. Harris and P. E. Morris (eds), *Everyday Memory, Actions and Absentmindedness*. Academic Press: New York.

Battig, W. F. (1979), 'The flexibility of memory', in L. S. Cermak and F. I. M. Craik (eds), *Levels of Processing in Human Memory*. Erlbaum: Hillsdale, NJ.

Bekerian, D. A. and Baddeley, A. D. (1980), 'Saturation advertising and the repetition effect', *Journal of Verbal Learning and Verbal Behavior, 19*, 17-25.

Bekerian, D. A. and Bowers, J. M. (1983), 'Eyewitness testimony: were we misled?' *Journal of Experimental Psychology: Learning and Cognition, 9*, 139-45.

Bower, G. H. (1983), 'Affect and cognition', *Philosophical Transactions of the Royal Society of London, Series B, 302*, 387-402.

Bowers, J. M. and Bekerian, D. A. (1984), 'When will post-event information distort eyewitness testimony?' *Journal of Applied Psychology, 69*, 466-72.

Cattell, J. M. (1895), 'Measurements of the accuracy of recollection', *Science, 2*, 761-6.

Colegrove, F. W. (1899), 'Individual memories', *American Journal of Psychology, 10*, 228-55.

Coughlan, A. K. and Hollows, S. E. (1986), *The Adult Memory and Information Processing Battery (AMIPB)* A. K. Coughlan: Leeds.

Doyle, A. C. (1887), *A Study in Scarlet*. Ward Lock: London.

Ebbinghaus, H. (1885), *Uber das Gedachtris*. Dunker: Leipzig. (Trans. H. Ruyer and C. E. Bussenius, *Memory*. Teachers College Press: New York, 1913.)

Fodor, J. A. (1983), *The Modularity of Mind: An Essay on Faculty Psychology*. MIT Press: Cambridge, Mass.

Harris, J. E. (1980), 'Memory aids people use: two interview studies', *Memory and Cognition, 8*, 31-8.

Harris, J. E. (1984), 'Remembering to do things: a forgotten topic', in J. E. Harris and P. E. Morris (eds), *Everyday Memory, Actions and Absentmindedness*. Academic Press: New York.

Herrmann, D. J. (1984), 'Questionnaires about memory', in J. E. Harris and P. E.

Morris (eds), *Everyday Memory, Actions and Absentmindedness*. Academic Press: New York.

Hunter, I. M. L. (1985), 'Lengthy verbatim recall: the role of text', in A. W. Ellis (ed.), *Progress in the Psychology of Language*, Vol. 1. Erlbaum: London.

Loftus, E. F. and Loftus, G. R. (1980), 'On the permanence of stored information in the human brain', *American Psychologist, 35*, 409-20.

Malpass, R. S. and Devine, P. G. (1981), 'Guided memory in eyewitness identification', *Journal of Applied Psychology, 66*, 343-50.

Morris, P. E. (1979), 'Strategies for learning and recall', in M. M. Gruneberg and P. E. Morris (eds), *Applied Problems in Memory*. Academic Press: London.

Morris, P. E. (1984), 'The validity of subjective reports on memory', in J. E. Harris and P. E. Morris (eds), *Everyday Memory, Actions and Absentmindedness*. Academic Press: New York.

Morris, V. (1983), *Factors influencing the accuracy of witness reports*. Ph.D. thesis, University of Lancaster.

Morris, P. E., Gruneberg, M. M., Sykes, R. N. and Merrick, A. (1981), 'Football knowledge and the acquisition of new results', *British Journal of Psychology, 72*, 479-83.

Morris, V. and Morris, P. E. (1985), 'The influence of question order on eyewitness accuracy', *British Journal of Psychology, 76*, 365-71.

Morris, P. E., Tweedy, M. and Gruneberg, M. M. (1985), 'Interest, knowledge and the memorizing of soccer scores', *British Journal of Psychology, 76*, 415-25.

Neisser, U. (1978), 'Memory: What are the important questions?' in M. M. Gruneberg, P. E. Morris and R.N. Sykes (eds), *Practical Aspects of Memory*. Academic Press: London.

Neisser, U. (1981), 'John Dean's memory: A case study', *Cognition, 9*, 1-22.

Neisser, U. (1982), *Memory Observed*. W. H. Freeman: San Francisco.

Nickerson, R. S. and Adams, M. J. (1979), 'Long-term memory for a common object', *Cognitive Psychology, 11*, 287-307.

Postman, L. and Keppel, G. (eds) (1969), *Verbal Learning and Memory*. Penguin: Harmondsworth.

Reason, J. T. (1984), 'Absentmindedness and cognitive control', in J. E. Harris and P. E. Morris (eds), *Everyday Memory, Actions and Absentmindedness*. Academic Press: New York.

Reason, J. T. and Embrey, D. E. (1985), *Human factors principles relevant to the modelling of human errors in abnormal conditions of nuclear and major hazardous installations*. Report prepared for the European Atomic Energy Community. Human Reliability Associates: Parbold, Lancs.

Reason, J. T. and Lucas, D. (1984), 'Using cognitive diaries to investigate naturally occurring memory blocks', in J. E. Harris and P. E. Morris (eds), *Everyday Memory, Actions and Absentmindedness*. Academic Press: New York.

Reason, J. T. and Mycielska, K. (1982), *Absentminded? The Psychology of Mental Lapses and Everyday Errors*. Prentice-Hall: Englewood-Cliffs, NJ.

Rubin, D. (ed.) (1986), *Autobiographical Memory*. Cambridge University Press: New York.

Ryle, G. (1949), *The Concept of Mind*. Hutchinson: London.

Schank, R. C. (1982), *Dynamic Memory*. Cambridge University Press: Cambridge.

Smyth, M., Morris, P. E., Ellis, A. W. and Levy, P. (1987), *Cognition in Action* Erlbaum: Hillsdale, NJ.

Stern, W. (1904), 'Wirklichkeitsversuche', *Beitrage zur Psychologie der Aussage, 2*, 1-31. (Trans. U. Neisser, 'Realistic experiments', in U. Neisser (ed.) (1982), *Memory Observed*. W. H. Freeman: San Francisco.)

Tulving, E. (1983), *Elements of Episodic Memory*. Oxford University Press: Oxford.

Tulving, E. (1984), Précis of 'Elements of episodic memory', *The Behavioral and Brain Sciences*, *7*, 223-68.

Underwood, B. J. (1957), 'Interference and forgetting', *Psychological Review*, *64*, 49-60.

Underwood, B. J., Boruch, R. F. and Malmi, R. (1978), 'Composition of episodic memory', *Journal of Experimental Psychology: General*, *107*, 393-419.

Wells, G. L. and Loftus, E. F. (eds) (1984), *Eyewitness Testimony: Psychological Perspectives*. Cambridge University Press: Cambridge.

Wilkins, A. J. and Baddeley, A. D. (1978), 'Remembering to recall in everyday life: an approach to absentmindedness', in M. M. Gruneberg, P. E. Morris and R. N. Sykes (eds), *Practical Aspects of Memory*. Academic Press: London.

5 Understanding

Alan Garnham

Introduction

Psycholinguistics, the study of the mental mechanisms and processes that underlie our ability to use language, found its major new direction in the early 1960s. Before that time the psychology of language had been studied primarily in so-called 'verbal learning' experiments in which subjects learned lists of words. Then George Miller introduced into psychology Chomsky's (1957) transformational generative grammar – a linguistic theory primarily about the structure of sentences (the grouping of the words in them), and attention began to focus on how we understand sentences rather than how we remember lists of words. Miller's move was consistent with Chomsky's own view that a linguistic description of a language (a *grammar*) was embodied in the mind of a speaker of that language and was used in both understanding and production.

Perhaps the most important fact to grasp about the operation of the language processor is that the mechanisms, representations and processes postulated in psycholinguistic theories are not, in general, accessible to consciousness. As readers and listeners, we are aware of the content of what we have read or heard, but not of how our understanding came about. Introspective evidence is, therefore, of little use in formulating psycholinguistic theories. We have to investigate objectively the structure of the task that the language understanding system performs – the extraction of information from discourse and text – and use experimental techniques to test theories about how it performs that task.

Since the early 1960s psycholinguistics has seen many changes, but processing models of language understanding and production have remained a central concern. Because of the importance of sentence

The final draft of this chapter was prepared while the author was a Visiting Fellow at the Max-Planck Institut für Psycholinguistik, Nijmegen. I would like to thank Guy Claxton and Jane Oakhill for their comments on previous drafts.

structure in transformational grammar, early work on language understanding examined its role in comprehension. The failure of this early research to produce a satisfactory theory of text comprehension led to a switch in interest to the role of meaning in comprehension and, as it became apparent that there are many aspects of meaning, it was also realised that focus on the sentence, rather than the discourse or text, was a mistake.

The processing models of the 1970s were often vaguely formulated, and much of the empirical research was exploratory. Many meaning-based manipulations affected ease of comprehension, but the experimental results rarely suggested detailed processing mechanisms.

An important advance was the recognition of the relevance of models of language use developed in artificial intelligence (AI). These models take the form of computer programs for understanding and/or producing language. This research fleshed out the assumption, implicit in the cognitive 'information processing' approach to psycholinguistics, that computers and computer programs provide appropriate models for human cognitive functioning. Computer programs are, of necessity, detailed and explicit. However, the goals of AI research projects – the production of working programs – are not the same as those of psycholinguistics, which aims to discover general principles about the way we use language. Because AI programmers are often forced to use 'tricks' to make a program work, it may be unclear what contribution a piece of AI research makes to our understanding of language use. (For a fuller discussion of the AI approach to language understanding see Garnham, 1988, Chapter 5.)

Over the past few years there has been a resurgence of interest in the role of sentence structure in comprehension, informed in part by work carried out in the 1970s (especially Kimball, 1973). Another development has been the emergence of cognitive science, an interdisciplinary blend of cognitive psychology, artificial intelligence, linguistics and philosophy. Cognitive science brings these disciplines together in an attempt to solve the difficult problems of human (and machine) cognition, including those of language use. The aim of this chapter is to give an account of recent work on syntactic analysis, and to describe, in a way informed by the ideas of cognitive science, the role of meaning in comprehension.

Parsing

A sentence is not simply an unstructured sequence of words, and if it is to be understood, the words must be grouped into larger units. This process of grouping is not understanding itself, but is a preliminary to it – the units formed by grouping the words together typically have simple meanings. They refer to people, animals and objects, abstractions (such as justice, or the number two), places, events, states and processes. To take a simple example, in the sentence

The red ball bounces over the wall.

the three words 'the red ball' form a group in a way that, for example, the words 'ball bounces over' do not. When the sentence is used in an appropriate context 'the red ball' will refer to a particular coloured spherical object. Similarly, 'the wall' refers to another object, 'over the wall' to a direction of movement and 'bounces over the wall' to something that objects can do. These groups of words are typically *phrases*, and they may be subclassified as, among other things, noun phrases ('the red ball', 'the wall'), prepositional phrases ('over the wall'), and verb phrases ('bounces over the wall'). As these examples show, one phrase may be part of another. So, sentences have a *hierarchical* structure, which can be exhibited either by labelled bracketing or by a tree diagram.

[[the red ball]~NP~[bounces[over[the wall]~NP~]~PP~]~VP~]~S~

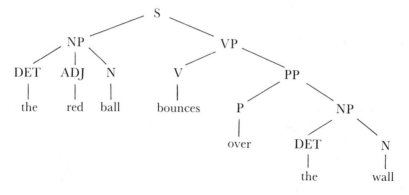

In the tree diagram the lexical categories of the words (whether they are nouns, N, verbs, V, prepositions, P, or determiners, DET) are also shown. Linguists call the characteristics of a sentence exhibited in such a tree diagram its *syntactic structure* (cf. Chomsky, 1957).

Psycholinguists must answer several questions about the *computation* of syntactic structure, or *parsing* as this process is usually known. The first question is to what extent syntactic structure is used in normal comprehension. One might be tempted to claim: if the meaning of a sentence depends on the way its words are grouped, then surely the syntactic structure must be computed. However, there are ways in which part of the computation might be avoided, at least for *some* sentences. Consider, for example:

The chemist mixed the medicine.
The medicine was mixed by the chemist.

The first of these sentences is an *active* sentence, and the second is the corresponding *passive*. In a passive sentence, unlike the more usual active, the person who performs the action, in this case mixing, is referred to not by the noun phrase that precedes the verb (the subject noun phrase) but by a noun phrase that is part of a prepositional 'by' phrase towards the end of the sentence. Generally speaking, in order to avoid misunderstanding passive sentences – to avoid taking:

The boy was seen by the girl.

to have the same meaning as:

The boy saw the girl.

a fairly complete syntactic analysis must be performed in which the passive form of the verb is identified along with the 'by' phrase that introduces the passive subject. However, in the sentences about the chemist, a trick can be used to avoid most of this analysis. Once the low-level groupings 'the chemist' and 'the medicine' have been identified, and 'mixed' has been recognised as the main verb, the meaning of the sentence is virtually fixed, as the following argument shows. First, in any mixing one thing does the mixing and another gets mixed. Second, things that mix must be either animate beings or natural forces. Medicine cannot mix. It can, therefore, be deduced that it was the chemist who did the mixing, and the medicine that got mixed. The meaning of the sentence has been worked out without a full syntactic analysis. However, such methods of interpretation must be used with care. One function of syntax is to allow implausible events to be described, so syntactic analysis may only be by-passed when all but one reading is *impossible*, not merely when there is only one *plausible* meaning. For example,

The doctor was examined by the patient.

means something quite different from

The doctor examined the patient.

but if we considered just the meanings of the words, and ignored the finer details of syntax we might misinterpret the first sentence as meaning the second. In general, the language understanding system must be able to compute syntactic structure, even if that computation can sometimes be by-passed.

The second psychological question about parsing is a difficult one to answer. Given that syntactic structure often *is* computed, how does the output of the parser relate to descriptions of syntactic structure proposed by linguists? This question leads to several more specific ones. First, does the psychological parser build up a complete tree for each sentence? Given our very poor memory for the verbatim details of sentences, the answer to this question is probably no. We may compute trees a clause at a time but, for many types of English sentence, holding even this much in memory is unnecessary. It is usually possible to work through a sentence from left to right computing syntactic relations as one goes along, using them straight away to work out meaning, and then forgetting them. A complete syntactic tree may never be constructed.

The second more specific question is whether linguists' generalisations about syntactic structure are represented in the brain or mind and, if they are, whether they take the same form there as they do in linguistics textbooks. Chomsky, whose work on syntactic structure formed the basis for modern psycholinguistics, maintained that linguistics is a branch of cognitive psychology, and that it gives a straightforward account of the knowledge that a native speaker/hearer uses in understanding and producing language. However, no satisfactory theory of language use has ever been based on this assumption, and it can be argued (e.g. Clark and Malt, 1984) that because linguists ignore truly psychological constraints on language use, linguistic formulations of syntactic rules may not parallel those used by the language understanding system.

To make this point more concrete I will give an example of how psychological considerations could influence the mental representation of syntactic rules. In some recent syntactic theories (e.g. Gazdar, Klein, Pullum and Sag, 1985) the fact that many syntactic rules have a similar form is captured by a metagrammar – a set of higher-level rules for generating one syntactic rule from another. In such theories the most satisfactory way of describing syntactic regularities is by stating a few basic syntactic rules and then giving metarules for generating other rules from them. Suppose, however, that in the human mind storage space is cheap and computation expensive. (This is just a supposition, but the relative capacities of long- and short-term memory stores suggest it may be true.) Under such circumstances it would make sense to store all the low-level syntactic rules – the basic ones and those derived via the metarules – directly. The metarules would then simply be generalisations that *could* be made by an observer outside the system (e.g. a linguist). Thus a linguistic description of the rules and a description of the way they are stored in the language understanding system may not coincide.

An alternative to Chomsky's view that linguistic rules are stored in the mind is that a grammar specifies the *outputs* that the language understanding system either *does* compute or *should* compute as it processes sentences. This idea is not inconsistent with the possibility, discussed above, that complete syntactic trees are never computed. The claim is simply that a sentence's syntactic tree specifies the syntactic relations among its parts that are (or should be) computed during comprehension. Since people misunderstand, and since syntactic analysis may sometimes be by-passed (see above), it is clear that the 'does compute' version of this theory is untenable and only a 'should compute' or 'could compute' interpretation is possible.

The two psychological questions about parsing considered so far have been very general ones. I now turn to some more specific questions, which only make sense on the assumptions that (i) the language understanding system has access to linguistic rules in some form, and (ii) in many cases syntactic analysis cannot be by-passed and a full parse is produced. These questions are about how the parser operates. The first, which has been posed in both psychology and AI, is whether the parser works *top-down*, *bottom-up* or in some mixed mode. The terms *top-down* and *bottom-up* can be understood with reference to the hierarchical tree structures that syntactic rules assign to sentences. A top-down parser is one that builds such trees from the top downwards. That is to say it starts with the S (sentence node) that spans the whole sentence, and uses its knowledge of syntax to look for the parts of the sentence. In English the most usual structure for a sentence is a noun phrase (NP) followed by a verb phrase (VP). This fact can be captured by a syntactic rule that is usually written S → NP VP. Other rules of English syntax are NP → DET N, NP → DET ADJ N, VP → V PP, PP → P NP. A top down parser, trying to find a sentence, starts by looking for an NP. It tries to find an NP by looking for a DET(erminer) followed by a N(oun). If the sentence it is trying to parse is:

The red ball bounces over the wall.

it will fail, and it will have to try again for the NP by looking for a DET followed by an ADJ followed by an N. This time it will succeed, and it can then look for the VP to complete the sentence.

A bottom-up parser constructs the tree in the other direction. It first looks up the lexical categories of the words in the sentence, and then sees what structure it can build over them. In the sentence above, 'the' is a DET, 'red' an ADJ, and 'ball' an N. A DET and an ADJ do not go together to form a phrase, but a DET an ADJ and an N form an NP. A bottom-up parser can, therefore, build an NP over 'the red ball'. Eventually it will build a VP over 'bounces over the wall', and then it will be able to put the NP and the VP together to form a sentence.

A top-down parser is efficient for predictable structures, but will often make 'mistakes' of the kind illustrated above – trying out the wrong rule before the right one – when there are a lot of options. It may also have problems with rules such as DET → NP's, which is required, in conjunction with NP → DET N, to analyse NPs such as:

Mary's sister's dog's collar.

A top-down parser using both of these rules could go on postulating NPs for ever, because when it looks for the determiner specified in the second of the rules, it tries to find yet another NP, and this process can be repeated over and over again. In English the beginnings of constituents are less predictable than their ends. For this reason it has been suggested (Johnson-Laird, 1983) that the human syntactic processor might be a left-corner parser, which starts at the bottom left-hand corner of each constituent that it tries to parse, and works bottom up until it can predict the tail of the constituent, which it processes top down.

Finally, perhaps the most interesting set of questions about parsing concern what happens when the parser encounters an ambiguity. Some sentences are structurally ambiguous, for example:

The old men and women left.

'old' could qualify 'men and women' or just 'men', and this ambiguity is reflected in two possible groupings of the words in the sentence: [old [men and women]] or [[old men] and women]. Many more sentences have *local ambiguities* that are resolved by the end of the sentence. For example, a sentence that begins 'the girl the boy'...could have at least two kinds of continuation.

The girl the boy and the dog went to the park.
The girl the boy helped thanked him.

The first four words of the sentence could have two different structures:

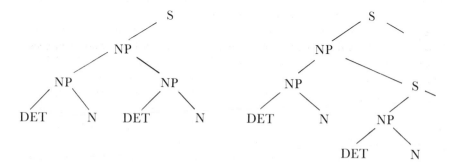

What happens when the understanding system is faced with such an ambiguity? There are three possibilities. (1) It waits until it has (or thinks it has) sufficient information to resolve the ambiguity before deciding on one of the structures. (2) It develops both analyses until one can be ruled out either for syntactic reasons – a later part of the sentence is incompatible with the structure – or semantic reasons – the structure has a meaning that either makes no sense or is highly implausible. (3) It picks on one analysis, and develops only that one, unless it becomes uninterpretable or implausible. A further question in each case is: what sort of information does the parser use to resolve its problem? Does it use only syntactic information? Does it use knowledge about the world to decide what is a plausible interpretation, or does the parser itself not resolve the problem? Perhaps it passes all possible parses on to the semantic processor, and leaves that to decide between them on its own.

This question has been addressed recently in the psycholinguistic literature. Support has been obtained for the third hypothesis – that one analysis is selected and developed, but there have been conflicting views about how that analysis is chosen. On the one hand experiments that examined subjects' eye movements, carried out at the University of Massachusetts (Ferreira and Clifton, 1986; Frazier and Rayner, 1982; Rayner, Carlson and Frazier, 1983), appear to indicate that the chosen analysis is always the syntactically most frequent one. The plausibility of the readings has no influence on which structure is considered first. On the other hand Crain and Steedman's (1985) research suggests that various aspects of the meaning of a sentence, including its relation to context, determine which structure is built. We await a resolution of this conflict.

Interpretation

As was emphasised earlier, the syntactic analysis of a sentence is a step towards understanding it, but it is not understanding itself. Furthermore, not all aspects of the message conveyed by a sentence are determined by its structure. Some depend on its relation to context, both linguistic (the preceding dialogue or text) and non-linguistic (who says it to whom, where and when it is said). The remaining part of this chapter will discuss those aspects of the interpretation of text that have interested psycholinguists.

The fundamental psycholinguistic questions about text comprehension are (1) what information do people extract from texts? and (2) how do they extract it? In the early years of modern psycholinguistics attention focused on syntax, because of the importance that Chomsky has placed on it in linguistic theory, and Miller (see e.g. Miller and McKean, 1964) proposed that what people remember of sentences is basically their syntactic structure. This idea is difficult to reconcile with our poor memory for verbatim detail, and was soon proved false. Chomsky (1965) proposed that every sentence has two syntactic structures, a superficial one – the one I have been discussing so far – and an underlying one in which all clauses are fully explicit and have a canonical subject-verb-(object) form. However, people can remember neither of these (Sachs, 1967; Johnson-Laird and Stevenson, 1970), unless they are specifically instructed to, or if the precise form of a sentence is important for the point that it makes, as it might be in a joke (e.g. Keenan, MacWhinney and Mayhew, 1977).

If people do not remember syntax, what do they remember? The simple answer, and the one in accord with common sense, is that they remember content. However, it is necessary to spell out in more detail what is meant by a text's content. In the early 1970s psycholinguists talked about the *semantic representation* of a text. But linguists now use the term semantics in a more restricted sense. The semantics of a (declarative) sentence determines the set of situations that it could correctly describe, but people get more information than that from most of the sentences that they hear – they know what particular situations those sentences are about, and what their *import* or *significance* is in the context that they are used (Johnson-Laird, 1977).

Mental models

We have proposed (Garnham, 1981; Johnson-Laird and Garnham, 1980; and especially Johnson-Laird, 1983) that representations of discourse be called *mental models* of parts of the real or imaginary worlds. This name reflects two facts about such representations. First, they contain information about particular situations in the world. Second, as a host of studies have shown (e.g. Bransford, Barclay and Franks, 1972; Barclay, 1973; Anderson and Hastie, 1974; Garnham, 1981), their structure parallels that of the world rather than that of sentences. Mental models contain tokens standing for individuals and events, but they do not usually encode how those individuals or events were described on particular occasions – whether someone was referred to as 'George Washington' or 'the first president of the United States' (Anderson and Bower, 1973), as 'the man standing by the window' or 'the man with the martini' (Garnham, 1981); whether an event was described as 'the buying of the fur coat at the furrier's' or 'the buying of the fur coat from the furrier' (Garnham, 1981). We assume that mental models are similar to representations of the world produced by perception, thinking, and other cognitive processes, an idea first mooted by Johnson-Laird (1970).

Each person constructs one mental model corresponding to each text that they read or dialogue that they take part in. This fact partly explains why potentially highly indeterminate phrases, such as 'the woman', have, in context, clear referents. If there is only one woman in the mental model of a text, then 'the woman' can refer unambiguously to her. The set of possible referents for a simple noun phrase or a pronoun is further restricted by the fact that some parts of a mental model are *in focus* or *foregrounded*. Only items in focus can be referred to by simple noun phrases, as opposed to ones with complex qualifiers, such as relative clauses or strings of adjectives.

Integrating information from different parts of a discourse

A mental model is built up as a discourse progresses. From each clause the basic information is extracted, and then integrated with the representation of the preceding text. The basic information in a sentence concerns the items mentioned in it, and the relations stated to hold between them. It can be computed from the syntactic structure of the sentence and the meanings of the words in it. Within the sentence an item may only be identifiable as 'the woman' or even 'she', but given the mental model of the preceding text as context, such expressions receive a more specific interpretation.

One important aspect of integrating information from different parts of a text is determining which items are the same as those previously mentioned, and which are new. An expression that has the same meaning as some part of the preceding text is called an *anaphor*, and determining its meaning is known as *resolving* it. Many anaphors, such as definite pronouns and definite noun phrases, refer back to things that have already been introduced. Other anaphors refer to another thing of the same kind as one that was previously mentioned. An example is the indefinite pronoun 'one' ('I had a chocolate ice cream. My sister had a vanilla one'). Another is the elliptical verb phrase ('I bought a house. My brother did, too'.).

Some general rules for the resolution of anaphors can be formulated. Definite pronouns (he, she, it, they) are either accompanied by 'pointing' gestures, and refer to some element of (non-linguistic) context, or their antecedents are explicit in the preceding text and, except under special circumstances, agree in number and gender. Definite noun phrases also *usually* refer back, often to an item introduced by a parallel indefinite noun phrase ('a bird', 'the bird'). However, the exact form of the noun phrase may differ – often the second is less specific ('the robin', 'the bird' or 'the blue car', 'the car'). Sometimes the first occurrence is implicit ('John went for a walk. The park was beautiful'.). A definite noun phrase may also be used at the beginning of a story as a literary device to create an effect of familiarity.

There are some syntactic constraints on the relation between an anaphor and its antecedent, particularly when a pronoun precedes a full noun phrase. For example, 'she' and 'Pam' cannot be coreferential in:

She sat down, when Pam had finished the painting.

There are also certain *preferred* configurations for anaphor and antecedent. Unlike the syntactic constraints, these preferences can be overridden, but sentences that conform to the preferences are easier to interpret. Examples of these constraints are that *near* antecedents are preferred to *far* ones (e.g. Clark and Sengul, 1979), pronouns are more readily interpreted if their antecedents are in subject position (e.g. Frederiksen, 1981), definite noun phrase anaphors are most natural if they are in subject position and their antecedents in object position (Yekovich, Walker and Blackman, 1979).

Inference

We have already seen that an inference may be necessary to interpret an anaphoric expression. In the 'park' example the existence of a park that John walked in must be inferred, if the second sentence is to be interpreted correctly. Inferences are frequently required to integrate information from different parts of a text. Another example in which an inference is needed to resolve an anaphor is:

Sue sold her car to Jenny because she had decided to take up cycling.

For definite noun phrases inferences usually establish the existence of a referent on the basis of general knowledge – there is likely to be a park suitable for walking in that John could go to. For definite pronouns inferences are used to choose between two possible referents – to decide whether taking up cycling would typically be accompanied by buying or selling a car.

Both everyday observations (e.g. our ability to answer questions in conversation that depend on inferences) and psychological experiments (e.g. Haviland and Clark, 1974; Garnham and Oakhill, 1985) show that inferences necessary to resolve anaphors are made as texts are read. There are also more general relations between the events in a text – spatial, temporal, logical, causal, intentional and moral (cf. Miller and Johnson-Laird, 1976) – that are usually implicit, but which we must compute as we read the text, because they are essential for a full understanding of it. However, psycholinguists have barely begun to study how these relations are determined. The only secure claim that can be made about them is that they almost always depends on knowledge of comparatively large-scale regularities in the way the physical and social worlds work.

There are other inferences that can be made from a text, but which are not essential to understanding it. For example, if we read that:

John stirred the sugar into his cup of tea.

it is reasonable to assume that he used a spoon, even though the sentence does not say so. If a spoon had not been used we would have expected explicit information to the contrary. However, the inference that a spoon was used will not, in general, be necessary for a coherent representation of the text. Are such highly probable inferences made during the initial processing of a discourse, or only later, if they are needed, for example, to answer a question (Did John use a spoon?)? In the early 1970s it was assumed that they were made immediately, because if people are asked if John used a spoon, or even if they are asked if they remember the sentence:

John stirred the sugar into his cup of tea with a spoon.

they say 'Yes' (e.g. Johnson, Bransford and Solomon, 1973; Paris and Lindauer, 1976). However, more recent work (e.g. Corbett and Dosher, 1978; Singer, 1979) is not consistent with this idea, and suggests that *merely elaborative* inferences are not made when texts are read. If they can be made from the text, then they can be made from an adequate memory representation of it. Garnham (1982) has proposed a theory – the omission theory – that reconciles data consistent with the two views. This theory states that material inferable with high probability from a text, whether explicit or implicit, is omitted from a memory representation of its *content*. In the short term, memory for the *surface form* of the text favours the explicit information, but in the longer term memory for surface form becomes unavailable, and people are unable to remember whether inferable information was presented or not.

Text structure

So far I have discussed relatively low-level connections between parts of a text. However, we have expectations about the overall structure of texts, and these expectations help us to understand them. How should those expectations be characterised, and how do they affect the way we understand texts? One suggestion is that the structure of stories should be described in the same way as the structure of sentences, using a *story grammar* (e.g. Lakoff, 1972; Rumelhart, 1975; Mandler and Johnson, 1977; Thorndyke, 1977). There are many problems with this suggestion. While it is true that texts are structured, story grammarians have not focused on structure that is specific to texts, but have concentrated on the hierarchical structure of goals, subgoals and attempts to fulfil them that is typical of simple folk tales. However, this structure is not story-specific, and it seems unnecessary to propose a story-specific repository of information to process it, when our knowledge of how people typically behave, both in and out of stories, can be used instead.

The significance of discourse

Finally, psycholinguists must explain how people determine the *significance* of texts, rather than simply working out what they describe. There are several aspects of text significance. First, people write and read texts for specific purposes. A book is read differently when it is being skimmed for a specific fact from when it is being studied in detail as a course text. More specifically, Anderson and Pichert (1978; Pichert and Anderson, 1977) showed that people remember different facts from a text if they read it from the perspective of a homebuyer than if they read it from the perspective of a burglar. However, these results could not be explained entirely in terms of how the text was encoded, because the effect could be partly reversed by a change in perspective at the time of recall.

Second, I have talked so far mainly about descriptive texts. However, much of our language, especially our spoken language, is not descriptive. It comprises questions, requests, commands, promises and so on. To understand a sentence it is necessary to grasp not only its descriptive content, in the sense of the situation that it is about, but also to determine whether it is intended as a description, a question or whatever – to work out what *speech act* it is being used to perform (cf. Austin, 1962; Searle, 1969). In many cases this computation is straightforward, because the form of a sentence is a good guide to its import. Interrogative sentences are typically questions, imperatives are usually commands. However, it is possible to use sentences for functions other than their normal ones – to perform *indirect* speech acts. Interrogatives frequently convey requests, for example:

Can you tell me the time?

In many cases the force of an indirect speech act is derived from its literal meaning. For example, Clark (1979; Clark and Schunk, 1980) showed that people are highly sensitive to the politeness of indirect requests, which depends on their literal meaning.

Would you mind telling me where Jordan Hall is?

is more polite than:

Shouldn't you tell me where Jordan Hall is?

Clark and Schunk argue that the politeness of an indirect request depends on how strongly the literal meaning suggests 'benefits' to the listener (rights that he or she has). 'Would you mind...' can be countered with a legitimate refusal, whereas 'Shouldn't you...' suggests an obligation to supply the information. However, Gibbs (e.g. 1983) has argued that the more stereotyped indirect speech acts are understood directly. An extreme example of such a speech act is 'How do you do?'

Third, the literal meaning of a sentence may provide only a very indirect guide to the information that it is intended to impart. Grice (1975, 1978) characterises conversation as a cooperative activity, and claims that the intended message of a contribution to a conversation can be determined from its literal meaning plus a set of maxims that follow from general principles about cooperative activities. So, if A, whose car has broken down, says to B 'I'm out of petrol' and B replies 'There's a garage round the corner', B implicates, but does not state, that the garage is open, and can supply the needed petrol. B is obeying an injunction to be relevant. Grice's claim is not that conversation is always cooperative – most obviously people tell lies. However, cooperation is the norm, and extra information can be gleaned from a conversation if its participants can assume that they are cooperating.

Knowledge representation

The preceding sections have shown that understanding language requires extensive use of stored 'knowledge': knowledge about words, about syntactic, semantic and pragmatic rules and about the world. The scare quotes indicate that only some of this information is knowledge in the usual sense. So, although we can become aware, for example, of the facts that enable us to resolve potentially ambiguous pronouns (see above), we cannot bring into consciousness our 'knowledge' of the syntactic rules of English. It is not knowledge in the everyday sense. From a psycholinguistic point of view this distinction is unimportant. What is crucial is that psycholinguistic theories should be able to draw on an account of how knowledge of all kinds is stored and organised in memory.

The difficult part of this task is to explain how 'semantic' information is stored. Knowledge about the pronunciation and spelling of words, and knowledge about syntax is comparatively circumscribed and poses few problems. Knowledge about word meanings and about the world, on the other hand, is enormously complex, yet we use it in language processing with apparent ease. There must, therefore, be an efficient mechanism for finding knowledge in *semantic memory*.

The simplest way of storing facts in semantic memory would be to list them using a uniform notation such as predicate calculus. Finding facts in such a list could be very time-consuming, unless they were grouped under headings such as facts about horses, facts about road accidents, facts about Ronald Reagan. Unfortunately, even when facts in such a database are grouped, finding the ones that are relevant to understanding a particular text can be hard. It is, therefore, usually assumed that semantic memory is structured in ways that make it easier to search.

The simplest kind of structure that has been proposed is the *associative* (or *semantic*) *network* (e.g. Quillian, 1968), which comprises a set of *nodes* connected by *links* (or associations). Associative networks can be used to represent word meanings, in which case there is a node corresponding to each word, and the links stand for relations between their meanings, such as the *subset* (ISA) relation that links 'dog', 'cat', 'horse', 'cow' and many other words to 'animal'. Networks can also be used to represent states of affairs, with nodes standing for people, places and objects, and links for relations between them. It is possible, therefore, that the mental models discussed earlier in this chapter are encoded in associative networks.

An associative network brings together information about a topic – a word, or a person, for example – by grouping it around a single node. However, any higher-order organisation remains *implicit* in the network structure. Related pieces of information tend to be near one another. For some purposes it is useful to make higher-order memory structures explicit. As with associative links, the justification is that, by treating some types of relations as special, more efficient use of memory can be made.

The best known example of a higher-order memory structure that has been proposed for text comprehension is the *script* (Schank and Abelson, 1977). Scripts describe stereotypical sequences of events, such as a visit to the cinema or a flight on an aeroplane. Stories that mention cinema visits may describe them only sketchily. Nevertheless, readers will be able to say, for example, that tickets were bought in the foyer, even if the ticket buying was not explicitly mentioned. They use their script-based knowledge to derive this information.

Scripts are also used 'on-line' in story comprehension. They become *activated* when certain *keywords* appear in a text. These words include those, such as *cinema*, that are part of the name of the script, as well as related words such as *film*. If an episode in a story begins 'We decided to go and see a film...' the cinema-visit script is made available to help with the interpretation of the subsequent text. However, keywords must not activate scripts indiscriminately, regardless of context. The cinema-visit script is unlikely to be relevant to an episode beginning 'We decided not to go to the cinema...'.

Once a script has been activated its structure is, at least according to Schank and Abelson's theory, imposed on the text, and this imposition may enable the language understanding system to forego a detailed low-level analysis of the text. For example, in a story about a visit to a restaurant, an early sentence containing the words 'waiter' and 'table' may, without further ado, be assumed to describe the waiter showing the people visiting the restaurant to a table – an action that forms part of the script.

So-called *declarative* methods of representation, such as associative networks and scripts, are best suited to encoding facts. However, much of our knowledge is not of knowledge of facts, but *procedural* knowledge of how to do things. First, many texts describe people performing actions – putting their procedural knowledge to use. Second, as Austin (1962) pointed out, people do things with words, such as getting married, making promises and naming ships. In comprehension, procedural knowledge of how to perform speech acts may be used 'in reverse' to work out what a speaker was trying to do.

A simple way of representing procedural knowledge is in a *production system* (Newell and Simon, 1972). A production system is a set of rules, called *productions*, that have the form:

IF <condition> THEN <action>

So, for example, information about how to wash clothes might be encoded as a production system, and one production in that system might be:

IF there are both coloureds and whites
THEN wash the coloureds and the whites separately

Finally, mental models of discourse are representations of facts about the real or an imaginary world. They are less permanent than semantic memory itself, but a theory of knowledge representation may suggest an account of what mental models are and of how they are related to memory structures such as associative networks, scripts and production systems.

Future directions

The present is a period of intense activity in the study of language understanding, and it is unlikely that this activity will abate in the next decade. There will be increased cooperation between psychologists and those in related fields, especially linguistics, computer science and artificial intelligence, as the field of cognitive science takes shape. Perhaps the main lesson that psychologists must learn is that vaguely formulated theories will no longer do. There is a need both for sets of general explanatory principles, such as psychologists have attempted to provide in the past, and for accounts of how those principles can be used to 'construct' detailed language understanding mechanisms of the sort that might be embodied in AI programs. Interestingly, AI researchers are now emphasising the need to formulate the principles on which their programs are based, rather than simply providing the mechanisms (see e.g. Winston, 1984).

One development in AI that *may* have an important influence on language understanding research is *connectionism* (see e.g. Feldman and Ballard, 1982). Ordinary 'serial' computers can only carry out one operation at a time. They are very different from the human brain – a large collection of small processors (neurons), any number of which can be 'computing' at the same time. Connectionist models attempt to mimic this aspect of the machinery that underlies cognitive functioning in humans. They comprise many simple processors that exchange excitatory and inhibitory signals along the connections from which the models get their name. In the field of language understanding, connectionist models of parsing (Waltz and Pollack, 1985) and of certain aspects of semantic memory (McClelland and Rumelhart, 1985) have already appeared. However, the large-scale implementation of such models awaits the availability of a new generation of computers with a large number of interconnected, but largely independent, processors. In the connectionist literature such computers are referred to as *massively parallel hardware*. Extravagant claims are being made for connectionist models, but it remains to be seen what their long-term impact will be.

Turning to the more specific topics of this chapter, there seems little doubt that syntax will remain a growth area in psycholinguistics over the next few years. Experimental research will continue to address the problems discussed above: when is a full syntactic analysis performed, and how is it performed when it is? Since the failure of the early syntax-based theories of comprehension, parsing has been unduly neglected in psycholinguistics. However, psycholinguists are now realising that syntactic processing plays a crucial role in comprehension, even though it cannot explain all aspects of the way we process texts.

A more general issue that will have to be faced is how the large body of work on parsing in computer science can be used in constructing psychological theories. Computer scientists study parsing because they have to make computers parse programming languages, and it has recently been suggested (e.g. by Gazdar, Klein, Pullum, and Sag, 1985) that natural languages are more like programming languages, at least from the point of view of parsing, than was previously thought.

Along with the growth of interest in parsing, experiments on meaning will continue to flourish. Psychologists who study meaning are in a very different position from those who work on parsing. Over the last fifteen to twenty years many basic findings have been established. What is needed now is an increase in the sophistication of this work, in two main respects. First, theories of language understanding must take more account of the complexities of language discovered by linguists, logicians and others. The closer cooperation between disciplines, promoted by cognitive science, removes any excuse that psycholinguists may have had for ignoring texts that are linguistically complex, but which people have little difficulty in producing or understanding. Second, as mentioned above, psycholinguistic theories themselves will have to increase in sophistication.

Major developments are likely in the study of how we understand extended discourse, as opposed to very brief texts. One important topic will be the way in which the plans of the participants contribute to the structure and content of conversation, a matter that has already received some attention in AI (e.g. Power, 1979; Cohen and Perrault, 1979). This study will highlight the neglected fact that many aspects of language understanding are purpose-relative – what is extracted from a text depends on the reason that it is being studied. The recognition of this fact should lead to clearer ideas about what it means to say that someone has understood what they have heard or read. Another area of interest that psycholinguistics will increasingly come to share with AI is that of topic selection, focus, and foregrounding (see e.g. Grosz, 1981; Sidner, 1983). Both Grosz and Sidner provide accounts of how the focused part of a discourse changes as the discourse progresses, but a question still to be answered is why we need to concentrate our attention on only a small part of a text at any time. In many ways it would be better if the whole of the discourse (so far) was equally accessible.

The explanation of focusing probably lies in the fact that language understanding makes use of psychological systems, in particular limited capacity short-term memory stores, such as those described by Halliday and Hitch (this volume), that evolved for other purposes. This brings me to a final new direction for psycholinguistics. Even after a quarter century of cognitive psychology, psycholinguistic theories need to be better integrated with those from related areas of psychology. Language use involves memory (see Morris, this volume), attention and other cognitive systems, and at least a broad familiarity with how these systems work is essential for psycholinguistic theorising. In the past there have been too many instances of psycholinguistic results being misinterpreted because of a naive view of, say, how a memory cue accesses a memory trace.

Whatever the precise future of psycholinguistics, it is sure to be an exciting one. Our use of language sets us apart from other animals, and understanding this ability remains one of the most important, and difficult, challenges that psychology can offer.

References

Anderson, J. R. and Bower, G. H. (1973), *Human Associative Memory*. Winston: Washington, DC.

Anderson, J. R. and Hastie, R. (1974), 'Individuation and reference in memory: Proper names and definite descriptions', *Cognitive Psychology*, 6, 167-80.

Anderson, R. C. and Pichert, J. W. (1978), 'Recall of previously unrecallable information following a shift in perspective', *Journal of Verbal Learning and Verbal Behavior*, *17*, 1-12.

Austin, J. L. (1962), *How to Do Things with Words*. Oxford University Press: Oxford.

Barclay, J. R. (1973), 'The role of comprehension in remembering sentences', *Cognitive Psychology*, 5, 229-54.

Bransford, J. D., Barclay, J. R. and Franks, J. J. (1972), 'Sentence memory: a constructive versus interpretive approach', *Cognitive Psychology*, 3, 331-50.

Chomsky, N. (1957), *Syntactic Structures*. Mouton: The Hague.

Chomsky, N. (1965), *Aspects of the Theory of Syntax*. MIT Press: Cambridge, Mass.

Clark, H. H. (1979), 'Responding to indirect speech acts', *Cognitive Psychology*, 11, 430-77.

Clark, H. H. and Malt, B. C. (1984), 'Psychological constraints on language: a commentary on Bresnan and Kaplan and on Givon', in W. Kintsch, J. R. Miller and P. G. Polson (eds), *Methods and Tactics in Cognitive Science*. Erlbaum: Hillsdale, NJ.

Clark, H. H. and Schunk, D. H. (1980), 'Polite responses to polite requests', *Cognition*, 8, 111-43.

Clark, H. H. and Sengul, C. J. (1979), 'In search of referents for noun phrases and pronouns', *Memory and Cognition*, 7, 35-41.

Cohen, P. R. and Perrault, C. R. (1979), 'Elements of a plan-based theory of speech acts', *Cognitive Science*, 3, 177-212.

Corbett, A. T. and Dosher, B. A. (1978), 'Instrument inferences in sentence encoding', *Journal of Verbal Learning and Verbal Behavior*, 17, 479-91.

Crain, S. and Steedman, M. J. (1985), 'On not being led up the garden path: the use of context by the psychological parser', in D. Dowty, L. Karttunen and A. Zwicky (eds), *Natural Language Parsing*. Cambridge University Press: Cambridge.

Feldman, J. A. and Ballard, D. H. (1982), 'Connectionist models and their properties', *Cognitive Science*, 6, 205-54.

Ferreira, F. and Clifton, C. (1986), 'The independence of syntactic processing', *Journal of Memory and Language*, 25, 348-68.

Frazier, L. and Rayner, K. (1982), 'Making and correcting errors during sentence comprehension: eye movements in the analysis of structurally ambiguous sentences', *Cognitive Psychology*, 14, 178-210.

Frederiksen, J. R. (1981), 'Understanding anaphora: rules used by readers in assigning pronominal referents', *Discourse Processes*, 4, 323-47.

Garnham, A. (1981), 'Mental models as representations of text', *Memory and Cognition*, 9, 560-5.

Garnham, A. (1982), 'Testing psychological theories about inference making', *Memory and Cognition*, 10, 341-9.

Garnham, A. (1988), *Artificial Intelligence: An Introduction*. Routledge & Kegan Paul: London.

Garnham, A. and Oakhill, J. V. (1985), 'On-line resolution of anaphoric pronouns: effects of inference making and verb semantics', *British Journal of Psychology*, 76, 385-93.

Gazdar, G., Klein, E., Pullum, G. and Sag, I. (1985), *Generalized Phrase Structure Grammar*. Blackwell: Oxford.

Gibbs, R. W. (1983), 'Do people always process the literal meaning of indirect requests?, *Journal of Experimental Psychology: Learning, Memory, and Cognition*, 9, 524-33.

Grice, H. P. (1975), 'Logic and conversation', in P. Cole and J. L. Morgan (eds), *Syntax and Semantics 3: Speech Acts*. Seminar Press: New York.

Grice, H. P. (1978), 'Further notes on logic and conversation', in P. Cole (ed.), *Syntax and Semantics 9: Pragmatics*. Academic Press: New York.

Grosz, B. (1981), 'Focusing and description in natural language dialogues', in A. K. Joshi, B. L. Webber and I. A. Sag (eds), *Elements of Discourse Understanding*. Cambridge University Press: Cambridge.

Haviland, S. E. and Clark, H. H. (1974), 'What's new? Acquiring new information as a process in comprehension', *Journal of Verbal Learning and Verbal Behavior, 19*, 168-75.

Johnson, M. K., Bransford, J. D. and Solomon, S. (1973), 'Memory for tacit implications of sentences', *Journal of Experimental Psychology, 98*, 203-5.

Johnson-Laird, P. N. (1970), 'The perception and memory of sentences', in J. Lyons (ed.), *New Horizons in Linguistics*. Penguin: Harmondsworth.

Johnson-Laird, P. N. (1977), 'Psycholinguistics without linguistics', in N. S. Sutherland (ed.), *Tutorial Essays in Psychology*, Vol. 1. Erlbaum: Hillsdale, NJ.

Johnson-Laird, P. N. (1983), *Mental Models: Towards a Cognitive Science of Language, Inference, and Consciousness*. Cambridge University Press: Cambridge.

Johnson-Laird, P. N. and Garnham, A. (1980), 'Descriptions and discourse models', *Linguistics and Philosophy, 3*, 371-93.

Johnson-Laird, P. N. and Stevenson, R. (1970), 'Memory for syntax', *Nature, 227*, p. 412.

Keenan, J. N., MacWhinney, B. and Mayhew, D. (1977), 'Pragmatics in memory: a study of natural conversation', *Journal of Verbal Learning and Verbal Behavior, 16*, 549-60.

Kimball, J. (1973), 'Seven principles of surface structure parsing in natural language', *Cognition, 2*, 15-47.

Lakoff, G. P. (1972), 'Structural complexity in fairy tales', *The Study of Man, 1*, 128-90.

McClelland, J. L. and Rumelhart, D. E. (1985), 'Distributed memory and the representation of general and specific information', *Journal of Experimental Psychology: General, 114*, 159-88.

Mandler, J. M. and Johnson, N. S. (1977), 'Remembrance of things parsed: story structure and recall', *Cognitive Psychology, 9*, 111-51.

Miller, G. A. and Johnson-Laird, P. N. (1976), *Language and Perception*. Cambridge University Press: Cambridge.

Miller, G. A. and McKean, K. A. (1964), 'A chronometric study of some relations between sentences', *Quarterly Journal of Experimental Psychology, 16*, 297-308.

Newell, A. and Simon, H. A. (1972), *Human Problem Solving*. Prentice-Hall: Englewood Cliffs, NJ.

Paris, S. G. and Lindauer, B. K. (1976), 'The role of inference in children's comprehension and memory for sentences', *Cognitive Psychology, 8*, 217-27.

Pichert, J. W. and Anderson, R. C. (1977), 'Taking different perspectives on a story', *Journal of Educational Psychology, 69*, 309-15.

Power, R. J. (1979), 'The organization of purposeful dialogues', *Linguistics, 17*, 107-52.

Quillian, M. R. (1968), 'Semantic memory', in M. Minsky (ed.), *Semantic Information Processing*. MIT Press: Cambridge, Mass.

Rayner, K., Carlson, M. and Frazier, L. (1983), 'The interaction of syntax and semantics during sentence processing: eye movements during the analysis of semantically biased sentences', *Journal of Verbal Learning and Verbal Behavior, 22*, 358-74.

Rumelhart, D. E. (1975), 'Notes on a schema for stories', in D. G. Bobrow and A. M. Collins (eds), *Representation and Understanding: Studies in Cognitive Science*. Academic Press: New York.

Sachs, J. S. (1967), 'Recognition memory for syntactic and semantic aspects of connected discourse', *Perception and Psychophysics, 2*, 437-42.

Schank, R. C. and Abelson, R. P. (1977), *Scripts, Goals, Plans and Understanding*. Erlbaum: Hillsdale, NJ.

Searle, J. R. (1969), *Speech Acts: An Essay in the Philosophy of Language*. Cambridge University Press: Cambridge.

Sidner, C. L. (1983), 'Focusing in the comprehension of definite anaphora', in M. Brady and R. C. Berwick (eds), *Computational Models of Discourse*. MIT Press: Cambridge, Mass.

Singer, M. (1979), 'The temporal locus of interference effects in the comprehension of brief passages: recognizing and verifying implications about instruments', *Perceptual and Motor Skills*, *49*, 539-50.

Thorndyke, P. W. (1977), 'Cognitive structures in comprehension and memory of narrative discourse', *Cognitive Psychology*, *9*, 77-110.

Waltz, D. L. and Pollack, J. B. (1985), 'Massively parallel parsing: a strongly interactive model of natural language interpretation', *Cognitive Science*, *9*, 51-74.

Winston, P. H. (1984), *Artificial Intelligence*, 2nd ed. Addison-Wesley: Reading, Mass.

Yekovich, F. R., Walker, C. H. and Blackman, H. (1979), 'The role of presupposed and focal information in integrating sentences', *Journal of Verbal Learning and Verbal Behavior*, *18*, 535-48.

6 Problem-solving: representation and discovery

David W. Green

Introduction

Research on problem-solving has looked at problems that exemplify general features such as mental search. The way a problem is worded might be a variable in such work – indeed we shall see that it is – but the research effort is directed at the way a problem is solved once this textual representation has been formed. Nonetheless, understanding a problem and solving it are closely related (see Greeno, 1977; Rumelhart, 1980). As we begin to tackle a problem we start to understand what it really amounts to. In a similar vein, in order to solve a problem we must retrieve relevant information. How we do so, and how that information is represented so that we can do so, is an important issue. But the focus of research on problem-solving has been on the effects of different kinds of knowledge on the representation of the problem itself.

A variety of methods exist for studying the way problems are solved. Sternberg, (1977) used a standard reaction time method in formulating a description of how individuals solve simple analogies of the form 'A is to B as C is to ?'. An alternative approach, and one that is suitable for more complex problems, requires individuals to think aloud while solving a problem (see Byrne, 1983). Such a method yields a rich source of data. It is restricted to tasks in which individuals can describe in words what they are currently attending to (see Ericsson and Simon, 1980). Since it does not yield a complete description of what a person is doing, considerable effort and ingenuity is required in order to fill in the gaps (see Lindsay and Norman, 1972).

Detailed simulations have been constructed on the basis of such protocols (e.g. Simon and Newell, 1971) and they are very useful in exploring thinking that extends over a long time period. Flower and Hayes (1984)

I thank Guy Claxton, Nigel Harvey and Peter Wason for helpful comments on an earlier draft of this chapter.

have used it to explore expository writing. It is also useful in assessing the thinking of experts in, for example, medical diagnosis (Kuipers and Kassirer, 1984), fault-finding (Rasmussen and Jensen, 1974) and process control (Bainbridge, 1979). Such studies find a practical application in the development of expert systems, i.e. computer programs that capture knowledge about a particular area of expertise and then apply that knowledge to solving a problem. Where a problem requires some physical action, the sequence of actions a person takes can also be treated as a protocol. Typically, individuals seek to explore a novel problem in a rather *ad hoc* manner before embarking on a more planned approach.

Our understanding of problem-solving over long periods is very restricted. Longitudinal case studies are not common and so our grasp of certain phenomena (e.g. the flash of insight) is based largely on the anecdotal reports of scientists, writers and inventors.

A brief resumé of conceptualisations of problem-solving

In Piaget's view (Piaget, 1972), adults solve problems according to the principles of hypothetico-deductive logic. However, it became clear both from work on human reasoning in the sixties and from research on human judgement (see, for example, Shaklee, 1979) that such a claim is incorrect. Indeed, it is perhaps as well that we do not think according to the canons of formal logic for our thinking would be maladapted to the world in which we live (Hunt, 1982) where relevance is more important than logical equivalence. We simplify reality and act according to these simplifications. Our rationality is 'bounded' (Simon, 1957).

The focus of current research has shifted away from a concern with how well individuals do in comparison with some formal description to an attempt to characterise what they actually do and the form of the representations that are used. Such an interest has led to the notion that our decision-making is based on certain heuristics i.e. rules of thumb (Tversky and Kahneman, 1974) and that our capacity to reason effectively is crucially dependent upon relatively specific, rather than context-free, problem representations. Examples of such work cited in the next section attempt to make clear the importance of problem content in determining the ease with which a problem is solved and the way that it is solved.

The effects of problem-content in novel problems

Problem-solving can be viewed as a process of moving through a problem-space in which an initial state of ignorance is transformed into a goal state where the solution to the problem is known. These states are really states of knowledge or belief about states of affairs in some real or imagined world. The transition from one state to another is accomplished by applying various operators or procedures whose conditions of application match those of the current state.

For any given state a number of operators may apply yielding a variety of subsequent states. One way to reach a goal would then be to search all of these possible states. But such exhaustive search is rarely possible. Instead, the search through the set of possibilities must be constrained. One heuristic for constraining search is to attempt to reduce progressively the difference between the initial state and the goal state. This means-end approach works well for certain classes of problems, such as the Tower of Hanoi problems which require a subject to move a set of discs from one location to another under certain constraints, but is maladapted to other problems such as Luchin's water-jar problems (see Sanford, 1985, p. 300).

For problems with known answers there may be only one path which allows the goal (answer) to be obtained in the fewest possible moves. The longer such a path, the greater the time required to solve the problem. This is not to say that in solving a problem humans mentally represent some complete and formally defined problem space and find a path through it. Limitations of memory and attention preclude us holding such a space in mind except in the simplest case. In fact, Atwood and Polson (1976) showed that individuals attempt to evaluate only three alternatives when searching in a means-end fashion.

More generally, the mathematical or formal complexity of a problem is not a good predictor of its psychological difficulty. Problems which are different versions of the same formal problem (problem isomorphs) are solved in significantly different times (e.g. Kotovsky, Hayes and Simon, 1985). The guise in which a problem is presented is crucial.

The study cited above used the Tower of Hanoi problem. But the finding is not exceptional. A similar result is found when individuals are asked to solve logically-equivalent versions of Wason's selection task. The original version of the task (Wason, 1968) required individuals to determine the truth or falsity of a rule which related vowels and numbers, under the restriction that vowels always appeared on one side of a card and numbers on the other, (viz. If there is a vowel on one side of a card then there is an even number on the other). Presented with four cards showing, respectively, A, D, 4, and 7, most students chose to inspect cards displaying A and 4. Whereas an odd number on the other side of the A card would refute the rule, the presence of a consonant on the other side of the 4 card is immaterial. Only by establishing the absence of a counter-example, i.e. a vowel and an odd number, can the rule actually be proved true. Hence only cards marked with A and 7 must be selected. Ten per cent or less of university students solve the original version. However, presented with another version of the problem, most students succeed. In this version, created by D'Andrade (cited in Rumelhart, 1980, and Mandler, 1983), individuals are asked to imagine that they are store managers who have to determine whether a particular rule is being upheld. In the store receipts for articles costing more than 30 dollars require the department manager's signature. Given the rule 'If any purchase exceeds 30 dollars, then the receipt must have the signature of the department manager on the back', which receipts would need to be turned over? (a) A purchase of 15 dollars, (b) a purchase of 45 dollars, (c) an unsigned receipt, (d) a signed receipt? In this scenario 70 per cent of the subjects chose the correct cards (receipts) whereas only 15 per cent solved an isomorphic version which substituted an arbitrary rule about labels (see Evans, 1982, Griggs, 1983, and Wason, 1983, for detailed commentaries on such work). It is worth observing here that such results refute the view that successful reasoning about conditionals involves context-free inference rules, or even the retrieval of specific experiences. Instead, reasoning is facilitated when suitable knowledge structures (or schemata) are evoked. Wason and Green (1984) showed that reasoning is improved when the conditional refers to the properties of a single object ('If there is a triangle, then it is coloured red') rather than to two separate entities ('All triangles have a red patch above them'). In the former case a single object schema is evoked permitting a unified representation of the content. Cheng and Holyoak (1985) have proposed, more specifically, that individuals reason using context-sensitive structures derived from everyday experience. One such structure, a permission schema, specifies the conditions for allowable action. In this case, if the rationale for the conditional evokes the schema then the selection task is successfully solved.

The guise of a problem can also affect the way individuals attempt to solve it. Tversky and Kahneman (1973) showed individuals a diagram consisting of a series of six-letter columns. Each comprised five Xs and an O in one of the six places. This fact was not stated explicitly but was an implicit part of the representation. They were required to estimate the percentage of pathways starting from the top which consisted of six Xs, five Xs and one O, four Xs and two Os and so on. Overall, the percentages assigned had to add up to 100 per cent. In this version of the problem, individuals estimated that there were more paths consisting of six Xs compared to those with five Xs. Their estimates were based on the ease of constructing the pathways. Because paths of six Xs were more available, they assumed that they were more numerous. Their decisions were based on the *availability* heuristic. In a second version of the problem, individuals were told that five-sixths of the cards in a card game were marked with an X and that one-sixth were marked with an O. Here, the proportion of Xs to Os was explicitly stated. Individuals had to estimate the percentage of plays in a game in which all six players would receive an X card and none a card marked with an O; the percentage of plays in which five players would receive an X card and one player an O card and so forth, as previously. In this problem, the estimates were based on the extent to which a play was representative of the pack of cards as a whole. Hence, individuals estimated a higher percentage of plays consisting of five Xs to one O. Their estimates were based on the *representativeness* heuristic.

Formally identical problems then are by no means psychologically equivalent. In order to understand what makes a problem easy or difficult, we need to know the nature of the representation of the problem that individuals actually use. The fact that some abstract characterisation of the problem is not a useful predictor means that we cannot tell without further information whether or not a person will succeed in solving the same problem presented in a different guise: i.e. transfer of learning becomes an important issue. Indeed the question of how we call up, construct and manipulate representations is of vital importance. This general issue has been the focus of intensive research and the following sections sample this effort. But why should an abstract characterisation be inadequate? It may be that we have simply looked in the wrong place. In evolutionary terms the primary function of thought is to guide action in a world of objects and other people. Perhaps the place to start is with the idea of a mental model.

Mental models

In order to achieve the goal of guiding and controlling action it is necessary that the world of thought represent, and be able to emulate, possible actions in the world. The content of awareness might then be thought of as a model of the world (Yates, 1985) and the essential function of mind to be the construction of such models (Johnson-Laird, 1983). Indeed in the literature the notion of a mental model is used to refer both to what we know and to what we construct on the basis of what we know. It is not necessary for us to be consciously aware of such models. The critical feature is that the mental entities and their manipulation symbolise things and operations in the external world (Craik, 1943). Granted that an ability to model the three-dimensional structure of the physical world is important, it is perhaps unsurprising that mental imagery should be for many the most obvious phenomenal experience of the modelling power of the mind. It is now recognised that such representations are not epiphenomenal. They allow certain kinds of operations to be carried out that are more time-consuming or more error-prone on other more abstract representations. The mind makes use of a wide variety of representations and indeed invents representations so that certain goals can be achieved more easily (see Sloman, 1984). The crucial property of such representations is, however, that they symbolise certain objects, actions or events.

As might be expected, experimental work has confirmed that providing individuals with a suitable model of a new device improves their ability to operate it and to understand it (Kieras and Bovair, 1984). But the fact that we can model aspects of the world does not entail that our models are scientifically accurate. In the case of motion, for instance, our knowledge acquired through experience with moving objects leads us to develop accounts which are effectively pre-Newtonian (McCloskey, 1983). Such models allow us to predict the outcomes of physical interactions in the street, for example, but mislead us when we are asked to depict the fall of an object from a plane. What is perhaps equally interesting, and more important educationally, is that even subjects who had taken physics courses still adhered to their naive theory. Instruction, unless it is specifically designed to modify preconceptions, may be distorted to fit them (see section on Expertise below). There is a link here to work on prejudice and attitude change.

The idea of a mental model has considerable appeal and is applicable to a wide range of problems. It is far removed from the notion that the mind operates like some calculating device according to the canons of formal logic. Johnson-Laird (1983) has proposed that the difficulties experienced in solving syllogisms (i.e. problems of the form 'Some As are Bs: Some Bs are Cs: Does it follow that some As are Cs?') reflect both the difficulty of constructing an internal model of the problem and the ease with which it can be manipulated. In this proposal (see, for example, Johnson-Laird and Steedman, 1978) mental tokens are established for each of the terms mentioned in a premise. In the case of 'Some As are Bs' an arbitrary number of A tokens are linked to B tokens and at least one A and one B token are left unattached. In representing the second premise a subset of the B tokens are linked to C tokens.

The process of determining whether a conclusion actually follows from the stated premises involves an attempt to break the links that have been formed in order to see whether the resulting model remains consistent with the premises and yet yields a different conclusion. Errors can occur in initially representing the premises (e.g. failing to represent that some B tokens are unattached) or in a failure to test out all the possibilities. Such a difficulty may stem from the fact that the material cannot be represented in a unified manner (Wason and Green, 1984; Oakhill and Johnson-Laird, 1985a). This may be so not only because such representations impose less load on working memory but also because they make it possible to see what needs to be tested, i.e. what counts as a counter-example.

A further factor accounting for reasoning errors is our beliefs. We are more likely to accept invalid conclusions if we believe them (Evans, Barston and Pollard, 1983). We are also more likely to produce them (Oakhill and Johnson-Laird, 1985b). In syllogistic reasoning such beliefs act to stop further exploration. In the context of scientific research, on the other hand, the belief in a particular hypothesis may spur the search for confirming results and discourage the destructive testing of alternatives.

Testing representations

Studies in the previous section do not really offer a window on the process of testing representations. One task which allows us to study the process of forming and testing hypotheses was developed by Wason (1960). In the 2-4-6 Task individuals are required to discover a simple rule which relates three numbers exemplified by the triad 2-4-6. The task requires individuals on each trial to produce three numbers. Typically, individuals formulate a hypothesis (e.g. that numbers must increase by 2) and then produce three numbers (e.g. 8-10-12) that are consistent with that hypothesis. We are more likely, it seems, to seek to confirm our hypotheses, than to disconfirm them. Indeed, despite evidence to the contrary, we may persist in maintaining what is logically the same hypothesis expressed in different terms (Wason, 1960). Recent work has sought to explore some of the factors that affect the likelihood of discovering a rule which is not simply sufficient to generate correct triples but is also necessary – Wason's rule was that the numbers increased in order of magnitude.

In Wason's original study, students were required to announce the rule when they thought that they had grasped it. They were then told if they were right or not. In such circumstances, instructing them to disconfirm their hypotheses does not improve performance (Tweney et al., 1980). However, such instructions are effective if individuals are left to test out the rules they announce for themselves (Gorman and Gorman, 1984). It is as if disconfirmation can be a hindrance rather than a help at certain stages in problem-solving. Indeed, in a study of complex problem-solving (Mynatt, Doherty, and Tweney, 1978) those who were most successful did not abandon their hypotheses too readily. Problem-representation is also important in this task. Individuals are better able to solve the problem when they are required to discover two rules which are complementary (Tweney et al., 1980). One rule corresponded to Wason's original 2-4-6 rule and the other to its complement, i.e. any triple that did not ascend in order of magnitude. Such rules facilitate a unified representation of the problem (Gorman, Stafford and Gorman, 1987) and allow individuals to solve even more difficult versions of the problem. In confirming the first rule one is testing the limits of the other.

The findings of such research are, of course, open to criticism that they do not apply to the solving of actual scientific problems. The experiments generally involve a task which is like a game rather than a passion and the sessions are over in hours rather than in years. A case study of Faraday (Tweney, Doherty and Mynatt, 1981) is illuminating in this regard. Faraday, it seems, would first seek to confirm his hypotheses – progressively refining his observations. A *confirmation heuristic* (Gorman, Tweney and Siegel, 1984) makes sense in an environment where true experimental signals need to be distinguished from noise. Only when he felt sure of the effects did he proceed to a phase of rigorous disconfirmation. Not all scientists are quite so rigorous, but then the manner in which hypotheses are established and confirmed is not simply an individual matter. Scientists operate within a social context in which the ability to advocate a position is arguably more important than the truth of it. Indeed, the forceful espousal of a viewpoint and an unwillingness to abandon it, characterised successful NASA scientists interviewed by Mitroff (1981).

Viewed overall, however, the process of testing representations is clearly important to discovery. We need to know when to abandon a line of enquiry and when to develop other representations of an issue that may be more revealing. It is not possible to specify precisely when we should abandon a line of enquiry, that is, interrupt search in the problem-space. At some point we perceive the costs of continuing to outweigh the benefits. We may, for instance, restructure when stuck or when we are overloaded by the demands of the problem as we perceive them to be (see Ohlsson, 1984a).

It follows from such considerations that we need to distinguish between the problem as presented, the problem as we describe it to ourselves, and the problem space itself. Through time the same presented problem may evoke different problem spaces because we describe it in different ways (see also Sanford, 1985, pp. 306-7).

Expertise

Intuitively, the kind of representation we construct for a particular problem will depend upon the knowledge we bring to bear upon it. Even in relatively simple problems, such as the Maier's horse-trading problem (e.g. Maier and Burke, 1967), individuals may bring different knowledge to bear. In this problem, individuals are asked to work out the profit a man makes in the horse-trading business. He buys a horse for 60 dollars and sells it for 70 dollars. He then buys it back for 80 dollars and sells it again for 90 dollars. Those who see it as two distinct transactions involving income and expenditure solve it easily whereas those who are guided by the surface form of the text erroneously assume that after making the sum of 10 dollars on the first transaction this sum is lost in purchasing the horse back again.

As an individual acquires expertise in a field naive representations are either supplanted or cease to be functional. For chess masters, a chess board is a set of patterns of attack and defence (DeGroot, 1965; Chase and Simon, 1973). It is as if their knowledge of the game was stored as a set of patterns, like words, in some internal dictionary and that perceiving the board was like seeing a page of text in a language one knew.

Differences between experts and novices have been demonstrated in other areas. Thus, novices represent a physics problem in terms of its wording rather than in terms of the forces or type of problem it actually addresses (Chi, Feltovich and Glaser, 1981). More specifically, Larkin (1983) has shown how novices represent problems in mechanics in terms of objects that exist in the real world (e.g. blocks and pulleys) and that their understanding involves emulating operations that correspond to actions that could be carried out in the real world. Experts, on the other hand, construct, in addition, a physical representation that contains fictitious entities (forces and momenta) in which operations correspond to the laws of physics. Other differences exist which are perhaps a consequence of the shift in representation. In solving textbook problems, students beginning physics work backward from the unknowns to the givens, whereas experts work forward (Larkin, McDermott, Simon and Simon, 1980).

The fact that experts have a more developed representation of a given domain does not mean that they cannot be affected by the presentation of a problem. For example, even an experienced mechanic may seriously underestimate the probability of faults arising from a particular source given a fault-tree (a graphic device which indicates possible reasons for a fault) that does not reveal the full details explicitly (Fischhoff, Slovic and Lichtenstein, 1978).

Expertise develops over time. Clearly, naive representations cease in some sense to control problem-solving in the expert. (For an overview of research on the conceptual structures individuals bring to bear when learning science, see Driver and Erickson, 1983.) But it seems unwise to conclude that they cease to exist or that the nature of these naive representations does not constrain the mental representation of expert knowledge. Meeting different task demands certainly seems to affect what is readily accessible in working memory (Green, 1975) but it may not fully determine what is represented. Under stress, perhaps, more naive representations come to dominate.

This issue of expert representations is complicated by the range of representations which must be deployed. In fault diagnosis, for example, an expert needs to possess not only a model of how the system operates (a functional model), but also needs to know how the physical components connect together (a physical model or connectivity description) and how a component may fail (fault models). In addition, an expert requires a strategy for diagnosis (see, for example, Atwood, Brooks and Radlinski, 1986). Such variety suggests that alternative formats may exist for representing such knowledge.

It is helpful to distinguish between a format based on propositional or language-like elements and their interconnections which may be used to capture causal or functional knowledge and one which uses patterns which may be better suited to capture visuo-spatial data such as the size, shape and proximity of components in a machine (see Bainbridge, 1987). But an adequate theory of representational types and formats remains to be developed (see also, Sloman (1984)).

Developing and changing representations

Functional fixity and set

One of the principal goals of a theory of problem-solving is to characterise the dynamics or manner in which problems are solved. A central metaphor is that problem-solving is a form of search through a mental space. But problems are sometimes solved when they are seen in a new way – when the nature of the search space is changed. Such a change means that different operators become applicable and hence the possibilities for action are altered (see Ohlsson, 1984a). Difficulties in attaining such a change in representation may account for certain types of mental block, whereas successful restructurings may account for the 'flash of insight'. The ease of solving a problem is, as we have seen, a question in some cases of possessing the relevant knowledge. In other cases, we may know what we need but be unable to use or retrieve it, at least for a while.

Thus, if an object has been recently used in one way, it tends to be less available for use in some other way. Duncker (1945) termed this effect 'functional fixedness' and it has been confirmed in a number of subsequent studies (e.g. Adamson, 1952; Birch and Rabinowitz, 1951). The effect does tend to fade with time (Adamson and Taylor, 1954) and it can be alleviated by calling attention to relevant parts of the object (Glucksberg and Danks, 1968). When using an object, it is mentally represented under a particular description such that certain features relevant to that use are preeminent. It is a form of encoding specificity. Achieving an alternative description involves making other features more salient. A matchbox has to cease to be a container for matches, for example, and become a support for a candle. Precisely, how such redescriptions are achieved is open to question (see Ohlsson, above, for a recent suggestion) but it is undeniable that restructuring can occur when an alternative function is mentally available (Saugstad and Raaheim, 1960). There is an applied link here to therapies involving cognitive restructuring where experiences are 'relabelled'.

Once a problem has been solved then the procedure for solving it can become automated. It can then be immediately elicited by problems of the same form. Once we have constructed a mental tool we may deploy it rather than constructing a new one which might be better adapted. Our solutions can also become fixed. Such a process presumably accounts for the effects of 'set' (cf. Luchins, 1942). In the Luchins' studies individuals are required to solve a series of problems involving quantities of liquid. These can all be solved in the same somewhat laborious way. Critical trials permit a more direct solution yet individuals frequently fail to avail themselves of it. Such a phenomenon, which seems to indicate the powerful effects of habit, and a failure to be open to experience, really needs to be considered in a wider context.

Efficient and rapid functioning often requires the development of relatively automated sequences of behaviour ('macro-operators') which no longer require conscious attention. The technical terms of a discipline, for example, serve to label such operators. In using technical language we are able to communicate effectively with those who are also familiar with those terms. But difficulties arise when we seek to explain ideas to the uninitiated or when a problem resists an approach in such terms. Efficiency in some contexts must be purchased by relative inefficiency in others. But let us return to the issue of restructuring. What means exist for restructuring a domain?

Analogy

The perception and creation of analogies has always played a vital role in our understanding of ourselves and the universe. Indeed analogy permeates our language (see, for example, Lakoff and Johnson, 1980). The mind is considered as a container ('he's out of his mind') and understanding is treated as a form of perception ('I see what you're saying'). And it is fair to say that the recognition of some deep analogy has produced some amazing scientific achievements (see Dreistadt, 1968). Unfortunately, there are no rules for telling how well some set of ideas will function as a model for another realm of phenomena. But it would be helpful to know the conditions for noticing and applying an analogy.

Some current theories (e.g. Gick and Holyoak, 1980, 1983) suppose that analogies are mapped on the basis of very abstract structural features. Such a claim seems to fly in the face of evidence cited earlier on the critical role of problem content (Johnson-Laird, personal communication): isomorphic versions of the same problem are not handled with equal facility. Indeed there is little or no transfer from one to the other. Experimental evidence (e.g. Gick and Holyoak, 1980) indicates that individuals rarely use a prior analogy unless it is hinted that they should do so, or unless there is some either identical or closely similar element in common (Keane, 1987). It seems reasonable to suppose along with Schank (1982) that we do tend to establish ways of construing our lives which are relatively abstract and thematic. But some specific cues are required if a particular event, incident or problem is to trigger a particular memory or the kinds of context-sensitive schema proposed by Cheng and Holyoak (1985, see above). One area where analogical reasoning is used routinely and where suitable analogs are available is reasoning concerned with common law in the United Kingdom. Judges reason by analogy from old cases to new cases (see Adam and Taylor, 1987).

A suitable analogy helps structure a domain of enquiry. Precisely how such a process occurs is not well understood. Dreistadt (1968) proposed that it allowed previously unintegrated material to be formed into a structure. Analogy may be useful then because it allows a unified model or representation of the target domain.

Since it also serves to emphasise certain kinds of relationship it may facilitate solving one class of problems and impede the solution of another class. Gentner and Gentner (1983) provide experimental evidence for this claim in a study that explores the effect of different analogies on solving problems to do with electricity.

It would be wrong to assume that analogies can always be simply applied. Some provisional recognition of relevance may take place on the basis of similar or identical features in the two domains but it may take considerable effort to find suitable correspondences. Schön (1979) cites an interesting case of a group of researchers seeking to improve the performance of a new paintbrush made with synthetic bristles. Instead of depositing paint evenly on the surface it tended to make the paint 'glop'. Schön records that at one point someone observed that a paintbrush is a kind of pump. This observation led the group to puzzle out the ways in which a paintbrush could be a pump. Whereas before the brush's bristles had been central, they came to see the spaces or channels between the bristles as focal. Paint was seen not to adhere to the bristles but to flow through the channels. The act of bending the brush served to compress channels and thereby to pump liquid rather to spread paint onto the surface. They went on to invent methods of smoothing out the way the synthetic bristles bent so as to make the brush pump paint more evenly. Eventually they developed a theory of 'pumpoids' encompassing both normal pumps and paintbrushes. This process of mapping one area of knowledge onto another involved considerable regrouping and renaming of the participants' knowledge of paintbrushes as well as their concept of a pump. It was not an immediate process but took place over an extended period of time. The analogy served to restructure the target domain through a process of redescription. The net effect was to enhance the possibilities for action (see Ohlsson, above).

A similar process may be at work in shorter time spans as postulated in interactionist accounts of the comprehension of metaphors (see Green, 1980) and may require as Miller (1979) proposed the identification of an underlying comparison.

Recently, in an attempt to characterise the nature of central processes, such as problem-solving, Fodor (1983) likened them to the process of accepting and rejecting hypotheses in the scientific world. He assumed in drawing this analogy that all knowledge is available for evaluation and hence that central processes differ in some radical way from sensory processes. Such simultaneous availability conflicts with the idea that problem solving involves a search for relevant information. It also conflicts with the findings that we have difficulty restructuring our representations.

How accurate a description of scientific research is Fodor's view in any case? Although information is perhaps potentially available in the scientific world, there are constraints on the communication of information and greater constraints perhaps on the interpretation of that information. Indeed it is interesting to note that the analogy has been drawn the other way. The scientific process has been likened to the process of perception (e.g. Gregory, 1981). Of course, an analogy is fruitful not simply because of the correspondences between two domains, but also because it highlights certain differences that can then lead to reformulation of the theory (see Carroll and Mack, 1985).

Problem-solving and expository writing

If restructuring is crucial to successful problem-solving, what are the conditions for such restructuring? The Gestaltist account supposed a period of 'unsuccessful' activity (see Ohlsson, 1984b). Indeed a number of anecdotal reports suppose that the creative process goes through a number of phases, viz. accumulating information, repeated attempts at solving the problem, incubation, insight and verification (see Wallas, 1926). In some accounts, incubation is a period during which significant problem-solving occurs below the level of conscious awareness. Perkins (1981), on the other hand, has proposed that anecdotal examples of 'flashes of insight' are akin to noticing and recognising. Both are the outcomes of a process of pattern-recognition which some hold to underlie all forms of mental activity (e.g. Anderson, 1983). On this view a single account can be given of everyday phenomena such as recognising a face in a crowd and acts of creativity.

Problem-solving involves working on representations of problems. For some individuals these representations are not, at least initially, linguistic or in any conventional symbol system. One of the major factors limiting our ability to solve problems may derive from the difficulty in translating such an internal code into conventional expression. Thought may certainly construct models of the world but these constructions can be fleeting and chaotic. The effort required to refine and to develop them can be considerable. Indeed, a certain openness to experience and a tolerance for disorder often typifies those who are most creative (Barron, 1963) and able to extract significant order out of noise. In a similar vein, Harding (1974), citing Thurstone, refers to genius as the capacity to deal with impulses when they are still only roughly affective states.

Hadamard (1954) writes of ideas meeting and combining at various depths and as being more or less scattered. These descriptions are intuitively appealing. The idea of depth relates to the relative ease of expressing ideas. Some ideas may already be in the format of words or propositions, others may be experienced in terms of images, sounds or feelings. As Flower and Hayes (1984) observed, the mapping of thought into expression involves a multiplicity of representations which differ in the ease with which they can be expressed in words. The view that ideas may be more or less scattered may reflect the fact that they are not arrayed in some discursive structure (Hebb and Bindra, 1952). It is necessary to render them coherent with respect to the medium of expression. Thus ideas vary in their expressibility and in their coherence with respect to a given medium of expression.

Problem-solving may be restricted, and expository writing disliked, because individuals are unable to tolerate the experience of disorder or to confront the apparent lack of coherence of their thoughts when these are written down (Green and Wason, 1982). Such difficulties may lead to procrastination or to writing block. Other reactions are also possible. We may resort to jargon in order to manage the impressions others gain of us. One way around such difficulties is to distinguish between a phase of externalising thought (confirming what one feels) and evaluating it (cf. Elbow, 1973; Wason, 1970).

The crucial property of an externalised representation is that it permits *further* discovery to take place. The effort to put concepts into words, for instance, can lead to an effort to clarify the concepts themselves (Scardamalia, Bereiter and Steinbach, 1984). Although expository writing offers a resource for discovery it is not necessarily used as such. Hence changes in a person's research ideas, for example, often derive solely from the outcome of empirical studies, rather than from the laboratory of the page (Green, 1986a).

We are only at the beginning of research into the way a person's conception of a problem evolves over time. In such a context, writing can be viewed as a kind of thought protocol. The role of affective and motivational factors which seem so apparent in expository writing are also demonstrable in other areas of cognitive processing.

Stress, problem-solving and information-processing

If we are anxious we usually make more errors and we are more distractable (see Eysenck, 1984 for further details). Individuals can, of course, be more or less anxious about being tested. Those who are more anxious perform more poorly (Mandler and Sarason, 1952) but their performance improves when the situation (solving anagrams) is presented as non-threatening (Sarason, 1961). Such research is not easily integrated into our account of human problem-solving because it concerns variables that relate to the state of the subject. How are we to include the effects of anxiety, time of day, sleep loss, heat and loud noise in an account which is couched in terms of the manipulation of symbols? Mandler (1979) has suggested one way. Arousal, for instance, is treated as a physiological variable, which nonetheless has cognitive effects because attending to an increased level of arousal demands attention and hence limits our capacity to deal with the task in hand. We certainly do not wish to abandon the insight that symbol manipulation is fundamental to intelligence (cf. Simon, 1969; 1980), but it seems important not to lose sight of the fact that the nature of the machine is also important. The machine places constraints on, and creates opportunities for, information-processing. It is a question then of trying to integrate these so-called energetic variables with our concepts of human information-processing in order to construct an adequate psychological theory.

In fact, such concepts already implicitly contribute to our descriptions. Words are assumed to possess a certain 'level of activation' and the consequences of presenting words in a certain context are attributed to a 'spread of activation'. Hitch (1986) has proposed that energetic concepts be treated as variables attached to certain information-processes. It is supposed here that carrying out mental operations requires resources of various kinds (see, for example, Sanders, 1983). Given that naming or problem-solving requires resources we can consider the nature of these resources. At the very least we need the means to activate responses and processes and also the means to inhibit them. If the resources to activate or to inhibit responses are insufficient then cognitive processing will be impaired, even though the processes themselves are intact. Stress, we suppose, affects the resources available to control processing. Under stress, for example, it is more difficult to speak a language one knows less well. Indeed deficits in such resources offer a way to explain some of the effects of major stressors such as brain-damage on speech (see, for example, Green, 1986b for an account of speech performance in bilinguals with brain-damage).

If we take these notions seriously then we have to consider discovery in energetic terms. In order to restructure a problem its current mental organisation has to be inhibited. The time course of discovery may then reflect the ease or difficulty in effecting such control. A particular problem may be solvable by some pre-existing routine or pattern but such a solution may not be noticed until that pattern comes to dominate other currently active patterns.

Conclusion

What are the major developments in problem-solving during the past few years? In my view there have been a number of interrelated developments. Research has become more concerned with the actual processes involved in solving problems rather with the measurement of human performance against some formal yardstick. There has also been an effort to set research on problem-solving and reasoning within a framework that recognises the fundamental function or task of thought – the intelligent guidance of action. A key concept here is the notion of a mental model. In addition, attempts have been made to interrelate apparently disparate phenomena in a single kind of process account. Thus, restructuring (a central concept in earlier Gestaltist accounts of discovery) can be explained in the same terms as those used to account for mental search. One of these terms is the notion of a mental operator that consists of a set of conditions which if met, permit or trigger a certain action. Such operators are effectively pattern-recognition elements. Since pattern-recognition is arguably crucial to all forms of human action, we are offered a way to explain extraordinary acts of creativity, for example, in terms of mundane, rather than special processes. The move towards integration and process accounts arises both from within the discipline – researchers after all need to establish a wider sense of coherence for their work on human information-processing – and because of concurrent developments in the field of artificial intelligence with its emphasis on computational solutions.

Certain other trends are emerging which are part of a move towards wider integration. These trends have their origins in a concern for the nature of the 'machine' on which mental programs run. Machines need energy to run and so it is necessary to be explicit in our theorising about this energetic dimension. The idea of excitatory and inhibitory resources is one way to capture this dimension and it offers a link to research in neuroscience that specifies the physical correlates of such resources. The way in which problems are solved or computed is also affected by the computational properties of the machine. Recently, researchers (Rumelhart, Smolensky, McClelland and Hinton, 1986) have explored the implications of treating the brain as a parallel processor of information (see also Allport, 1985 for an extension into the area of dysphasia). One consequence of such work is that certain mental structures (e.g. schemas) can be seen as essentially emerging from more elementary components during the course of problem-solving. Such a view promises to revolutionise our understanding of knowledge representations and their use in problem-solving.

References

Adam, A. E. and Taylor, A. D. (1987), 'Modelling analogical reasoning for legal applications', in M. A. Bramer (ed.), *Research and Development in Expert Systems III*. Cambridge University Press: Cambridge.

Adamson, R. E. (1952), 'Functional fixedness as related to problem-solving: a repetition of three experiments', *Journal of Experimental Psychology, 44*, 228-91.

Adamson, R. E. and Taylor, D. W. (1954), 'Functional fixedness as related to elapsed time and set', *Journal of Experimental Psychology, 47*, 122-216.

148   *David W. Green*

Allport, D. A. (1985), 'Distributed memory, modular subsystems and dysphasia', in S. Newman and R. Epstein (eds), *Current Perspectives in Dysphasia*. Churchill Livingstone: Edinburgh.

Anderson, J. R. (1983), *The Architecture of Cognition*. Harvard University Press: Cambridge, Mass.

Atwood, M. E., Brooks, R. and Radlinski, E. R. (1986), 'Causal models: the next generation of expert systems', *Electrical Communication, 60*, 180-4.

Atwood, M. E. and Polson, P. G. (1976), 'A process model for water jar problems', *Cognitive Psychology, 8*, 191-216.

Bainbridge, L. (1979), 'Verbal reports as evidence of the process operator's knowledge', *International Journal of Man-Machine Studies, 11*, 343-68.

Bainbridge, L. (1987), 'Types of representation', in L. P. Goodstein, H. B. Anderson and S. E. Olsen (eds), *Mental Models, Tasks and Errors*. Taylor and Francis: London.

Barron, F. (1963), 'The needs for order and disorder as motives in creative activity', in C. W. Taylor and F. Barron (eds), *Scientific Creativity: Its Recognition and Development*. Wiley: New York and London.

Birch, H. G. and Rabinowitz, H. S. (1951), 'The negative effects of previous experience on productive thinking', *Journal of Experimental Psychology, 41*, 121-5.

Byrne, R. (1983), 'Protocol analysis in problem-solving', in J. St. B. T. Evans (ed.), *Thinking and Reasoning: Psychological Approaches*. Routledge & Kegan Paul: London and Boston.

Carroll, J. M. and Mack, R. L. (1985), 'Metaphor, computing systems and active learning', *International Journal of Man-Machine Studies, 22*, 39-57.

Chase, W. G. and Simon, H. A. (1973), 'Perception in chess', *Cognitive Psychology, 4*, 55-81.

Cheng, P. W. and Holyoak, K. J. (1985), 'Pragmatic reasoning schemas', *Cognitive Psychology, 17*, 391-416.

Chi, M. T., Feltovich, P. J. and Glaser, R. (1981), 'Categorisation and representation of physics problems by experts and novices', *Cognitive Science, 5*, 121-52.

Craik, K. (1943), *The Nature of Explanation*. Cambridge University Press: Cambridge.

DeGroot, A. D. (1965), *Thought and Choice in Chess*. Mouton: The Hague.

Dreistadt, R. (1968), 'An analysis of the use of analogies and metaphors in science', *Journal of Psychology, 68*, 97-116.

Driver, R. and Erickson, G. (1983), 'Theories in action: some theoretical and empirical issues in the study of students' conceptual frameworks in science', *Studies in Science Education, 10*, 37-60.

Duncker, K. (1945), 'On problem-solving', *Psychological Monographs, 58*, 5: whole issue no. 270.

Elbow, P. (1973), *Writing without Teachers*. Oxford University Press: London.

Ericsson, K. A. and Simon, H. A. (1980), 'Verbal reports as data', *Psychological Review, 87*, 215-51.

Evans, J. St. B. T. (1982), *The Psychology of Deductive Reasoning*. Erlbaum: Hillsdale, New Jersey.

Evans, J. St. B. T., Barston, J. and Pollard, P. (1983), 'On the conflict between logic and belief in syllogistic reasoning', *Memory and Cognition, 11*, 295-306.

Eysenck, M. W. (1984), *A Handbook of Cognitive Psychology*. Erlbaum: Hillsdale, New Jersey.

Fischhoff, B., Slovic, P. and Lichtenstein, S. (1978), 'Fault trees: sensitivity of estimated failure probabilities to problem representation', *Journal of Experimental Psychology: Human Perception and Performance, 4*, 330-4.

Flower, L. S. and Hayes, J. R. (1984), 'Images, plans and prose: the representation of meaning in writing', *Written Communication*, *1*, 120-60.

Fodor, J. A. (1983), *The Modularity of Mind*. MIT Press: Cambridge, Mass.

Gentner, D. and Gentner, D. R. (1983), 'Flowing waters or teeming crowds: mental models of electricity', in D. Gentner and A. L. Stevens (eds), *Mental Models*. Erlbaum: Hillsdale, New Jersey.

Gick, M. L. and Holyoak, K. J. (1980), 'Analogical problem-solving', *Cognitive Psychology*, *12*, 306-55.

Gick, M. L. and Holyoak, K. J. (1983), 'Schema induction and analogical transfer', *Cognitive Psychology*, *15*, 1-38.

Glucksberg, S. and Danks, J. (1968), 'Effects of discriminating labels and of nonsense labels upon availability of a novel function', *Journal of Verbal Learning and Verbal Behaviour*, *7*, 72-6.

Gorman, Michael E. and Gorman, Margaret E. (1984), 'A comparison of disconfirmatory, confirmatory and control strategies in Wason's 2-4-6 task', *Quarterly Journal of Experimental Psychology*, *36A*, 629-48.

Gorman, Michael E., Stafford, A. and Gorman, Margaret E. (1987), 'Disconfirmation and dual hypotheses in a more difficult version of Wason's 2-4-6 task', *Quarterly Journal of Experimental Psychology*, *39A*, 1-28.

Gorman, M. E., Tweney, R. D. and Siegel, H. (1984), 'Towards a psychology of discovery and justification', manuscript based on a paper before the Annual Meeting of the Society for Philosophy and Psychology.

Green, D. W. (1975), 'The effects of task on the representation of sentences', *Journal of Verbal Learning and Verbal Behaviour*, *14*, 275-83.

Green, D. W. (1980), 'Psycholinguistics: cognitive aspects of human communication', in G. Claxton (ed.), *Cognitive Psychology: New Directions*. Routledge & Kegan Paul: London.

Green, D. W. (1986a), 'Writing, jargon and research', *Written Communication*, *3*, 364-81.

Green, D. W. (1986b), 'Control, activation and resource: a framework and a model for the control of speech in bilinguals', *Brain and Language*, *27*, 210-23.

Green, D. W. and Wason, P. C. (1982), 'Notes on the psychology of writing', *Human Relations*, *35*, 47-56.

Greeno, J. G. (1977), 'Natures of problem-solving abilities', in W. K. Estes (ed.), *Handbook of Learning and Cognitive Processes*. Academic Press: New York.

Gregory, R. L. (1981), *Mind in Science: A History of Explanations in Psychology and Physics*. Cambridge University Press: Cambridge.

Griggs, R. A. (1983), 'The role of problem content in the selection task and THOG problem', in J. St. B. T. Evans (ed.), *Thinking and Reasoning: Psychological Approaches*. Routledge & Kegan Paul: London.

Hadamard, J. (1954), *The Psychology of Invention in the Mathematical Field*. Dover: New York.

Harding, D. W. (1974), *Experience into Words*. Penguin Books: Harmondsworth.

Hebb, D. O. and Bindra, D. (1952), 'Scientific writing and the general problem of communication', *American Psychologist*, *7*, 569-73.

Hitch, G. J. (1986), 'The integration of energetics into information processing models: some pretheoretical issues', in R. Hockey, A. Gaillard and M. Coles (eds), *Energetics and Human Information Processing*. Dordrecht: Nijhoff.

Hunt, M. (1982), *The Universe Within: A New Science Explores The Human Mind*. Harvester Press: Brighton.

Johnson-Laird, P. N. (1983), *Mental Models*. Cambridge University Press: Cambridge. Excerpted in A. M. Aitkenhead and J. M. Slack (eds) (1985), *Issues in Cognitive Modelling*. Erlbaum: Hillsdale, New Jersey.

Johnson-Laird, P. N. (1986), personal communication.

Johnson-Laird, P. N. and Steedman, M. J. (1978), 'The psychology of syllogisms', *Cognitive Psychology, 10*, 64-99.

Keane, M. (1987), 'On retrieving analogues when solving problems', *Quarterly Journal of Experimental Psychology, 39A*, 29-41.

Kieras, D. E. and Bovair, S. (1984), 'The role of a mental model in learning to operate a device', *Cognitive Science, 8*, 255-73.

Kotovsky, K., Hayes, J. R. and Simon, H. A. (1985), 'Why are some problems hard? Evidence from Tower of Hanoi', *Cognitive Psychology, 17*, 248-94.

Kuipers, B. and Kassirer, J. P. (1984), 'Causal reasoning in medicine: analysis of a protocol', *Cognitive Science, 8*, 363-85.

Lakoff, G. and Johnson, M. (1980), 'The metaphorical structure of the human conceptual system', *Cognitive Science, 4*, 195-208.

Larkin, J. H. (1983), 'The role of problem-representation in physics', in D. Gentner and A. L. Stevens (eds), *Mental Models*. Erlbaum: Hillsdale, New Jersey.

Larkin, J. H. McDermott, J., Simon, D. P. and Simon, H. A. (1980), 'Models of competence in solving physics problems', *Cognitive Science, 4*, 317-45.

Lindsay, P. H. and Norman, D. A. (1972), *Human Information Processing*. Academic Press: New York and London.

Luchins, A. S. (1942), 'Mechanization of problem-solving', *Psychological Monographs, 54*, 248.

McCloskey, M. (1983), 'Naive theories of motion', in D. Gentner and A. L. Stevens (eds), *Mental Models*. Erlbaum: Hillsdale, New Jersey.

Maier, N. R. F. and Burke, R. J. (1967), 'Response availability as a factor in the problem-solving performance of males and females', *Journal of Personality and Social Psychology, 5*, 304-10.

Mandler, G. (1979), 'Thought processes, consciousness and stress', in V. Hamilton and D. M. Warburton (eds), *Human Stress and Cognition: An Information Processing Approach*. Wiley: London.

Mandler, G. and Sarason, I. (1952), 'A study of anxiety and learning', *Journal of Abnormal and Social Psychology, 47*, 166-73.

Mandler, J. M. (1983), 'Structural invariants in development', in L. S. Liben (ed.), *Piaget and the Foundation of Knowledge*. Erlbaum: Hillsdale, New Jersey.

Miller, G. A. (1979), 'Images and models, similes and metaphors', in A. Ortony (ed.), *Metaphor and Thought*. Cambridge University Press: Cambridge.

Mitroff, I. I. (1981), 'Scientists and confirmation bias', in R. D. Tweney, M. E. Doherty and C. R. Mynatt (eds), *On Scientific Thinking*. Columbia University Press: New York.

Mynatt, C. R., Doherty, M. E. and Tweney, R. D. (1978), 'Consequences of confirmation and disconfirmation in a simulated research environment', *Quarterly Journal of Experimental Psychology, 30*, 395-406.

Oakhill, J. V. and Johnson-Laird, P. N. (1985a), 'Rationality, memory and the search for counter-examples', *Cognition, 20*, 79-94.

Oakhill, J. V. and Johnson-Laird, P. N. (1985b), 'The effects of belief on the spontaneous production of syllogistic conclusions', *Quarterly Journal of Experimental Psychology, 37a*, 553-69.

Ohlsson, S. (1984a), 'Restructuring revisited II: An information processing theory of restructuring and insight', *Scandinavian Journal of Psychology, 25*, 117-29.

Ohlsson, S. (1984b), 'Restructuring revisited I: summary and critique of the Gestalt theory of problem-solving', *Scandinavian Journal of Psychology, 25*, 65-78.

Perkins, D. N. (1981), *The Mind's Best Work*. Harvard University Press: Cambridge, Mass.

Piaget, J. (1972), 'Intellectual development from adolescence to adulthood', *Human Development, 15*, 1-12.

Rasmussen, J. and Jensen, A. (1974), 'Mental procedures in real-life tasks: a case study of electronic trouble shooting', *Ergonomics, 17*, 293-307.

Rumelhart, D. E. (1980), 'Schemata: the building blocks of cognition', in R. J. Spiro, B. C. Bruce and W. F. Brewer (eds), *Theoretical Issues in Reading Comprehension*. Erlbaum: Hillsdale, New Jersey.

Rumelhart, D. E., Smolensky, P., McClelland, J. L. and Hinton, G. E. (1986), 'Schemata and sequential thought processes in the PDP model', in D. E. Rumelhart, J. L. McClelland and the PDP Research Group (eds), *Parallel Distributed Processing: Explorations in the Microstructure of Cognition*, Vol. II. MIT Press: Cambridge, Mass.

Sanders, A. F. (1983), 'Towards a model of stress and human performance', *Acta Psychologica, 53*, 61-97.

Sanford, A. J. (1985), *Cognition and Cognitive Psychology*. Weidenfeld & Nicolson: London.

Sarason, I. (1961), 'The effects of anxiety and threat on the solution of a difficult task', *Journal of Abnormal and Social Psychology, 62*, 165-8.

Saugstad, P. and Raaheim, K. (1960), 'Problem-solving, past experience, and availability of functions', *British Journal of Psychology, 51*, 97-104.

Scardamalia, M., Bereiter, C. and Steinbach, R. (1984), 'Teachability of reflective processes in written composition', *Cognitive Science, 8*, 173-90.

Schank, R. C. (1982), *Dynamic Memory: A theory of Reminding and Learning in Computers and People*. Cambridge University Press: Cambridge.

Schön, D. A. (1979), 'Generative metaphor: a perspective on problem-solving in social policy', in A. Ortony (ed.), *Metaphor and Thought*. Cambridge University Press: Cambridge.

Shaklee, H. (1979), 'Bounded rationality and cognitive development: upper limits on growth?', *Cognitive Psychology, 11*, 327-45

Simon, H. (1957), *Models of Man*. Wiley: New York.

Simon, H. (1969), *The Sciences of the Artificial*. MIT Press: Cambridge, Mass.

Simon, H. (1980), 'Cognitive science: the newest science of the artificial', *Cognitive Science, 4*, 33-46.

Simon, H. and Newell, A. (1971), *Human Problem-Solving*. Prentice-Hall: Englewood Cliffs, New Jersey.

Sloman, A. (1984), 'Why we need many knowledge representation formalisms', paper given at BCS Expert System Conference, Warwick.

Sternberg, R. J. (1977), *Intelligence, Information-Processing and Analogical Reasoning: The Componential Analysis of Human Abilities*. Erlbaum: Hillsdale, New Jersey.

Tversky, A. and Kahneman, D. (1973), 'Availability: a heuristic for judging frequency and probability', *Cognitive Psychology, 5*, 207-32.

Tversky, A. and Kahneman, D. (1974), 'Judgment under uncertainty: heuristics and biases', *Science, 185*, 1124-31.

Tweney, R. D., Doherty, M. E., Worner, W. J., Pliske, D. B., Mynatt, C. R., Gross, K. A. and Arklin, D. L. (1980), 'Strategies of rule discovery in an inference task', *Quarterly Journal of Experimental Psychology, 32*, 109-23.

Tweney, R. D., Doherty, M. E. and Mynatt, C. R. (1981), 'The problem of generalisation', in R. D. Tweney, M. E. Doherty, and C. R. Mynatt (eds), *On Scientific Thinking*. Columbia University Press: New York.

Wallas, G. (1926), *The Art of Thought*. Harcourt and Brace: New York.

Wason, P. C. (1960), 'On the failure to eliminate hypotheses in a conceptual task', *Quarterly Journal of Experimental Psychology, 12*, 129-40.

Wason, P. C. (1968), 'Reasoning about a rule', *Quarterly Journal of Experimental Psychology, 20*, 273-81.

Wason, P. C. (1970), 'On writing scientific papers', *Physics Bulletin, 21*, 407-8.

Reprinted in J. Hartley (ed.) (1980), *The Psychology of Written Composition*. Kogan Page: London.

Wason, P. C. (1983), 'Realism and rationality in the selection task', in J. St. B. T. Evans (ed.), *Thinking and Reasoning: Psychological Approaches*. Routledge & Kegan Paul: London.

Wason, P. C. and Green, D. W. (1984), 'Reasoning and mental representation', *Quarterly Journal of Experimental Psychology, 36A*, 597-610.

Yates, J. (1985), 'The content of awareness is a model of the world', *Psychological Review, 92*, 249-84.

7 Cognitive neuropsychology

Ruth Campbell

Cognitive neuropsychology does not yet have an entry in the excellent *Penguin Dictionary of Psychology* (Reber, 1985); yet the nine syllables have an impressive ring and formed the title of a limpid address to the prestigious 1984 Attention and Performance meeting (Coltheart, 1985). These are just the sort of words to be glimpsed in the academic poser's airplane reading or overheard at a (particularly pretentious) party. Is this all that they stand for, or do the two words add up to an important component of the exploration for a useful understanding of human thought, perception and action?

Cognitive neuropsychology is the study of cognitive functions in the context of impaired cerebral processes. One thing it can do is elucidate normal psychological processes by examining impaired ones. This is a useful exercise in a very particular way. A psychological skill might comprise separate, functionally independent, subcomponents which can be mapped by the usual sorts of laboratory experiments with the usual sorts of subject. However, evidence for the existence of one or other component of a mental skill could come from the discovery that, following brain damage, a particular component no longer works. This is a standard method in animal neuropsychology, where cerebral lesioning is part of the armoury of the experimenter. In human neuropsychology, with some notable exceptions (for instance, Sperry's (1974) studies on the human split-brain), we rely less on surgical intervention to produce functional cerebral impairment and more on acts of nature (blood clots, aneurisms) or man (war wounds or accidents) to direct our explorations of how minds work.

Often, then, the neuropsychologist examines behavioural function in a *clinical* setting, as one of a team of experts. The primary aim here is to gain information that may help in the diagnosis, treatment and prognosis of

Thedi Landis and Marianne Regard commented wisely and generously on this chapter. The work in which we are all engaged (see p. 167) is supported by a Twinning Grant (TW/85/851/2) from the European Science Foundation.

153

patients who may have suffered a stroke or other cerebral trauma. However neuropsychologists have long been aware that sometimes cerebral trauma can lead to behaviours that are interesting because of the light they shed on normal psychological functions and on theories about such functions. With the rise of information theoretic and cognitive psychology, and their emphases on isolating the nature and number of component functions of higher mental phenomena, the role of evidence from impaired function can be very telling. Neuropsychology is *cognitive* to the extent that it purports to clarify the mechanisms of cognitive functions such as thinking, reading, writing, speaking, recognising and remembering, using evidence from neuropathology. Essentially, such evidence is disconfirmatory; that is, if the claim is made (from normal experimental evidence) that function X is necessary for function Y to proceed effectively and a patient can be demonstrated with no X, but good Y, there must be something wrong with the contingencies expressed in the original theory.

This is a powerful experimental technique; it was used with devastating effect when Shallice and Warrington reported a patient, KF, who, after a motorcycle accident which caused cerebral damage, was no longer able to repeat simple, short lists of words that were spoken to him, although his speech comprehension and production were rather good (Warrington and Shallice, 1969; Shallice and Warrington, 1970). This patient was well able to remember the gist of what was to be remembered; only his *verbatim* recall was impaired. In the theoretical terms current at that time, KF could access long-term memory, while his ability to perform short-term memory tasks was grossly deficient. One of the motivations for identifying two memory systems, one short- and one long-term, was that short-term memory was thought to serve as a 'gatekeeper' to long-term memory; intact short-term memory was thought to be necessary for the rather slow consolidation processes needed by long-term memory mechanisms to become effective. Since KF performed very badly on tasks that tap short-term memory (immediate verbal recall tasks of various sorts) while new information was effectively registered and maintained for later access from long-term memory (or else how could he recall gist?), this view of the relationship between long- and short-term memory, and/or of the tasks thought to tap these processes, could not be correct.

Such powerful disconfirmations of psychological theory from clinical sources are rare; yet a single case can suffice (as in Popper's example of the black swan which, once discovered, falsifies the claim that 'all swans are white') to weaken any strong, causal theory. Nevertheless, such demonstrations may depend on the investigator's awareness of the issues, rather than the uniqueness of the patient's disorder. KF's particular problems in repeating lists of speech sounds put him into the clinical pigeonhole labelled 'conduction aphasia'. This is not a particularly rare consequence of brain lesion and the key symptom – that of an immediate repetition failure – was predicted and then demonstrated by Carl Wernicke in 1874; yet the use of such evidence to shake theories of normal memory function had to await Warrington and Shallice's demonstration.

Beyond disconfirmation: cognitive neuropsychology can make theories explicit

While disconfirmation is all very well it does not necessarily get one very far in postulating useful theories. At least one recent line of investigation in cognitive neuropsychology, however, does make theories explicit. This is to do with the processes involved in reading single words (and non-words) aloud. In 1966 Marshall and Newcombe reported a patient, GR, with a peculiar reading problem. In reading lists of unrelated words this patient made a great number of errors of different sorts. Sometimes his errors were semantically related to the target word (he misread ANTIQUE as 'vase'; CAUTION as 'danger' and NEEDLE as 'thimble'), sometimes his errors looked more like failures to process particular letters adequately (NEXT as 'exit'; GENTLE as 'Gentleman'). This patient was very bad at reading simple nonsense words aloud, like SLINT or PARM, and was very poor at reading function words like AS, IF, THAN. Such paralexias (misreadings) and alexias (failures to read the item at all) indicated to the authors that this patient had a particular problem in reading words in terms of their letter-sound correspondences. He could not use the 'phonic route' in reading single words aloud. Later studies confirmed and defined this pattern of single-word misreading in more than a dozen patients (*deep dyslexia*; see Coltheart, Patterson and Marshall, 1980) and differentiated it from a 'purer' disturbance of phonic reading, where no semantic errors are made to target words (*phonological dyslexia*; see, for example, Patterson, 1982) and from a complementary acquired reading impairment, *surface dyslexia*, where single word reading seems to be characterised by over-reliance on the phonic route (see Patterson, Marshall and Coltheart, 1985).

Much more important than the labels, however, is what they mean. These patients demonstrate functional dissociations in reading aloud; that is, one patient (a surface dyslexic) might read non-words perfectly well, yet misread simple, familiar, but irregularly-spelled words like WORD (it would be regularised to rhyme with BOARD). While another, a phonological dyslexic, would have no trouble reading irregular words like WORD, SWORD or YACHT, but would be stumped by a simple non-word like YORD. When a patient (or anyone) performs task A well but task B badly, and another patient (or anyone) can be shown with the reverse pattern of impairment on the two tasks, the term used is *double dissociation of function*. It indicates that the hypothetical psychological processes tapped by the two tasks are independent, for how else could such complementary disturbances be explained? Double dissociation of function provides the strongest evidence for independent components of any psychological skill. It is a term, and a method, strictly derived from clinical neuropsychology.

This approach can be applied in a non-clinical setting. Bryant and Impey (1986) find that a large group of normal 10-year-old children include several who read irregular words well, but non-words badly, and also some who read non-words well and irregular words badly. Such children fall squarely into the 'phonological dyslexia' and the 'surface dyslexia' categories. These authors suggest that, since such variability can be demonstrated in normal learning readers, it may not be necessary to posit the loss of one or other route in reading in acquired dyslexic cases but rather to assume reversion to an earlier developmental stage; one in which the child showed an uneven command of phonic rules and irregular word reading skills. Such a suggestion carries with it the implication that patterns of acquired reading disorder are telling us nothing new about reading (a conclusion suggested by those authors).

However, to me it suggests that, even before readers are very skilled, the reading of single words in English proceeds by two somewhat independent means; a process used for reading words which is relatively insensitive to the letter-sound correspondences in the word, so regular and irregular words are easily read, and another process which can be used to read non-words and which, if used to read words will lead to 'regularisations' of them. And, surely, it is just this reliance on two rather different processes that is what we should expect of anyone trying to master the delicate relationship, in English, between letters and how they sound in words. Of course, this 'dual route reading' hypothesis has been held by a number of researchers in normal acquisition of reading, whose subjects are school children and young, normal adults (e.g. Baron, 1979; Baron and Treiman, 1980). But with normal, skilled readers, relative reliance on the phonic route and relative reliance on the word-reading route is rarely as pronounced as it can be following lesions. It could be argued that normal skilled reading demands that both routes be used with *some* aptitude: patients give us a clearer picture of a necessary functional separation of the two reading processes.

However Bryant and Impey's demonstration does serve as a very useful warning: labelling a person 'phonological dyslexic' or anything else can be a hindrance, rather than an aid, to understanding the particular reading pattern. In this case the pattern is not statistically abnormal (unless we say that all 10-year-olds are 'dyslexic') and this can mislead us into ignoring the real usefulness of the dissociated skills, namely the demonstration of independent functional components of those skills.

Note, also, that such double dissociations do not tell us *how* two separable processes come into being. In reading, for example, there is considerable controversy concerning the origin of word reading mechanisms. Do we read words, and potential words (non-words) by the use of analogical mechanisms on words we can already read, or do we derive a set of grapheme-phoneme correspondence rules from the words that we know in order to read new ones (see Marcel, 1980; Seidenberg, Waters, Barnes and Tanenhaus 1984; Patterson and Morton, 1985; Kay, 1985)? The preferred answer to this question leads to radically different views about the nature of the impairments that lead to surface and phonological dyslexia; and these are surprisingly hard to resolve experimentally (but see Kay and Lesser, 1985). Demonstrating double dissociations is only a first step; the mechanisms that give rise to them remain to be elucidated.

Double dissociation of function: things, names, objects

The principle of double dissociation of function has been demonstrated in a number of fascinating cognitive disorders. A series of studies by Warrington and her colleagues (Warrington, 1982; Warrington and McCarthy, 1983; Warrington and Shallice, 1984) suggests our knowledge of objects in the world can be impaired as a function of the semantic category to be named, described or recognised. One patient, VER, for example (Warrington and McCarthy, 1983) can recognise, discriminate and describe the names of flowers and food, but not those of familiar inanimate objects, like household equipment or vehicles. By contrast, Warrington and Shallice (1984) describe four patients who all (for a while) showed the complementary problem; they were well able to describe a wheelbarrow but not (for instance) a cabbage. There appears, therefore, to be a double dissociation in the ability to access knowledge about animate objects like food, flowers and 'feathered friends' and equally familiar things like household objects, playthings or vehicles.

The suggestion is that these patients have separately damaged different parts of their semantic representational system; that the 'flower encyclo-paedia' is somewhere quite separate from the 'kitchen equipment encyclopaedia' and these encyclopaedias are in turn filed in separate 'animate' and 'inanimate' rooms in the Library of Mental Knowledge.

So far, so good: such classifications echo those that have been noted in cross-cultural studies and in studies of object-naming and knowledge in normal undergraduates (e.g. Rosch and Lloyd, 1978). But what underlies them? Warrington suggests that the basic distinction reflected in these impairments is that between sensory and functional knowledge: we know a cabbage from a cauliflower in terms of sensory differences (smell, sight, taste) rather than what we characteristically do with them. On the other hand, the important difference between a chisel and a screwdriver is their function; how we use them, not their sensory characteristics (both, indeed can look the same to the un-tooled). It is not clear quite how far this distinction as a key feature of the dissociation can be pushed; for instance, it is not immediately clear to me that the main distinction between a minicab and a London taxi is a functional, rather than a sensory distinction; while the distinction between an orange and a lemon seems to me to have as much to do with how one acts on the different fruits (peeling, cutting and using in cooking) as with their sensory characteristics. But it does suggest a mechanism that should have ramifications in other aspects of these patients' behaviour. For instance, if patients like VER are impaired in the comprehension of how things function they might perhaps show deficits in miming the actions one does with things (*ideo-motor apraxia* is the term for deficits in such actions) which are associated with their peculiar naming impairments for objects. By contrast, patients who could tell you what a wheelbarrow is, but not a cabbage, might be more likely to have problems with sensory qualities more generally – for example, in deciding whether mauve and violet name the same colour.

The general point I am making, however, is that, whatever underlies this particular dissociation can be tested, and should be for our explanations to have any power.

Now one thing that must be emphasised about these patients is that their complementary deficits were not particularly to do with the *visual* aspect of things (although, in some cases, they extended to them). It was in describing what spoken or written words meant that the pattern of dissociation arose so clearly. What would it mean if, rather than words, it was pictures, or the objects themselves, that prompted the same separations in different patients? One possibility, certainly, could be that it was at the highest level of object representation, one which is shared by words and the objects that they represent, that food and kitchen equipment are separately represented, but if the dissociated deficits were confined *just* to the visual presentation of objects and not to words that referred to them we would suspect either that visual and verbal semantic domains do not overlap much (see Beauvois, 1982; Warrington 1982) or, alternatively, that the dissociations were not in the object representations, but rather in the relative reliance of different classes of object on different sensory dimensions. Such an argument might go like this.

It is possible that colour (for example) might be a better discriminator of flowers than kitchen equipment: any failure in colour perception would then adversely affect flowers more than kitchen equipment. And it is possible (for example) that the ability to discriminate kitchen equipment might depend on the ability to judge how many surfaces there are on a given visual object. So, deficits which appear to be to do with classifications of objects – that is, deficits in the associative aspects of objects, deficits to do with what objects signify – do not really dissociate one from the other. It could be the weighting of the different *perceptual* mechanisms needed to identify the objects that differ with the category under scrutiny. So a patient who has poor food discrimination has a primary deficit in colour discrimination, while a patient who cannot recognise inanimate objects really has problems in computing some basic perceptual aspects of any stimulus, such as number of edges or amount of fine detail.

Now this particular argument was made up; there is no evidence that I know of that discriminating between flowers and kitchen hardware does depend, respectively, more on fine colour and surface discrimination, but the principle of this argument is widely seen in neuropsychology. And necessarily so; it would be unwise to accept an explanation for a disorder that has recourse to high-level, poorly understood functions, if it were possible to find a cause for the impairments that reflected damage at a simpler, lower level of analysis. Such reductive explanations are likely to be more powerful than high-level ones; they would predict, for instance, a constellation of impairments in the two, dissociated, disorders which the high-level explanation would not.

Faces: more arguments from dissociation

One area of investigation where this argument has been used is that of acquired disorders of face recognition. A number of cases have now been described where, following fairly specific cerebral damage, a patient loses the ability to recognise previously familiar faces. This failure, called *prosopagnosia*, does not necessarily involve recognition problems for other types of visually distinctive material, such as places or objects, although it can co-occur with such deficits. Nor is prosopagnosia a deficit in recognising the person, as an *amnesic* disturbance might be: the patient can identify the 'unrecognisable' person by other clues, such as voice, or typical clothing, or scent. It seems to be a deficit solely in recognising the visual configuration of the face as belonging to a particular individual.

Now it could be claimed (as it has been by many people, most recently and explicitly by Sergent, 1984) that such apparently isolated failures of recognition have, in fact, a perceptual base. In Chapter 2 of the present volume Bruce points out how the structural requirements for face identification are very different from those required for recognising objects adequately. Of all visually familiar objects faces are arguably the most visually complex and distinctive. Their distinctions, moreover, are often in terms of very small features; the length of a nose or the separation distance of the eyes (a configurational or structural property in Bruce's terms). Recognising a face adequately also demands that such small feature differences be properly integrated to give whole-face information, and that the ability to detect a face through its many non-rigid transformations (expression, ageing) be effective (see Bruce, p. 49). Where the *perceptual* demands of the recognition task are so great, it is argued, face recognition will fail before any other task shows clinical impairment. If this argument were true, it follows that discrimination between faces which are presented concurrently, as well as between faces that are presented sequentially, should be poor in prosopagnosics. And it could also be argued that recognition of *un*-familiar faces as being 'old' or 'new' in a forced choice task where a subset had previously been presented, should be as poor as familiar face recognition. As it happens, all prosopagnosics tested so far *are* somewhat impaired on such face discrimination tasks, but they do not all show the same degree of impairment, and, moreover, their performance on such tasks fails to predict the extent of their problem in recognising *familiar* faces (Benton and Van Allen, 1972). The clearest example of this comes from a study by Malone, Morris, Kay and Levin (1982). They report two prosopagnosic patients. Both presented with problems in recognising familiar faces, yet one recovered to the extent that his ability to match unfamiliar faces (visual discriminative skill) improved, and with it some familiar faces were, it seems, relearned; while the other, despite being quite good at discriminating between pictures of 'old' and 'new' unfamiliar faces, yet was unable to recognise previously familiar and famous faces. Thus familiar face recognition failure may reflect two, somewhat independent, components: an *apperceptive* failure, to do with the perceptual details necessary for adequate recognition, and an essentially *agnosic* failure, where the perceptual qualities of the stimulus may be adequately processed but they do not have access to sufficiently well specified representations of the face of that individual. Such representations, Bruce reminds us, must be very well formulated and we are still seeking a metric that might cope with individual face identities sufficiently well to be useful.

But how independent can such apperceptive and agnosic deficits be? T. Landis, M. Regard and I have recently had the opportunity to examine a woman with what seems to be an *agnosic* type of face recognition problem (Campbell, Landis and Regard, 1986). Frau D had a stroke when she was 61, three years prior to testing her, after which she was unable to recognise people by their face, though as soon as they spoke they became familiar to her. She could match simultaneously presented pictures of unfamiliar faces taken from different viewpoints in the test devised by Benton and Van Allen (1972), although she was abnormally slow at it.

We were interested to determine which aspects of facial processing were impaired and which were unimpaired in this patient. One thing that she could not do was to label photographs of facial expressions accurately and she was impaired at matching faces, and parts of faces, by their expression (prosop-affective agnosia). However, Frau D can perform another face processing task perfectly: Frau D can lipread.

So, when we mouthed single numbers to her, in her Swiss-German dialect, she told us just what numbers we were saying, even though she did not know who we were. She sorted piles of face photographs according to speech sound perfectly well despite being unable to identify the speaker and being poor at determining whether different views and different speakers were represented. Normal speaker-hearers are susceptible to a powerful illusion when a syllable like 'ga' is seen to be spoken in synchrony with a heard 'ba'. The impression is that one has heard 'da' being spoken, even though what one hears is 'ba' and not 'da' at all (McGurk and MacDonald, 1976). The influence of the seen 'ga', produced with the lips apart, seems to be sufficient to set the speech recognition system for a 'fused' auditory percept.

Frau D was highly susceptible to this illusion; she perceived seen and heard speech in an integrated way just as most people do. Yet (to drive the point home) she was unable to perform other tasks on the face pictures. So although she could tell you which picture of a mouth was saying 'oo' and which was saying 'ee', she could not tell you whether a photograph or a drawing of a face was of a sad or happy face, nor if it was of a man or a woman.

It seems to us that this is the clearest possible evidence that, while different face-processing tasks may rely, differentially, on different sorts of perceptual mechanism, a failure of the perceptual mechanism alone is unlikely to explain Frau D's dense prosopagnosia and her prosop-affective agnosia while leaving her lipreading completely unaffected. Lipreading uses just the same sort of perceptual information from the lower face as does matching facial expression; yet, for Frau D lipreading is no problem.

At this point, it might be argued that while the perceptual demands of lipreading are similar to those for face identification, the lipreading task itself is so easy that no-one would ever show any impairment on it. If such an argument could be upheld it would weaken the claim that prosopagnosia is a quite specific disturbance of knowledge about known faces. However, this claim cannot be upheld. Frau T, a patient we tested at the same time as Frau D, had no obvious problems in processing faces for identity or for expression, yet her lipreading was impaired and she failed to be susceptible to the auditory-visual blend illusion. Frau T, then, could recognise faces and facial expressions but could not lipread, while Frau D could lipread but not do anything else with faces. Here is the clearest possible sort of double dissociation. It tells us that different tasks that use the same part of the face as the basic visual stimulus do not share the same psychological components.

It therefore shows us, as other sorts of dissociable object recognition disorders cannot, that (for Frau D at least) a basic perceptual problem does not underlie her failure to recognise familiar faces or facial expressions. Her poor performance on the Benton and Van Allen face discrimination task need not reflect impaired perceptual discrimination but, as likely as not, a failure in the ability to use the sorts of categorical, organisational processes one needs to recognise familiar faces: these could affect unfamiliar as well as familiar face recognition. Watching her perform the Benton and Van Allen task bears this out; she examines each picture minutely and talks to herself as she does it – 'ah this one has a mole, and no lines...'; the ability to take the memorable, distinctive, properties of a face in 'at a glance' seems to have gone.

Functional and anatomical localisation; keeping the differences clear

The relationship of a particular function to a particular brain site is not simple. As psychologists repeat (sometimes ad nauseam, see Morton, 1983; Mehler, Morton and Jusczyk, 1984) the identification of a particular psychological component of a particular cognitive skill need not necessarily tell us anything about where in the brain such a skill exists; the level of description of the task is such that a psychological (functional) explanation is sufficient to itself. Such arguments can be supported by epistemological argument from Artificial Intelligence, famously Marr (1982), who stressed that different levels of explanation suit different cognitive phenomena. The separation between function and locale may suit psychology pure and simple, but neuropsychology cannot proceed without tackling this question.

One of the reasons why neuropsychologists have traditionally been concerned with defining cognitive functional impairments carefully is that such specification *can* often give very useful information about where in the brain damage has occurred. That is, a *functional* impairment can indicate an *anatomical* locus. Now the clinical imperative for refining such localising symptoms has lessened since direct imaging techniques, such as CAT and PET scans and MR, have become more widespread and the neurologist can see, directly, where damage has occurred. A new clinical imperative is to test the fit of older, functional-inference, predictions of anatomical locus of impairment with the direct visual evidence.

More important, it is becoming clear that, on some models of cognitive function at least, proximity of neural subsystems may be vital to functional integrity. It could be wrong to claim that two functions that are psychological neighbours (let us say the identification of a letter and the identification of a word of which it forms part) can be as effectively related in a system where they are not closely physically connected as in one where they are neuro-anatomical neighbours. This notion is a *theoretical* one: thus matrix models of information processing applied to visual identification (see Rolls, 1986) demand that all the processing units be intimately connected each with the other. This is recognised in many current AI formulations of psychological processing: in fact, the powerful, multiply parallel processing models developed over the last few years acknowledge this explicitly in their self-description as *connectionist* models (see Waltz, 1985). Thus, where regions of the brain of high physical interconnectedness are damaged, the resulting constellation of functional impairments may well tell us something useful about the nature of the psychological processes that are affected.

This could be seen as an affirmation of some aspects of older ideas about the relationship between brain and behaviour, the most explicit being that of A. R. Luria (see Luria, 1973 and De Renzi, 1982a). Luria's enterprise was to show that functional localisation in the brain followed the principle that functions closely associated with a particular sensory or motor area – which are indubitably localised in predictable fashion in human brains – would be anatomically close, too.

Thus, the first cortical site at which information from the eyes is represented (the primary visual areas) is in the occipital lobe, at the back of the brain. But this is primarily a *sensory* area; that is, if it is excised, the effect is akin to blindness. (See Campion, Latto and Smith, 1983, for current disputation on just how blind these lesions make one.) However, close by it, in the occipito-parietal regions, are regions concerned with vision, but not in this sensory fashion: Luria called such regions *secondary zones or areas*. What precise functions such secondary visual areas might subserve is not entirely clear: Luria says they 'play the role of synthesising visual stimuli, coding them and forming them into complex systems' (Luria, 1973, p. 115). This will not do for current psychological theorising, and the characteristics of such 'codes' and such 'complexity' are still open to discussion. If, for example, we were to apply Marr's (1982) theory of vision directly to brain sites it would be in these regions that we would seek evidence for 'the primal sketch', where stable, reasonably invariant representations of the visual world may start to be formulated (and see Chapter 2, this volume).

In any case, a useful neuropsychological predicate could be that functional associatedness is reflected in anatomical localisation, with close connected structures showing some commonality or similarity of function. In hierarchical, computational models of mental function, this would mean that whenever the output from one particular part of the system is needed for another function to run, they will be closely interconnected. As functions become less tied to particular sensory or motor constraints – when, for instance, one attempts to make high-level strategic plans about where to spend Christmas, or when one thinks about the Meaning of Life – the local activity of specific brain sites is likely to be less important than their efficient interaction.

This distinction between computational systems that are tight-linked and that run off reasonably automatically, and those that are not, is captured by Fodor (1983) in the distinction between vertical and horizontal faculties. Vertically organised faculties are those (hypothesised) psychological functions that can run on simple, serial, computational lines: they are encapsulated (hard to disturb or extend) and modular (they only apply to a limited sensory-motor domain). One example that Fodor thinks might be such a vertical faculty is face recognition; another – language. Horizontal faculties, by contrast, use inputs from vertical faculties to perform broader intellective functions: their characteristics are the precise opposite of vertical faculties.

Left-brain, right-brain

One of the paths which led to the current resurgence of psychological interest in the cerebral basis of higher mental functions lay in the discovery (Mishkin and Forgays, 1952) that one could tap localised functions in normal, intact, subjects *indirectly*. Because the cerebral control of sensory and motor function is quite discretely lateralised it is possible to test which cerebral hemisphere is more able at a particular task. Thus, a single word presented to the right of a central visual fixation spot is more likely to be correctly read than one presented to the left of centre. This is because the right visual field (RVF) projects directly to the left hemisphere (LH), and in most people, this hemisphere is the cerebral site of language processing. Because the corpus callosum connects the two sides of the brain, such a RVF advantage would not be a complete one; only relative accuracy and speed of word detection would be better for RVF than LVF presentations. There are, however, a few patients in whom the corpus callosum is surgically excised (split-brain patients), and they can read with their RVF, but not at all (or hardly at all) with their LVF.

Following fast upon language studies in split-brain and normal subjects came demonstrations of a somewhat complementary advantage for non-linguistic processing in the RH of normal people. Thus faces are often faster recognised in the LVF than the RVF; so, too, emotional expression. These RH advantages, however, did not appear as reliable as those of the LH for language processing. Many further examples of hemispheric specialisation and related matters are discussed very clearly by Springer and Deutsch (1984).

An innocent question

Does the demonstration of normal hemispheric lateralisation of function taken together with the evidence from patients, mean that language is a modular function and is located in the left hemisphere, while face processing is modular and in the right hemisphere? Ten years or so ago, a consensus opinion would have been likely to answer Yes to the first question and No to the second. Yes to the first, because the clinical evidence was overwhelming that, when there was LH damage, language suffered in a broadly predictable way, while no such claims held for RH damage. No to the second, because careful post-mortem anatomical study (Meadows, 1974) showed that all patients who had been prosopagnosic had lesions both in the left and the right hemisphere, and because there was some evidence for LH contributions to face processing in normal people. This evidence has since been extended and confirmed (see Sergent, 1985). The LH may be better at some aspects of face processing – particularly when the information to be extracted is of small detail and/or of high spatial frequency. Yet this bilateral sharing of some visual aspects of face processing need not mean that familiar face recognition is a bilaterally distributed function.

Current imaging techniques, like CAT and PET-scan, allow us to see brain damage in situ. A number of patients have now been shown (Frau D among them) who are indisputably prosopagnosic and who show no CAT or PET-scan evidence of LH damage (Landis, Cummings, Christen, Bogen and Imhof, 1986; De Renzi, 1986). At the moment, then, we might infer that while face recognition can use information that is handled by either hemisphere it is possible that there *is* a specific RH locale involved in the recognition of familiar faces. That is, a RH module for familiar face *recognition* may be a viable idea, although there are alternative ways of processing faces in order to discriminate between them.

A similar argument might temper the idea that language processing is strictly modular and LH located. For example, Hirst, LeDoux and Stein (1984), showed that RH, not LH, patients have great difficulty in pragmatic linguistic comprehension. If you ask such a patient 'Can you open the door?' he is likely to respond 'Yes I can' but do nothing about it. He has mistaken your request for a question of information. Unless we discount pragmatic aspects such deficits cannot be encompassed in a LH language module. Similar, rather subtle, linguistic deficits have been observed in RH patients. They can tend to be very 'literal-minded', failing to pick up metaphoric meanings in speech, (Winner and Gardner, 1977) and may lose some structural relationships between words, such as antonymy (Gardner, Silverman, Wapner and Zurif, 1978). The ability to deliver and comprehend speech with the correct rise and fall of intonation is also adversely affected by RH damage (see Ross, 1981).

Right hemisphere reading?

Further indications of some circumscribed RH language comprehension might be inferred from the semantic errors in reading that can occur in LH-damaged patients. Where they can read words, LH-damaged aphasic patients tend to be able to read emotionally-laden ones; and it is these words – the few that they can sometimes read correctly – that also tend to give rise to semantic errors (so *kill* might be read as 'die', while an abstract and non-emotive word like *stay* may not elicit any response at all; Landis, Graves and Goodglass, 1982). Now, it could be that such responses are those of a damaged LH system not an intact RH system. Landis, Regard, Graves and Goodglass (1983), however, point out that such errors tend to increase with the size of the LH lesion; that is, the *worse* the LH damage, the *more* semantic errors in reading tend to be produced. They argue that an impaired LH should get dumber as the lesion size increases, not more fluent (even if wrong). So these semantic errors reflect RH reading. These results certainly give cause for thought, despite some question about their robustness (see Marshall and Patterson, 1983; but also Jones and Martin, 1984).

Others, too, have proposed that the RH may have a limited reading system. For example, Coltheart (1983) sifts the evidence from various hemispheric abnormalities in relation to reading and concurs that the RH may be producing the semantic errors of deep dyslexic reading. Patterson and Besner (1984) unpick the strands of this argument, both on experimental and inductive grounds: the major problem is that 'deep dyslexic reading', characterised by semantic errors and by word class effects, does not seem to be typical of other readers, normal or impaired, when their RH appears to be doing the reading. We could up-end the proposed RH reading solution and ask instead, why should impaired LH reading generate such peculiar reading errors?

One possibility is that reading may not be as tightly organised, as modular, in its functional architecture as was generally believed. It is provocative that a characteristic of highly interconnected, parallel organised, distributed processing systems (see for example Allport, 1985), is that quite local damage may produce global effects, and that such damage shows as 'graceful degradation' depending on the extent of information loss. That is, greater damage leads not so much to additive, stepwise loss of functional subcomponents but to a more gradual loss in general sensitivity to the task demands. If semantic reading errors are considered to be such effects, then this might mean the LH is indeed the reading hemisphere, but that it is not fully modular in its subcomponent architecture. So Patterson and Besner could be right about LH reading, while Landis et al. could be right about LH damage producing semantic errors as the damage gets greater.

Now, since RH damage affects the ability to comprehend pragmatic and structural aspects of speech, and since there is not yet any evidence that this shows 'graceful degradation' with cerebral loss, it is possible that these important structural aspects of language might be modular, but bilaterally or even RH located. Paradoxically, we have arrived at the possibility (no more than that) that the LH may read, but not in a modular way, and that the RH may be deeply involved in language processes and in a modular fashion! The point of all this, though, is to indicate how a seemingly straightforward and innocent question 'Is language modular and LH organised?' cannot be answered affirmatively, despite overwhelming evidence for a major LH contribution to language skills, and despite the effectiveness of experimental and neuropsychological techniques for splitting various language tasks into seemingly clear subcomponents. We need to reformulate the possible relationships between brains and language more clearly to respect the counter-evidence, and we ignore such evidence, and the usefulness of brains in elucidating language, at our peril.

Left-right differences in one (visual) function

The two patients mentioned earlier are relevant to the question of lateralisation of function. Frau D, you remember, could lipread, but could not recognise faces: Frau T could recognise faces, but not lipread. Frau D's lesion was strictly right-sided, while Frau T had a strictly left-sided lesion. These lesions were in comparable sites and of similar size; anatomical mirror images. Both were in parieto-tempero-occipital regions. In Luria's system, these are secondary visual (association) areas. If these areas are functionally unlateralised then both ladies should show similar symptoms. But they do not, and so, even at this relatively peripheral neural processing stage, the left and right secondary association areas are already specialised to subserve rather different functions. A damaged RH does not prevent Frau D lipreading; the required LH secondary association areas are intact. Indeed, since Frau T cannot lipread, we might confidently assert that the LH parieto-tempero-occipital regions subserve a lipreading function which cannot be taken over by RH analysis.

However, such confidence would be misplaced. The picture is more complicated. In a study of undergraduate lip-picture to speech sound matching, I found that the RH, not the LH, was better at the task. Students matched lip-pictures to speech sounds more accurately when the picture appeared in their LVF not the RVF (Campbell, 1986). If the LH was the 'lip-reading hemisphere' this should not happen; RVF matching should be better.

There are a number of more or less ad hoc ways to reconcile these findings; that the RH-damaged patient could lipread but the LH-damaged one could not, while the RH for normal people is probably better than the LH at matching lip pictures to speech sounds. The most appealing to a psychologist is to fractionate the stages of lipreading and to say that the RH may be better at (let us say) getting the correct visual description of the mouth area from a face photograph, while only the LH is able to integrate this information with heard speech. Depending which part of the process one is testing one will get a different laterality pattern.

A traditional neuropsychologist, however, might take a different tack.

Frau T's deficit in lipreading might not be due to damage of a component of a LH lipreading system, but possibly to a failure of the necessary visual information in accessing a possible 'lipreading comprehension' site in the left hemisphere. That is, Frau T's deficit may be a *disconnection deficit*. Just such a disconnection account is traditionally (Dejerine, 1914) offered for Frau T's other presenting symptom: her reading failure. Frau T cannot read effectively; instead, her reading proceeds a letter at a time and often whole words are 'read' by identifying each letter, aloud, first. She can spell and can tell you what a word is if you tell her the letters. She can identify letters by touch and by sight. She can describe letter forms accurately by drawing them in the air. What she cannot do is map this knowledge onto the presented *written* word. The visual information from the letters in the word is 'disconnected' from her knowledge of letters in words. There is debate over exactly what such patients are able to abstract from the letters that they can read (see Patterson and Kay, 1982; Shallice and Warrington, 1980.)

Disconnection effects, where one can show that someone has all the necessary knowledge to perform a particular task but that the information is not getting through, are hard to conceive of in anything other than modular, serially linked types of structure; massively parallel, densely interconnected structures presumably would not allow such functional lesions to occur without the intervention of intermediate structures. Here are more paradoxes to be resolved if we are to understand the relationship between psychological functions and their localisation in any detail.

Exploring disconnection deficits in terms derived from artificial thinking machines might be a useful task for the future. Such impairments are proving amenable to psychological explanation and formulation (Patterson and Kay, 1982). Note that the term disconnection itself, like double dissociation, describes a state of affairs but hardly explains it. Just what is 'disconnected' or 'dissociated' is what the psychologist aims to find out.

By focusing on the apparent complementarity of Frau T and Frau D's problems a number of inferences and insights should have emerged. These ladies enable us, if we are careful, to integrate the data that they provide with that from other sources normal and pathological, to come to a number of conclusions about how speech and face recognition may be functionally and anatomically separated in human minds and brains. Just how far and in what manner such separations occur is the meat and drink of cognitive neuropsychology.

Coming round

By now the reader's head will be awash with dichotomies and contradictions: right and left hemispheres, modular and distributed systems, visual and verbal skills, objects and their perceptual qualities...where has this led us?

The point of this excursion was not to give a guided tour of the landmarks of a particular area of study, pointing out its monuments and edifices. Rather it was (to mix metaphors even further) to immerse you in the rather turbulent waters where psychology and neurology meet. Where water currents meet there is fog, but also the most productive fishing. Cognitive neuropsychology has the potential to provide a rich harvest of understanding of basic mental processes and their neurological bases. It will only progress if it respects both neurological and psychological principles; it is possible that models of machine thinking might provide some guidance in integrating these areas and the evidence that is being produced by them.

This is a field of growing interest and activity and I have been unable in this short chapter to deal with a range of current issues – for instance, I have not touched on disorders of memory (see Hirst, 1982), nor on problems in grammatical speech comprehension and production (see Howard, 1985), nor yet on problems in spatial knowledge and orientation (see De Renzi, 1982b) or attention to spatial position (Bisiach, Berti and Vallar, 1985). A cognitive-neuropsychological analysis of speech and other language production processes is very clearly made by Ellis (1985). But perhaps the most important thing about fishing in fog is to make sure that the radar and the foghorn are functioning. I hope that this chapter will have shown you how to set the machinery to sense potential dangers and to announce your presence.

References

Allport, D. A. (1985), 'Distributed memory, modular subsystems and dysphasia', in S. Newman and R. Epstein (eds) *Current Perspectives in Dysphasia*. Churchill-Livingstone: Edinburgh.

Baron, J. (1979), 'Orthographic and word-specific mechanisms in children's reading of words', *Child Development*, *50*, 60-72.

Baron, J. and Treiman, R. (1980), 'Use of orthography in reading and learning to read', in J. F. Kavanagh and R. L. Venezky (eds) *Orthography, Reading and Dyslexia*. The Parks Press: Baltimore.

Beauvois, M-F. (1982), 'Optic aphasia – a process of interaction between vision and language', *Philosophical Transactions of the Royal Society of London, Series B, 298*, 135-48.

Benton, A. L. and Van Allen, M. W. (1972), 'Prosopagnosia and facial discrimination', *Journal of Neurological Science 15*, 167-72.

Bisiach, E., Berti, A. and Vallar, G. (1985), 'Analogical and logical disorders underlying unilateral neglect of space', in O. Marin and M. Posner (eds), *Attention and Performance*, Vol. 11. Lawrence Erlbaum: New Jersey.

Bryant, P. E. and Impey, L. (1986), 'The similarities between normal readers and dyslexic adults and children,' *Cognition, 24*, 121-37

Campbell, R., Landis, T. and Regard, M. (1986), 'Face recognition and lipreading; a neurological dissociation', *Brain 109*, 509-21.

Campbell, R. (1986), 'The lateralisation of lipreading; a first look', *Brain and Cognition*, 5, 1-22.

Campbell, R. (in press), 'Lipreading', in H. Ellis and A. Young (eds), *Handbook of Face Processing*. North Holland: Elsevier.

Campion, J., Latto, R. and Smith, V. (1983), 'Is blindsight an effect of scattered light, spared cortex and near threshold vision?' *Behav. and Brain Sciences, 6*, 423-64.

Coltheart, M. (1985), 'Cognitive neuropsychology: the association address', in O. Marin and M. Posner (eds), *Attention and Performance*, Vol. 11. Erlbaum, N.J.

Coltheart, M. (1983). 'The right hemisphere and disorders of reading', in A. Young (ed.), *Functions of the Right Cerebral Hemisphere*. Academic Press: London.

Coltheart, M., Patterson, K. E. and Marshall, J. (eds) (1980), *Deep Dyslexia*. Routledge & Kegan Paul: London.

De Renzi, E. (1982a), 'Memory disorders following focal brain damage', *Philosophical Transactions of the Royal Society of London, Series B, 298*, 73-84.

De Renzi, E. (1982b), *Disorders of Space Exploration and Cognition*. Wiley: New York.

De Renzi, E. (1986), 'Prosopagnosia in two patients with CT-scan evidence of damage confined to the right hemisphere', *Neuropsychologica, 24*, 385-91.

Dejerine, J. (1914), *Semiologie des affections du système nerveux*. Masson: Paris.

Ellis, A. W. (1985), 'The production of spoken words: a cognitive neuropsychological perspective', in A. W. Ellis (ed.), *Progress in the Psychology of Language*, Vol. 2. Lawrence Erlbaum: London.

Fodor, J. (1983), *Modularity of Mind*. MIT Press: Cambridge, Mass.

Gardner, H., Silverman, W., Wapner, W. and Zurif, E. (1978), 'The appreciation of antonymic contrasts in aphasia', *Brain and Language, 6*, 301-17.

Hirst, W. (1982), 'The amnesic syndrome: descriptions and explanations', *Psychological Bulletin, 91*, 435-60.

Hirst, W., Le Doux, J. and Stein, S. (1984), 'Constraints on the Processing of Indirect Speech Acts: evidence from Aphasiology', *Brain and Language, 23*, 26-33.

Howard, D. (1985), 'Agrammatism', in S. Newman and R. Epstein (eds), *Current Perspectives in Dysphasia*. Churchill-Livingstone: Edinburgh.

Jones, G. and Martin, M. (1984), 'Deep dyslexia and the right hemisphere hypothesis for semantic paralexia: a reply to Marshall and Patterson', *Neuropsychologica, 23*, 685-8.

Kay, J. (1985), 'Mechanisms of oral reading: a critical appraisal of cognitive models', in A. W. Ellis (ed.) *Progress in the Psychology of Language*, Vol. 2. Lawrence Erlbaum: London.

Kay, J. and Lesser, R. (1985), 'The nature of phonological processing in oral reading: evidence from surface dyslexia', *Quarterly Journal of Experimental Psychology, 37A*, 39-82.

Landis, T., Graves, R. and Goodglass, H. (1982), 'Aphasic reading and writing; possible evidence for right hemisphere mediation', *Cortex, 18*, 105-12.

Landis, T., Regard, M., Graves, R. and Goodglass, H. (1983) 'Semantic paralexia: a release of right hemisphere function from left hemisphere control', *Neuropsychologica, 21*, 359-64.

Landis, T., Cummings, J. L., Christen, L., Bogen, J. E. and Imhof, H-G (1986), 'Are unilateral right posterior lesions sufficient to cause prosopagnosia? Clinical and radiological findings in six additional patients', *Cortex, 22*, 243-52.

Luria, A. R. (1973), *The Working Brain: An Introduction to Neuropsychology*. Penguin Books, Harmondsworth.

McGurk, H. and MacDonald, J. (1976), 'Hearing lips and seeing voices', *Nature*, *264*, 746-8.

Malone, D. R., Morris, H. M., Kay, M. C. and Levin, H. S. (1982), 'Prosopagnosia: a double dissociation between the recognition of familiar and unfamiliar faces', *Journal of Neurology, Neurosurgery and Psychiatry*, *45*, 820-2.

Marcel, A. J. (1980) 'Surface dyslexia and beginning reading; a revised hypothesis of the pronunciation of print and its impairments', in M. Coltheart, K. E. Patterson and J. C. Marshall (eds), *Deep Dyslexia*. Routledge and Kegan Paul: London.

Marr, D. (1982), *Vision*. W. H. Freeman: San Francisco.

Marshall, J. C. and Newcombe, F. (1966), 'Syntactic and semantic errors in paralexia', *Neuropsychologica*, *6*, 169-76.

Marshall, J. C. and Patterson, K. E. (1983), 'Semantic paralexia and the wrong hemisphere: a note on Landis, Graves, Regard and Goodglass', *Neuropsychologica*, *21*, 425-7.

Meadows, J. C. (1974), 'The anatomical basis of prosopagnosia', *Journal of Neurology, Neurosurgery and Psychiatry*, *37*, 489-501.

Mehler, J., Morton, J. and Jusczyk, P. W. (1984), 'On reducing language to biology', *Cognitive Neuropsychology*, *1*, 83-116.

Mishkin, M. and Forgays, J. D. (1952), 'Word recognition as a function of retinal locus', *Journal of Experimental Psychology*, *43*, 43-8.

Morton, J. (1983), 'Brain-based and non-brain-based models of language', in D. Caplan (ed.), *Biological Perspectives on Language*. MIT Press: Boston, Mass.

Patterson, K. E. (1982), 'The relation between reading and phonological coding', in A. W. Ellis (ed.), *Normality and Pathology in Cognitive Functions*. Academic Press: London.

Patterson, K. E. and Besner, D. (1984), 'Is the right hemisphere literate?' *Cognitive Neuropsychology*, *1*, 315-41.

Patterson, K. E. and Kay, J. (1982), 'Letter-by-letter reading; psychological descriptions of a neurological syndrome', *Quarterly Journal of Psychology*, *34A*, 411-41.

Patterson, K. E., Marshall, J. C. and Coltheart, M. (eds) (1985), *Surface Dyslexia*. Lawrence Erlbaum: London.

Patterson, K. E. and Morton, J. (1985), 'From orthography to phonology: an attempt at an old interpretation', in K. E. Patterson, J. C. Marshall and M. Coltheart (eds) (1985), *Surface Dyslexia*. Lawrence Erlbaum: London.

Reber, A. S. (1985), *The Penguin Dictionary of Psychology*. Penguin Books: Harmondsworth.

Rolls, E. T. (1986), 'Information representation, processing and storage in the brain: analysis at the single neuron level', in J-P. Changeux and M. Koniski (eds), *Neural and Molecular Mechanisms of Learning*. Springer: Berlin.

Rosch, E. and Lloyd, B. B. (1978), *Cognition and Categorisation*. Lawrence Erlbaum: Hillsdale, NJ.

Ross, O. (1981), 'The aprosodias', *Archives of Neurology*, *38*, 561-9.

Seidenberg, M., Waters, G. S., Barnes, M. A. and Tanenhaus, M. K. (1984), 'When does irregular spelling or pronunciation influence word recognition?' *Journal of Verbal Learning and Verbal Behavior*, *22*, 383-404.

Sergent, J. (1984), 'Inferences from unilateral brain damage about normal hemispheric functions in visual pattern recognition', *Psychological Bulletin*, *96*, 99-115.

Sergent, J. (1985) 'Influence of task and input factors on the hemispheric processing of faces', *Journal of Experimental Psychology: Human Perception and Performance*, *11*, 846-62.

Shallice, T. and Warrington, E. K. (1970), 'The independent functioning of the verbal memory areas: a neuropsychological study', *Quarterly Journal of Experimental Psychology, 22,* 261-73.

Shallice, T. and Warrington, E. K. (1980), 'Single and multiple component central dyslexic syndromes', in M. Coltheart, K. E. Patterson and J. C. Marshall (eds), *Deep Dyslexia.* Routledge & Kegan Paul: London.

Sperry, R. W. (1974), 'Lateral specialisation in the surgically separated hemispheres', in F. D. Schmitt and R. G. Worden (eds), *The Neurosciences Third Study Program.* MIT Press: Cambridge, Mass.

Springer, S. and Deutsch, G. (1984), *Left Brain, Right Brain,* 2nd edn. W. H. Freeman: New York.

Waltz, D. L. (ed.) (1985), 'Connectionist models and their applications', *Cognitive Science, 9,* (a special issue). Ablex: Norwood, NJ.

Warrington, E. K. (1982), 'Neuropsychological studies of object recognition', *Philosophical Transactions of the Royal Society of London, Series B, 298,* 15-34.

Warrington, E. K. and Shallice, T. (1969), 'The selective impairment of auditory-verbal short term memory', *Brain, 92,* 885-96.

Warrington, E. K. and McCarthy, R. (1983), 'Category specific access dysphasia', *Brain, 106,* 854-78.

Warrington, E. K. and Shallice, T. (1984), 'Category specific semantic impairments', *Brain, 107,* 829-54.

Wernicke, C. (1874), *Der Aphasische Symptomencomplex.* Cohn & Weigert: Breslau.

Winner, E. and Gardner, H. (1977), 'Comprehension of metaphor in braindamaged patients', *Brain, 100,* 717-29.

8 Relative universals: perspectives on culture and cognition

H. Valerie Curran

Introduction

A thousand previous days concluded with the same melodic incantations pierced irregularly by a half-scream, half-growl as the shaman struck a powerful blow with his arm or arrow at one of a multitude of humanoid spirits *(hekura)* radiant in their fiery halos, bellowing incandescent names, and partaking of the substance of human souls. I did not have to look up to know that the score of glistening men, streaked with green, *ebene*-laden mucus, were growing more aggressive and violent as the effect of the magical powder hit them, and their foreboding preoccupation with sickness and death became more complete...[They] were assembled to drive out the perceived, but mostly imagined, sickness that Dedeheiwa diagnosed as the effects of *hekura* sent by his enemies in Yeisikorowa-teri, a village far to the South. Dedeheiwa, as was his style, led the attack - very vigorously for a man his age. (Chagnon, 1974)

This passage is a description by the social anthropologist, Napoleon Chagnon, of a shaman's efforts to cure illness among the Yanomamo Indians of Southern Venezuela and Northern Brazil. When illness is caused by *hekura* sent by shaman in enemy villages, the cure is to drive back those spirits by fighting them with fists and weapons and by frightening them with terrifying displays of aggression. Chagnon's (1968, 1974) detailed books are full of examples of what, to most of us, seems very exotic and strange behaviour. We are told, for example, how Yanomamo consume the ashes of dead people in a soup so that the living may 'see' their departed friends and relatives who are in *hedu* (spirit world).

Having lived for years with a group of Yanomamo, using the main anthropological technique of participant observation, Chagnon learnt their language and their norms of behaviour and came to appreciate and respect what he calls their 'intellectual environment' – 'the richness and complexity of their theological concepts, myths and legends' (1968, p. 44).

From a different theoretical perspective, cognitive psychologists have not been concerned with theology, myths and legends. For them, these are examples of *products* of thought which should not be confused with the thought *processes* of individuals within a culture. Psychologists have been more concerned with questions about how the thought processes of people who have grown up in very different cultures resemble or differ from those of people reared and educated in urban, technological societies mainly in Europe and North America.

Psychologists are relatively recent students of culture compared with anthropologists and, as we shall see later, many of the issues of contemporary research on culture and cognition have parallels in early debates in anthropology (Price-Williams, 1981). Central to current debates is the extent to which it is possible or meaningful to study psychological processes as if they can be abstracted from the cultural contexts in which they developed and are used (Curran, 1984). There are two main schools of thought on this, which reflect the two main approaches to culture and cognition.

On the one hand, there is the 'cognitive universals' approach which is based on Piaget's theory of an invariant sequence of stages in the development of operational thinking. Pierre Dasen and his colleagues (e.g. Dasen, 1977, 1984; Dasen and Heron, 1981) have been foremost in extending and developing Piagetian theory in the cross-cultural domain. On the other hand, there is the 'context-specific' school, exemplified by Michael Cole and his associates (e.g. Cole, Gay, Glick and Sharp, 1971; Cole and Scribner, 1974; Laboratory of Comparative Human Cognition, 1983) which doubts that psychological processes can be studied in isolation, divorced from the cultural contexts in which they are used and tends more to the belief that 'mind and culture are different aspects of the same phenomenon' (LCHC, 1983, p. 349).

The universalists take their starting point from a psychological theory of cognitive development; the context-specific school argues that one should begin by observing everyday activities and problem-solving and model experiments on these observed *cultural practices*.

In this chapter, I shall illustrate these approaches in terms of research on logical processes. As Scribner (1977) notes: 'Of the many issues relating to culture and thought that have been a matter of scholarly concern in the last century, the question of whether industrialised and traditional peoples share the same logical processes has provoked the most bitter controversy.' The debate was initially centred within anthropology but over the years has shifted to psychology and especially to interpretation of Piagetian cross-cultural experiments. However, in a general book on cognitive psychology it is relevant to begin by examining the rationale for carrying out studies in diverse cultures and what contributions such work can make to the subject as a whole.

Aims of cross-cultural studies

The interest of psychologists in cross-cultural studies – apart from the opportunity to travel to exotic parts of the world – stems from three main contributions such work can make to mainstream cognitive psychology. First, there is the question of how general are our theories of cognition. As is widely acknowledged, the subjects most often used to test hypotheses in psychology come from a fairly limited range of backgrounds (e.g. college sophomores, undergraduates, Cambridge housewives). It makes sense, therefore, to test those theories on people from very different backgrounds in different cultures of the world.

Second, cross-cultural studies aim to relate cognition to culture and to describe the nature of their interaction. Most psychologists would agree that adult cognition has developed through organism-environment interaction. By allowing variation in the environments of people we study, cross-cultural research can investigate the influence of environment on cognition. Mainstream psychology is dependent on cultural information about subjects at most levels of research. There is no more a culture-free man than there can be a culture-free test. Researchers rely on cultural knowledge of their subjects when designing and interpreting experiments so that they know, for example, how instructions would be interpreted and what reinforcements are required to engage their co-operation. Experimenters know these things implicitly because they share their subject's cultural experiences. When they move outside their own particular culture this dependence on cultural information becomes explicit.

Third, cultures can sometimes provide opportunities for examining the effects of variables which are inaccessible within Western societies. This can happen in two ways. One uses cross-cultural variation to examine the effects of factors like language, physical environment or subsistence modes. Sometimes it may be crucial to a theory to use this kind of variation. A notable case in point is Rosch's (1977) work on the relation between language, thought and perceptual salience where testing her hypothesis required subject populations whose languages varied in the numbers of colours coded.

The second way uses intra-cultural variation in factors which do not vary substantially in the West. Many traditional societies in certain parts of the world are presently undergoing rapid social change. Technological innovations have been introduced in some parts but not others; formal education is available for some people but not all; nutritional programmes are being carried out only in limited areas. Such 'transitional state' societies allow comparisons to be made to assess the effects of such factors as schooling, literacy, urbanisation and nutritional levels on cognitive functioning. A large body of cross-cultural research has focussed on the effects of schooling (for a detailed review of this field, see Rogoff, 1981). In the West, after a child is about 5, years of schooling and age correlate highly until adulthood. Thus much developmental research inevitably confounds maturational changes and school experience. As the Laboratory of Comparative Human Cognition (1979, p. 830) points out: 'to some people it seems that cognitive-developmental research in the United States has been measuring *years of schooling*, using *age* as its proxy variable.' In these ways, cross-cultural studies can expand the range of variables examinable.

The potential of cross-cultural studies in the development of a general science of cognition and of general theories of cognitive development seems fairly clear, but as yet that potential has not been fulfilled. The area is fraught with methodological problems and with conceptual confusions about cultural variables, many of which also hampered nineteenth-century anthropological theorising about culture and logical processes.

Logic and magic: anthropological history

Early anthropologists had little doubt that different belief systems and customs were the products of different processes of thought. Given, for example, the intellectual world of the Yanomamo, where unobservable spirits 'cause' observable sickness and where communication with the dead 'happens', they would have argued that such beliefs are only tenable if people had ways of inferring cause and effect which were qualitatively very different from those of urban Europeans.

Evolutionary concepts of natural selection and inheritance of acquired traits were borrowed from biology and applied to both cultural and psychological phenomena such that both cultures and their individual members were placed on an evolutionary ladder (Tylor, 1874). Cultures were seen to range from at one end nomadic hunter-gatherers to, at the other, urban technological societies. Social development was imposed on a scale from savagery through barbarism to civilisation (Morgan, 1877). And reflections of these 'primitive' societies were 'primitive' mentalities. The thought processes of individuals were seen to range along a parallel evolutionary scale from the concrete, magical and childlike to the abstract, logical and scientific such that: 'out of savages unable to count up to the number of their fingers and speaking a language containing only nouns and verbs, arise at length our Newtons and Shakespeares' (Spencer, 1887, p. 471).

Views like Spencer's were pervasive until the turn of the century. The notion that 'ontogeny recapitulates phylogeny' encapsulated the idea that the development of a child proceeds through the same stages as the human race has passed through during its evolution.

Another main influence on early anthropology was Levy-Bruhl (1910, 1923) who argued for a primitive mentality which was holistic, affective and poetic. This mentality neither made nor aimed at making the distinctions between rationality and emotion, or between objective and subjective, which were basic to European logic. It was a prelogical thought which allowed for contradictions and inconsistencies.

There was also the influential work of Sir James Frazer (1922) who saw a broad psychological evolution from magical thought to religious belief, and from religious belief to scientific thought. Frazer considered magical thinking to arise from erroneous concepts of causality. Magical practices, he argued, followed a 'law of sympathy' which governed primitive thought. From this 'law' things which had a striking quality in common (e.g. the jerky movements of a red bush monkey and those of a person in an epileptic fit) were believed to affect one another (e.g. the Zande try to cure epilepsy by consuming the burnt skull of a red bush monkey). This 'imitative magic' was contrasted with 'contagious magic' where things which had been in close contact (such as a person and a lock of his hair) influenced each other (illness could be inflicted on the person by magical treatment of his hair).

Magic and logic reconsidered

All these early anthropologists formulated their ideas mainly in armchairs, on the basis of inadequate data such as reports by travellers and missionaries who seemed to record differences in cultures much more often than similarities. Later pioneers like Franz Boas (1911), who was one of the first anthropologists to conduct systematic and detailed fieldwork, pointed out that *what* people believe and *what* they think about implies nothing about *how* they think: given bizarre premises one can reason perfectly logically and end up with bizarre conclusions.

Misconceptions about 'primitive' mentality were compounded by misconceptions about 'civilised' thought. Technological man was not as rational and scientific in his thinking as he liked to think. As Bartlett (1923) pointed out, one error 'was not that the primitive or the abnormal are wrongly observed, but that the modern or normal are hardly observed at all' (p. 284). There are many examples of magical thinking in technological societies, not only in superstitions (cf. Malinowski, 1954) but also in the everyday way in which causes are attributed to events (cf. Shweder, 1977). Responses to medicines in the Western world can be almost as magical as Zande attempts to cure epilepsy with a monkey's burnt skull. For example, people feel either drowsy or alert, and have corresponding changes in pulse rate and blood pressure, depending on whether they are told that a tablet they took was a depressant or stimulant, even though the tablet contains no drug whatsoever (Griffiths, 1981). Griffiths also points out that many patients believe coloured capsules are more effective medicines than white tablets, even when each contains the same drug.

What is now accepted in modern anthropology is that magical thinking, religious belief and logical thinking are not separate rungs on any evolutionary ladder. Rather, all three can and do co-exist but to different proportions depending on the individual and on his cultural experience. And most social anthropologists nowadays assume psychic unity, that, as Levi-Strauss (1978, p. 19) asserts: 'the human mind is everywhere one and the same and that it has the same capacities.' But given that anthropology has no theory of cognition, on what basis is this assumption of psychic unity made? Twentieth-century anthropologists have often spent two or three years doing fieldwork, living with a group of traditional people, learning their language, participating in their way of life, observing daily activities and problem solving, understanding their explanations of the universe and so on. It is obvious to them that traditional peoples can think just as logically as they can but that their different interests and needs mean they think about different things. They may not have 'scientific' explanations of the world, but myths give them the illusion that they can and do understand how the world operates. Through learning to understand each culture within its own terms and respecting it as a coherent whole, logical, religious and magical thinking are seen to coexist depending upon the problem at hand.

Cognitive universals: Piagetian approaches

> There is no 'primitive mentality', but there may well be a 'pre-logic' in the sense of a pre-operational level of thought or of a level to begin with limited to concrete operations. (Piaget, 1968, p. 116)

Piaget (1968) criticises the approach of his fellow structuralist, Levi-Strauss, which he sees as not concerned with everyday reasoning or individual invention but 'installs itself from the start in finished products'. Like Boas before, Piaget asserts that the finished products of a culture – classification systems, mythologies and so on – cannot be used to gauge thought processes of individual members of society.

Piaget's theory of a universal and invariant sequence of stages in the development of the child's logical abilities has generated the largest single body of cross-cultural studies on cognition to date – and some of the most vehement debates (for detailed reviews, see Dasen, 1977; Dasen and Heron, 1981; Price-Williams, 1981; Saxe, 1983).

Cross-cultural Piagetian research has focussed largely on the concrete operational stage which among Swiss children begins around 7 years of age. This focus is partly because the physical materials required in concrete operational tasks (e.g. water, clay, sticks) can be found in every culture and partly because the child's or adult's responses can be scored as 'right' or 'wrong' and the circumstances can be standardised. Although this goes against the important clinical aspects of such tasks, few cross-cultural studies have used clinical techniques (cf. Nyiti, 1982). Research on the formal operational stage, which begins for Swiss children at about 12 years of age, is as yet less extensive, partly because it has proved more difficult to find culturally appropriate formal operational tasks.

Concrete operations

Children in other cultures have been found to achieve concrete operations sooner, at the same time or later than European and American children. In most studies of children who have not attended formal, Western-type schools, the general finding has been a developmental 'lag' of a few years behind schooled populations (cf. Ashton, 1975; Price-Williams 1981). In some studies, a significant proportion of adults has failed to give the appropriate responses in conservation tasks and the interpretation of this result has been controversial. Within a classic Piagetian framework, these adults would be categorised as non-conservers and it may even be argued that they had not reached the level of concrete operational thought (e.g. Hallpike, 1979). But as Cole (1975) and Goodnow (1980) point out, it is hard to imagine any society surviving in which many of its adults are functioning at a pre-operational level of thought.

One crucial distinction in interpreting such findings is that between competence and performance (Flavell and Wohlwill, 1969; Dasen, 1977). Someone's performance in a task does not necessarily reflect his true competence, or in other words, what he does not do does not imply what he cannot do. Imagine yourself as a Yanomamo confronted by a strange and probably white researcher who asks you odd questions while pouring water between containers. Reported cultural differences in performance may be due to artifacts of the testing situation and the specific assessments used.

Undoubtedly, many features of the assessment procedure affect a child's or adult's performance. Familiarity with the materials used, with the operations required, with materials and operations combined, and with the language used have all been found to be critical variables affecting performance: even slight alterations in the procedures used have produced dramatic changes in responses. In one early study, Greenfield (1966) found that Wolof (Senegalese) children had difficulty in the typical conservation of liquids task, tending to give non-conservation responses and often justifying these with 'magical' reasons such as claiming an increase in quantity because it was the experimenter who had poured the liquid. Irvine (1978) attempted to re-examine the difficulties encountered by Wolof children. She asked subjects to play the role of 'informant' and to help *her* understand the Wolof terms for equivalence and resemblance. Subjects having given the 'wrong' response in the standard conservation task went on in their role as 'informants' to clearly explain that while the level of water was 'more', the quantity was the 'same'. It is noteworthy that Irvine (1978) herself had spent some time living with Wolof and was familiar to the children she tested. As Irvine (1978) notes, the questioning in Piagetian (and other) experiments seems strange to people who have not experienced classroom exchanges or school tests. 'Outside the schoolroom, it is rare for a Wolof adult to ask another adult, or even a child more than six or seven years old, a question to which he or she already knows the answer. Where this kind of questioning does occur it suggests an aggressive challenge, or a riddle with a trick answer.' (p. 304). In two studies in which the psychologists were native speakers of the relevant languages and had expertise in clinical interviewing, developmental curves were found to be similar to European norms (Kamara and Easley, 1977; Nyiti, 1976).

One strategy for trying to assess competence as distinct from performance is to train subjects on tasks involving the relevant operations before assessing them on other, related tasks. Marked and rapid effects of training are interpreted as showing that the underlying or 'latent' competences existed and that their expression in performance was 'triggered' by the training. Training procedures have met with some success (Dasen, Lavellé and Retschitzki, 1979; Dasen, Ngini and Lavellé, 1979). However, rather than 'triggering latent competencies', training studies can simply be seen to help the subject to understand the experimental procedures, the nature of the problem being posed and what is expected of him. Even test-retest procedures can produce marked changes in performance (Dasen, 1984).

Cross-cultural studies have also found variation *within* the concrete operational stage in the order of acquisition of different concepts. Dasen (1977) expresses the commonsense notion that 'each cultural group is expected to develop specifically those skills and concepts which it most needs' (p. 184) and he has tried to account for within-stage variation in terms of an 'ecocultural framework' (Berry, 1976; Dasen, Berry and Witkin, 1979). This framework sees cognitive development as influenced by four major, interacting factors: physical ecology, economic activity, social organisation and child-rearing practices. A nomadic group who use spatial cues and depend on the ability to orient in space, were found to develop spatial concepts earlier than conservation, but the reverse was found with a sedentary group – they acquired conservation earlier than spatial concepts. Linking within-stage variation to environmental variation is a potentially interesting extension of Piagetian research.

Formal operations

Finding appropriate ways of assessing formal operational thought has posed problems cross-culturally. Piaget largely discussed formal thinking in the context of abstract logical propositions and the physical world. But as Jahoda (1980) points out, in non-literate groups, formal operations are used more in verbal exchanges in social contexts. Early studies generally failed to find evidence of formal operational thought among people who had not attended formal schooling (Ashton, 1975) but, like early studies of concrete operations, most were compounded by methodological problems. Saxe (1979) used an indigenous knowledge system, the birth-order system, to examine formal operational thought with a schooled group from Papua New Guinea and found a shift from concrete to formal operations between 13 and 19 years of age.

Piaget (1972) himself stated that formal operations is a universal stage but that it is acquired first, and perhaps only, in particular areas of specialisation or in terms of specific aptitudes. If this is so within relatively homogenous cultures of Europe and America it will be much more so within very different cultures.

It is not possible to use a few Piagetian tasks to determine even an individual's global 'intelligence' or 'level of development', let alone to ascertain the cognitive functioning of a whole cultural group. But as Dasen (1984) complains, such generalisations have been drawn as seen in Hallpike's (1979) re-introduction of the idea that you can talk about 'primitive' thought and that it can be characterised as pre-operational. This is clearly a step backwards into the themes of nineteenth-century anthropology. However, the ladder this time is cognitive-developmental rather than explicitly evolutionary.

European norms on Piagetian tasks are not a yardstick against which people of other cultures can be compared. To use them as such would be blatant ethnocentrism. The same task and the same procedure does not necessarily tap the same psychological processes in different cultural groups. As Greenfield (1976) argued, cross-cultural research has followed Piagetian procedures when it would do better to follow Piagetian theory. We shall return to these issues when we consider the important question of endpoints of development.

Contextualist approaches

> Cultural resources are ingredient, not accessory, to human thought
> (Geertz, 1962, p. 737).

The contextualist or 'context-specific' school of culture and cognition is exemplified by the work of Michael Cole, Sylvia Scribner and associates (e.g. Cole et al., 1971; Cole and Scribner, 1974; Laboratory of Comparative Human Cognition, 1983), although Cole traces his sociohistorical approach to Vygotsky (e.g. Vygotsky, 1978) and Luria (e.g. Luria, 1971). Cole et al.'s early and extensive research with Kpelle of Liberia led them to conclude that: 'cultural differences in cognition reside more in the situations to which particular cognitive processes are applied than in the existence of a process in one cultural group and its absence in another' (1971, p. 233).

At every point in their research (which included categorisation and conceptual processes, free recall, problem-solving and verbal reasoning), whenever they had demonstrated their subjects' failure to use a particular process in one situation, they went on to show their use of that same process in another situation. This early work was important in showing that apparent 'deficits' in cognitive functioning reported so often were more deficits in the methods used than in the people tested.

Cole et al. showed the illogicality of the 'deficit interpretation' of apparent group differences in cognition (cf. Cole and Bruner, 1971) in a similar way to that in which Labov (1969, 1970) had shown the illogicality of 'deficits' in linguistic abilities of black American youths. The results of many studies demonstrating the context-dependent nature of cognitive performance accord with the commonsense notion that people will be good at doing things that they are used to doing, and not so good at doing unfamiliar things. Non-literate rice farmers will obviously be more adept at classifying types of rice than at sorting geometric figures (as Irwin and McLaughlin, 1970, showed), just as North American students do not match Kpelle when it comes to sorting vine and forest leaves (as Cole et al. showed). One expects a butcher to be more adept at classifying cuts of meat than a carpenter, who in his turn will be more proficient when it comes to wood.

Rather than viewing the context-dependent nature of performance as due to experimental artifacts, Cole et al. argue that one should investigate how the changes in context relate to everyday cultural experience: 'Cultural variations in performance becomes an invitation to discover the relation of tested performance to prior cultural practice' (Laboratory of Comparative Human Cognition, 1983, p. 321).

Verbal reasoning studies

During the early 1930s Luria (1976) and his colleagues investigated cultural influences on verbal reasoning with people from remote regions of Uzbekistan, Central Asia. These areas were undergoing economic and social changes after the cultural revolution which involved collectivising agriculture and introducing courses in literacy and technology. Luria compared groups of people who differed in their degree of involvement with 'modern' institutions: non-literate men and women in remote villages where traditional farming methods were still used; young people involved in collective farming some of whom had minimal literacy training; women attending teacher training schools. Luria used verbal reasoning problems based on syllogisms, which involved giving two related premises (e.g. Precious metals do not rust. Gold is a precious metal.) and asking for a conclusion (Does gold rust or not?). Many of the non-literate adults did not appear to treat the two premises as being related, so that when they were asked only to recall the premises they produced responses like 'Do precious metals rust? Is gold a precious metal?' (Luria, 1982) as if the premises themselves were questions or questionable statements. Even subjects who did recall the syllogism correctly and who drew the correct conclusion added remarks like: 'Yes, I know this myself. I have a gold ring. I've had it for a long time. It does not rust!' (Luria, 1982, p. 207). The addition of 'I know this myself' is significant. When syllogisms involved premises or inferences which non-literate subjects did not themselves know to be true, they often refused to accept them and argued they could only judge on what they themselves had seen or knew from reliable people to be true.

> *Syllogism*: In the Far North, where there is snow, all bears are white. Novaya Zemlya is in the Far North and there is always snow there. What colour are the bears there?
> 'We always speak only of what we see; we don't talk about what we haven't seen.'
> E: 'But what do my words imply?' (The syllogism is repeated.)
> 'Well, it's like this: our tsar isn't like yours, and yours isn't like ours. Your words can be answered only by someone who was there, and if a person wasn't there he can't say anything on the basis of your words.'
> E: '...But on the basis of my words – in the North, where there is always snow, the bears are white, can you gather what kind of bears there are in Novaya Zemlya?'
> 'If a man was sixty or eighty and had seen a white bear and had told about it, he could be believed, but I've never seen one and hence I can't say. That's my last word. Those who saw can tell, and those who didn't see can't say anything!' (At this point a young Uzbek volunteered, 'From

your words it means that bears there are white.')
E: 'Well, which of you is right?'
'What the cock knows how to do, he does. What I know, I say, and
nothing beyond that!' (Luria, 1976, p. 108-9)

It seems in this transcript that the subject does not find the 'words' of the
experimenter an acceptable basis on which to make a conclusion and is
trying to communicate what his culture views as evidence and truth ('We
don't talk about what we haven't seen.'). Perhaps if the experimenter had
been sixty years old or more, and if he had seen a white bear, the subject
may have behaved differently: but nothing can be concluded about the
subject's logical thinking when he disputes the experimenter's criteria for
truth. Using other syllogisms however, when the premises accorded with
the practical experiences of non-literate adults – 'I know this myself' – their
reasoning followed the standard rules.

Luria's findings have been replicated with non-schooled children and
non-literate adults in several cultures (e.g. Cole et al., 1971; Scribner 1977;
Fobih, 1979; Sharp et al., 1979). Scribner (1977) uses the term 'empiric' to
refer to reasoning on the basis of the subject's own knowledge or experience
(external to the information contained in the problem) and the term
'theoretic' for reasoning on the basis of only the premises given. Examining
the use of empiric versus theoretic reasons, Scribner (1977) found that
theoretic reasons were almost always given for correct answers to the
syllogism whereas empiric reasons were associated with correct answers at
a rate only a little better than chance. This was true for both schooled and
non-schooled populations from various studies, which shows that when
non-literate people treat the syllogism as a self-contained problem they
reason in the same logical way as literate people. And although non-literate
subjects used empiric reasons most frequently, most of them responded
theoretically to some of the problems so clearly they could think logically;
the difference was in the acceptability of the information given.

Scribner (1977) suggests that the formal approach necessary to cope with
deductive problems is essentially a particular *genre* of language. It may be
that people become more familiar with that *genre* through schooling and
through reading and writing. An analogy may be seen in Zen Buddhism
where a master may pose a student such problems as 'What is the sound of
one hand clapping?', problems which to Western 'logical thinkers' appear
insoluble and even bizarre but which train Zen students to think in
culturally valued ways.

Another interpretation of empiric reasoning is that schooling may simply
teach acceptance of information, of premises, provided by an authority.
Some of the examples quoted as 'representative' of syllogisms used in
Scribner's (1977) paper almost invite an empirical bias: 'A dog and a horse
are *always* together. The horse is *here now*. Where do you think the dog

might be *now*?' Unless the experimenter made some elaborate arrangements with animals, in which case he would not be looking at reasoning but at observation, the premises are clearly untrue to anyone's way of thinking. Another example also quoted in Scribner (1977) uses the premise 'All women who live in Monrovia are married'. Monrovia is the capital city of Liberia and again the statement is obviously untrue. A more subtle example is a premise like 'All wealthy men have power', which depends on definitions of power. I should think Western undergraduates might produce a lot of empiric reasons with syllogisms like 'All psychology students are egocentric. You are a psychology student. Are you...?'

Conclusions remarkably similar to Scribner's about empiric and theoretic reasoning were, however, reached in a very different kind of study. Blurton-Jones and Konner (1976), an animal behaviourist and an anthropologist respectively, held 'seminars' with !Kung San (hunter-gatherers of the northern Kalahari desert, Botswana) about animal behaviour. Knowledge of animal behaviour is important to any hunting society and the extent of !Kung knowledge is impressive – 'the !Kung appear to know a good deal more about many subjects than do the scientists' (p. 328). Their knowledge was in terms of facts – about what animals actually do – rather than theories or explanations about why they behave that way, and !Kung were at pains to discriminate observed behaviour (data) from hearsay.

This empirical bias in terms of facts about animal behaviour should be considered with the excellence shown by !Kung in tracking, a skill which requires patterns of inference, hypothesis-testing, and discovery that tax the best inferential and analytic capacities of the human mind. As Lee (1979, p. 212) describes: 'The !Kung are such superb trackers and make such accurate deductions from the faintest marks in the sand that at first their skill seems uncanny. For example, both men and women are able to identify an individual person merely by the sight of his or her footprint in the sand. There is nothing mysterious about this. Their tracking is a skill, cultivated over a lifetime, that builds on literally tens of thousands of observations.'

One lesson to be learnt from these kind of observations is that the use of one method or one paradigm for investigating one cognitive process may well produce misleading results. An empirical bias may be shown in accumulating facts about animal behaviours; theoretical reasoning is clear in tracking skills. However many detailed variations are introduced into syllogisms or conservation tasks, they can only sample a tiny fraction of an individual's cognitive domain.

Cultural practices

Limitations of the context-specific approach derive from its lack of a theoretical framework which takes into account the situational dependence of cognitive functioning. There can be no psychologically meaningful 'theory of situations' (Curran, 1980) as the same situation is construed differently by different individuals. So as Jahoda (1980) points out, 'most of [Cole's] account consists of listing various possibilities like a seemingly endless trail vanishing at the distant horizon.' (p. 124)

What then is Cole's alternative to accumulating catalogues describing the performance of culture A in situation 1,2,3,4...? The Laboratory of Comparative Human Cognition (1983) suggest that cultural practices – learned systems of activities – should be the unit of analysis for the study of culture and thought. Where culture and mind can be seen operating together is in the activities organised by a culture for learning. As examples of such research, they cite the work of Lave and Greenfield (Lave, 1977; Greenfield and Childs, 1977; Greenfield and Lave, 1982) on cognitive aspects of informal education.

Lave's (1977) research was based on the traditional apprenticeship of Liberian tailors in the capital city of Monrovia. She spent months observing how apprentices' learning was structured or 'scaffolded' into an active, organised system. On the basis of her observations, Lave designed two sets of mathematical tasks which involved the same operations but one set resembled problems encountered in tailoring (e.g. estimation of sizes of waistbands on trousers) and the other set were similar to school mathematics problems. She gave the tasks to tailors aged 10 to 40 years who varied in their amounts of experience of school and of tailoring. Years of tailoring was the best predictor of performance on tailoring mathematics; years of schooling the best predictor for school mathematics. But neither schooling nor tailoring skills generalised much beyond the problems they were normally applied to.

Childs and Greenfield (1980) worked with Zinacantecan weavers in Mexico and found they could represent traditional weaving patterns with sticks but when it came to completing *unfamiliar* patterns, they were not as successful as non-weavers. Greenfield and Lave (1982, p. 207) conclude 'each of the diverse educational forms we investigated can lead to generalisation from existing problem-solving skills to problem situations that are related in definable ways. The limited nature of generalisation skills is characteristic of all of the educational forms discussed here – including schooling.'

If skills acquired in formal education are not generalisable much beyond the school-type problems they were used to solve, why do comparisons of non-schooled with schooled children so often show schooling to be a positive influence on cognitive functioning? One explanation is that the tasks used in cognitive psychology are closer to the school-problems than to problems encountered in informal education or in everyday activities. The experiments used to examine cognitive processes may be seen as models of skills used, in the contexts given in formal education. So rather than looking at the effects of schooling on cognitive development (or of literacy on adult cognition), studies may have been simply showing that people without formal, institutionalised education do not easily transfer their skills to school-type tasks.

End-points of development: ours or theirs?

A main aim of Piagetian studies in a cross-cultural context is to test the universality of the sequence of stages of logical development. In being exclusively concerned with logical development, Piagetian theory reflects the importance European and American cultures attached to logical thinking. The end point of development – formal operational thought – involves the kinds of hypothetico-deductive ways of reasoning that Western societies value for academic achievement and for scientific thinking. Clearly, not everyone values the same things and the ideal 'end-point' of development varies across cultures. As Wober (1969) pointed out long ago, we should not be asking 'How well do *they* do our tricks' but rather looking at the performance of people from different cultures on *their* own skills and in *their* own areas of expertise.

Research has found significant variations in what different cultures regard as intelligent behaviour (Goodnow, 1976; 1980; 1984) with many conceptions of intelligence including social as well as cognitive skills. Mundy-Castle (1974, 1983) distinguishes a 'social intelligence' (including tact, sensitivity and unselfconsciousness) from a more cognitively defined 'technical intelligence'. Keats (1983) summarises the intelligent person in China thus: 'The totality is of a responsible pragmatic socially oriented person who gets things right. He observes and memorises but his is not an enquiring mind nor a critical faculty' (p. 73). Several other studies have reported wide variations (Putnam and Kilbride, 1980; Super, 1983) and it is clear that what is intelligent to a cross-cultural psychologist may have little in common with what his or her subjects regard as intelligent.

Dasen (1984) has taken up the concept that the ideal 'end point' of a child's development will be similarly culturally relative and that: 'We should first determine what the ideal endpoint of development is, in each particular culture, and then study the developmental stages leading to this last state' (1984, p. 425). With this approach, the focus is on what Dasen calls Piaget's metatheory – the interactionist model of adaptation (assimilation and accommodation) – rather than Piaget's stage theory.

Dasen (1984) investigated concepts of intelligence among the Baoule of the Ivory Coast and found that 'what the Baoule do value are social skills: being helpful, obedient, respectful, but also being knowledgeable, taking responsibilities and showing initiative in tasks useful to the family and the community' (p. 430). He correlated ratings of children on Baoule intelligence, on school performance and on Piagetian tasks. Although the Piagetian tasks were fairly good predictors of school performance, they were not related to attributes valued by the traditional Baoule culture. 'There were even some indications that the attributes that define intelligence for the Baoule are negatively related to performance on operational tasks' (p. 430). So whatever the Piagetian tasks were actually measuring, it was not something valued within the culture of the subjects being tested. Again, the correlation of school performance with operational task performance suggests that what was being measured was nearer to what is valued in formal education.

The goals and values of much of formal education are not ones shared by everyone. Academic intelligence, as Neisser (1976) points out, is characterised by many Westerners as over-concerned with trivia, head-in-the-clouds and lacking in practical commonsense. Perhaps psychologists have unwittingly designed cognitive tasks to assess the kinds of intellectual abilities required in their own thinking? Neisser (1976, p. 138) writes: 'academic people are in the position of having focussed their professional activities around a particular personal quality, as instantiated in a certain set of skills. We have then gone on to *define* the quality in terms of this skill set, and ended by asserting that persons who lack these special skills are unintelligent altogether.'

Relative universals

Anthropologists in the nineteenth century formulated global theories of mind and culture. On the basis of inadequate data, they contrasted the magical, holistic, pre-logical thought processes of people in traditional societies with the logical, reductionist, scientific thinking of people in Europe and America. In the twentieth century, anthropologists accepted cultural relativity and realised that you have to understand a culture on its own terms, making detailed ethnographies of each society, before any global statements about 'culture' can be attempted.

Psychologists working cross-culturally are still torn between two aims. On the one hand, there is a desire for a global, universal understanding of culture and cognition. On the other hand, there is clearly the need for culturally-relative and culturally-sensitive conceptualisations of cognitive functioning and cognitive development. The parallels with anthropological history are clear. The use of experiments has produced data which is often unreliable, situation-dependent and ungeneralisable to everyday problem-solving activities. There are more problems encountered in trying to define and unpackage the independent variables: what is a culture? How urban is urban? Who and what decides which children attend school?

The context-specific school argue for a cultural practice approach which examines cognitive functioning in everyday activities and culturally organised learning situations. This approach is clearly culturally sensitive but Dasen (1983) complains it is 'mainly descriptive' and Jahoda (1983) maintains it is difficult to regard it as a goal of cross-cultural psychology.

The Piagetian school bases its approach on a (universal?) theory of logical development but have the problem of making their studies culturally sensitive. As Dasen (1983, p. 158) asks: 'Are we waiting for indigenous Piagets to arise? Or could it be that psychology is nothing but a Western paradigm anyway?' Certainly it seems that most of our experiments in cognitive psychology are cultural products of the Western world and its educational systems which cannot competently assess the thought processes of traditional peoples. We should take a lesson from anthropology and realise that global, universal theories of culture and mind cannot be attempted until we have a reliable, culturally relative understanding and in this endeavour, cultural practice research will make a start by inserting 'relative' before 'universals'.

References

Ashton, P. T. (1975), 'Cross-cultural Piagetian research: an experimental perspective', *Harvard Educational Review*, 45, 475-506.

Bartlett, F. C. (1923), *Psychology and Primitive Culture*. Cambridge University Press: Cambridge.

Berry, J. W. (1976), *Human Ecology and Cognitive Style*. Halstead: New York.

Blurton-Jones, N. and Konner, M. J. (1976), '!Kung knowledge of animal behaviour', in R. B. Lee and I. Devore (eds), *Kalahari Hunter Gatherers: Studies of the !Kung San and their Neighbours*. Harvard University Press: Cambridge, Mass.

Boas, F. (1911), *The Mind of Primitive Man*. Republished by Free Press: New York, 1965.

Chagnon, N. A. (1968), *Yanomamo: The Fierce People*. Holt, Rinehart & Winston: New York.

Chagnon, N. A. (1974), *Studying the Yanomamo*. Holt, Rinehart & Winston: New York.

Childs, C. P. and Greenfield P. M. (1980), 'Informal modes of learning and teaching: the case of Zinacanteco weaving', in N. Warren (ed.), *Studies in Cross-Cultural Psychology*, Vol. 2. Academic Press: New York.

Cole, M. (1975) 'An ethnographic psychology of cognition', in R. W. Brislin, S. Bochner and W. J. Lonner (eds), *Cross-Cultural Perspectives on Learning*. Halstead Press: New York.

Cole. M. and Bruner, J. S. (1971) 'Cultural differences and inferences about psychological processes', *American Psychologist*, 26, 867-76.

Cole, M., Gay, J., Glick, J. and Sharp, D. W. (1971), *The Cultural Context of Learning and Thinking*. Basic Books: New York.

190 H. Valerie Curran

Cole, M. and Scribner, S. (1974), *Culture and Thought: A Psychological Introduction.* Wiley: New York.

Curran, H. V. (1980), 'Cross-cultural perspectives on cognition', in G. L. Claxton (ed.), *Cognitive Psychology: New Directions.* Routledge & Kegan Paul: London.

Curran, H. V. (1984), 'Developmental perspectives on memory', in H. V. Curran (ed.), *Nigerian Children: Developmental Perspectives.* Routledge & Kegan Paul: London.

Dasen, P. R. (1977), 'Are cognitive processes universal? A contribution to cross-cultural Piagetian psychology', in N. Warren (ed.), *Studies in Cross-Cultural Psychology.* Academic Press: New York.

Dasen, P. R. (1983), 'Comment', in J. B. Deregowski, S. Dziurawiec and R. C. Annis (eds), *Expiscations in Cross-Cultural Psychology.* Swets & Zeitlinger: Lisse.

Dasen, P. R. (1984), 'The cross-cultural study of intelligence: Piaget and the Baoule', *International Journal of Psychology, 19,* 407-34.

Dasen, P. R., Berry, J. W. and Witkin, H. (1979), 'The use of developmental theories cross-culturally', in L. Eckensberger, Y. Poortinga and W. Conner (eds), *Cross-Cultural Contributions to Psychology.* Swets & Zeitlinger: Lisse.

Dasen, P. R. and Heron, A. (1981), 'Cross-cultural tests of Piaget's theory', in H. C. Triandis and A. Heron (eds), *Handbook of Cross-Cultural Psychology,* Vol. 4. Allyn & Bacon: Boston.

Dasen, P. R., Lavellé, M., Retschitzki, J. (1979), 'Training conservation of quantity (liquids) in West African (Baoule) children'. *International Journal of Psychology, 14,* 57-68.

Dasen, P. R., Ngini, L. and Lavellé, M. (1979), 'Cross-cultural training studies of concrete operations', in L. H. Eckensberger, W. I. Lonner and Y. Poortinga (eds), *Cross-Cultural Contributions to Psychology.* Swets & Zeitlinger: Lisse.

Flavell, J. H. and Wohlwill, J. F. (1969), 'Formal and functional aspects of cognitive development', in D. Elkind and J. H. Flavell (eds), *Studies in Cognitive Development.* Oxford University Press: New York.

Fobih, A. (1979), *The influence of different educational experiences on classificatory and verbal reasoning behaviour of children in Ghana.* Unpublished doctoral dissertation, University of Alberta.

Frazer, J. G. (1922), *The Golden Bough.* MacMillan: London.

Geertz, J. (1962), 'The growth of culture and the evolution of mind', in J. M. Sher (ed.), *Theories of Mind.* Free Press: New York.

Goodnow, J. J. (1976), 'The nature of intelligent behaviour: questions raised by cross-cultural studies', in L. Resnick (ed.), *The Nature of Intelligence.* Wiley: New York.

Goodnow, J. J. (1980), 'Everyday concepts of intelligence and its development', in N. Warren (ed.), *Studies in Cross-Cultural Psychology,* Vol. 2. Academic Press: New York.

Goodnow, J. J. (1984), 'On being judged "intelligent"', *International Journal of Psychology, 19,* 391-406.

Greenfield, P. M. (1966), 'On culture and conservation', in J. S. Bruner, R. R. Olver and P. M. Greenfield (eds), *Studies in Cognitive Growth.* Wiley: New York.

Greenfield, P. M. (1976), 'Cross-cultural research and Piagetian theory: paradox and progress', in K. Riegel and J. Meacham (eds), *The Developing Individual in a Changing World.* Vol. 1. Mouton: The Hague.

Greenfield, P. M. and Childs, C. P. (1977), 'Understanding sibling concepts: a developmental study of kin terms in Zinacatan', in P. Dasen (ed.) *Piagetian Psychology: Cross-Cultural Contributions.* Gardner: New York.

Greenfield, P. M. and Lave, J. (1982), 'Cognitive aspects of informal education', in

D. A. Wagner and H. W. Stevenson (eds), *Cultural Perspectives on Child Development*. Freeman: San Francisco.

Griffiths, D. (1981), 'Psychological aspects of the response to drugs', in D. Griffiths (ed.), *Psychology and Medicine*. Macmillan: London.

Hallpike, C. (1979), *The Foundations of Primitive Thought*. Oxford University Press: London.

Irvine, J. (1978), 'Wolof magical thinking: culture and conservation revisited', *Journal of Cross-Cultural Psychology*, 9.

Irwin, M. H. and McLaughlin, D. H. (1970), 'Ability and preference in category-sorting by Mano School children and adults', *Journal of Social Psychology*, *82*, 15-24.

Jahoda, G. (1980), 'Theoretical and systematic approaches in cross-cultural psychology', in H. C. Triandis and W. W. Lambert (eds), *Handbook of Cross-Cultural Psychology*, Vol. 1. Allyn & Bacon: Boston.

Jahoda, G. (1983), 'The cross-cultural emperor's new clothes: the emic-etic issue revisited', in J. B. Deregowski, S. Dziurawiec and R. C. Annis (eds), *Expiscations in Cross-Cultural Psychology*. Swets & Zeitlinger: Lisse.

Kamara, A. and Easley, J. A. (1977), 'Is the rate of cognitive development uniform across cultures?' in P. R. Dasen (ed.), *Piagetian Psychology: Cross-Cultural Contributions*. Gardner: New York.

Keats, D. (1982), 'Cultural bases of concepts of intelligence: a Chinese versus American comparison', in *Proceedings of Second Asian Workshop on Child and Adolescent Development*, Behavioural Science Research.

Laboratory of Comparative Human Cognition (1979), 'What's cultural about cross-cultural psychology?', *Annual Review of Psychology*, *30*, 143-72.

Laboratory of Comparative Human Cognition (1983), 'Culture and cognitive development', in P. Mussen (ed.), *Handbook of Child Psychology*, Vol. 1, 4th edition. Wiley: New York.

Labov, W. (1969), 'The logic of non-standard English', in F. Williams (ed.), *Language and Poverty*. Markham Press: Chicago.

Labov, W. (1970), 'The study of language in its social context', *Studium Generale*, *23*, 66-84.

Lave, J. (1977), 'Cognitive consequences of traditional apprenticeship training in West Africa', *Anthropology and Education Quarterly*, *8*, 177-80.

Lee, R. B. (1979), *The !Kung San: Men, Women and Work in a Foraging Society*. Cambridge University Press: Cambridge.

Levi-Strauss, C. (1978), *Myth and Meaning*. Routledge & Kegan Paul: London.

Levy-Bruhl, C. (1910), *How Natives Think*. Washington Square Press: New York, 1966.

Levy-Bruhl, L. (1923), *Primitive Mentality*. Beacon Press: Boston, 1966.

Luria, A. R. (1971), 'Towards the problem of historical nature of psychological processes', *International Journal of Psychology*, *5*, 259-72.

Luria, A. R. (1976), *Cognitive Development, its Cultural and Social Foundations*. Harvard University Press: Cambridge, Mass.

Luria, A. R. (1982), *Language and Cognition*. Wiley: New York.

Malinowski, B. (1954), *Magic, Science and Religion*. Doubleday: New York.

Morgan, L. N. (1877), *Ancient Society*. Reprinted by The World Publishing Co.: Cleveland, 1963.

Mundy-Castle, A. C. (1974), 'Social and technological intelligence in Western and non-Western cultures', University of Ghana, Legon *4*, 46-52.

Mundy-Castle, A. (1983), 'Are Western psychological concepts valid in Africa? A Nigerian Review', in S. Pilowsky (ed.), *Cultures in Collision*. Australian National Association of Mental Health: Adelaide.

Neisser, U. (1976), 'General, academic and artificial intelligence', in L. B. Resnick (ed.) *The Nature of Intelligence*. Lawrence Erlbaum: Hillsdale, New Jersey.

Nyiti, R. M. (1976), 'The development of conservation in the Meru children of Tanzania', *Child Development, 47*, 1122-9.

Nyiti, R. M. (1982), 'The validity of "cultural differences explanations" for cross-cultural variation in the rate of Piagetian cognitive development', in D. D. Wagner and H. W. Stevenson (eds), *Cultural Perspectives on Child Development*. Freeman: San Francisco.

Piaget, J. (1968), *Structuralism*. Routledge & Kegan Paul: London.

Piaget, J. (1972), 'Intellectual evolution from adolescence to adulthood', *Human development, 15*, 1-12.

Price-Williams, D. R. (1981), 'Anthropological approaches to cognition and their relevance to psychology', in H. C. Triandis and W. Lonner (eds), *Handbook of Cross-Cultural Psychology*, Vol. 3. Allyn & Bacon: Boston.

Putnam, D. B. and Kilbride, P. (1980), 'A relativistic understanding of intelligence: social intelligence among the Songhay of Mali and Samia of Kenya', paper presented at Society for Cross-Cultural Research, Philadelphia.

Rogoff, B. (1981), 'Schooling and the development of cognitive skills', in H. C. Triandis and A. Heron (eds), *Handbook of Cross-Cultural Psychology*, Vol. 4. Allyn & Bacon: Boston.

Rosch,. E. (1977), 'Human categorisation', in N. Warren (ed.), *Studies in Cross-Cultural Psychology*. Academic Press: New York.

Saxe, G. B. (1979), 'A comparative analysis of the acquisition of numeration: studies from Papua New Guinea', *The Quarterly Newsletter of the Laboratory of Comparative Human Cognition, 1*, 37-43.

Saxe, G. B. (1983), 'Piaget and anthropology', *American Anthropologist, 85*, 136-43.

Scribner, S. (1977), 'Modes of thinking and ways of speaking: culture and logic reconsidered', in R. O. Freedle (ed.), *Discourse Production and Comprehension*. Lawrence Erlbaum: Hillsdale, NJ.

Sharp, D. W., Cole, M. and Lave, C. (1979), 'Education and cognitive development: the evidence from experimental research', *Monographs of the Society for Research in Child Development, 44* (No. 178).

Shweder, R. A. (1977), 'Likeness and Likelihood in everyday thought; magical judgements about personality', *Current Anthropology, 18*, 637-58.

Spencer, H. (1887), *The Principles of Psychology*, Vol. 1. Appleton & Co: New York.

Super, C. M. (1983), 'Cultural variation in the meaning and uses of children's "intelligence"', in J. B. Deregowski, S. Dziurawiec and R. C. Annis (eds), *Expiscations in Cross-Cultural Psychology*. Swets & Zietlinger: Amsterdam.

Tylor, E. G. (1874), *Primitive Culture*. Murray: London.

Vygotsky, L. S. (1978), *Mind in Society: The Development of Higher Psychological Processes*. Harvard University Press: Cambridge, Mass.

Wober, M. (1969), 'Distinguishing centri-cultural from cross-cultural tests and research', *Perceptual and Motor Skills, 28*, 488.

9 Developmental applications of working memory

M. Sebastian Halliday and Graham J. Hitch

Introduction

Cognitive psychology has its origins in the information-processing approach and the assumption that human performance can be analysed by studying inputs and outputs and from this deducing the function of the intervening 'black box'. Cognitive psychologists have increasingly seen the digital computer both as a paradigm for human information-processing systems and as the means for testing models of such systems by simulation. However, computers have no individual developmental history; they are designed to be switched on and go, not like an organism, to grow. Since these mechanisms have played such a large theoretical role in cognitive psychology it is hardly surprising that developmental processes have been relatively neglected by most cognitive psychologists. This is unfortunate: the adult cognitive system cannot be adequately understood by studying it only in its mature state. To attempt to do so is as limiting as trying to understand the anatomy or physiology of a species while ignoring all information about ontogenesis or phylogenesis. The attempt may have some value but it is bound to be less interesting or rewarding than it would have been if these sources of evidence had been taken into account. Similarly a non-developmental model of cognition must be impoverished as compared to one which adopts a developmental perspective. In addition, as we shall argue below, any such model will be denied a valuable way of testing and refining ideas about cognitive function.

The study of cognitive development has run a very different course and has been dominated, at least until recently, by the influence of Piaget. Any description of his comprehensive and complex theoretical position lies outside the scope of this chapter. However it is worth noting two of its most pervasive characteristics, (1) an emphasis on structure, and (2) the related

We are grateful to the Economic and Social Research Council for supporting some of the research discussed here.

assumption that failures in performance can most readily be explained in terms of the absence of particular logical capacities. Thus cognitive differences observed in the course of development are attributed to major restructuring of the mental apparatus (most markedly in the transition from pre-operational to operational thought); while the inability of younger children to deal with Piagetian tasks which cause no problems to older ones is explained in terms of the absence of the appropriate logical abilities. Neo-Piagetian research has challenged these assumptions and in particular the second one (see e.g. Donaldson, 1978; Flavell, 1985; Meadows, 1983). It is now widely accepted that children's cognitive performance may be profoundly influenced by memory limitations (e.g. Bryant and Trabasso, 1971), by the social demand characteristics of the situation (e.g. Light, Buckingham and Robbins, 1979) or by the precise linguistic form in which a question is posed (e.g. McGarrigle and Donaldson, 1975). These factors are seen to be at least as important in understanding children's cognition and its development as the logical constraints emphasised by Piaget. As a result, explanations in terms of logical structure are being replaced by a concentration on the precise way in which a child tackles a particular cognitive task, making possible a rapprochement between the study of cognitive development and that of adult cognition. So long as structural explanations of children's thinking were dominant this was essentially unachieveable, since it was impossible to imagine a metamorphosis which could transform the Piagetian child into the information-processing adult of cognitive psychology. The realms of discourse were so different that the two areas of study had effectively cut themselves off from each other's theoretical insights and empirical findings. The new emphasis on function in developmental psychology has opened the way to information-processing analyses of children's thought that are much more easy to relate to adult models (e.g. Klahr and Wallace, 1976; Siegler, 1978; Sternberg, 1984; Young, 1976). Indeed in the latest edition of his influential book *Cognitive Development* John Flavell, the erstwhile expositor of Piaget, acknowledges that the information-processing approach is now perhaps the major influence on research in cognitive development.

In this context it is rather surprising to note that there is still relatively little direct application of adult models of cognition to the study of cognitive development. Researchers working with children tend naturally to be interested in the *changes* that occur in information-processing and this is often specified in terms of increasing sophistication of the type of rule that can be applied. Thus Siegler (1976, 1978) provides an analysis of a modified version of the well known Piagetian balance problem. In this task the child is presented with a balance arm which is locked in the horizontal position and has a number of weights suspended from it at various distances either side of the fulcrum. For any particular arrangement of weights the child has to predict which side of the balance will go down when it is unlocked. Initially the child appears to use a rule which only takes the number of weights on each side into account in making the judgement. Later both number of weights and distance from the fulcrum enter into the decision provided that the two are not in conflict. Finally both number and distance are used even when they are in conflict. Siegler's analysis is convincing and accounts, at least descriptively, for most of the patterns of performance seen among children over a wide age range. However, while this theory is certainly couched in information-processing terms, it is not easily translated into the categories most familiar to cognitive psychology. In particular, the emphasis is on the rules which determine performance rather than on the mechanisms which allow these rules to be applied. This type of emphasis is found in other developmental information-processing theorists (e.g. Case, 1984; Young, 1976). On the other side, cognitive psychologists have not, in general, extended their investigations to children. Partly this is undoubtedly due to the non-developmental origins of cognitive psychology, partly to the fact that the standard research methods in the cognitive psychologists' tool-kit are not well adapted to use with young children, who have too little patience to devote much time to such tasks as visual search or dichotic listening.

Despite these continuing obstacles to effective communication we would argue that there is much to be gained on both sides from the attempt to apply the methods and models of cognitive psychology to the study of development. Such models are, by psychological standards at least, well tried and tested; they should therefore offer powerful ways of analysing children's cognitive capacities. Secondly, as we noted above, it is very desirable that there should be a common frame of explanation for the cognitive system both in the course of growth and in its developed adult state. Since Piagetian theory has failed to provide this, the way is open for information-processing cognitive psychology to attempt a unified account. There is a natural tendency to see this in terms of what the information-processing approach can offer the study of development – or less positively as a sort of colonial expansion by cognitive psychologists. However, cognitive psychology has much to gain from taking the process of development seriously. This point was clearly expressed ninety years ago by James Mark Baldwin who wrote:

> The study of children is generally the only means of testing the truth of our mental analyses. If we decide that a certain complex product is due to the union of simpler elements, then we may appeal to the proper period of child life to see the union taking place. There is hardly a question of analysis now under debate which may not be treated by this method. (Baldwin, 1894)

A similar strategy of 'fractionation' has proved exceptionally fruitful in the growing association between cognitive psychology and neuropsychology (see chapter 7 in this volume). Since information-processing models are in general modular, the possibility exists that neurological patients may have lesions which are specific to, or at least concentrated in, a very limited part of the system. If this is so, careful analysis of the performance of patients with these rather specific lesions provides a powerful method of testing models of cognitive function, since different models assume different components of the system and patterns of connection among them, and therefore predict different patterns of disruption following brain damage. Neuropsychological fractionation has proved enormously successful in a variety of areas of research, most notably perhaps memory (Shallice, 1979a) and reading (Coltheart, 1982) and has become one of the staple tools of cognitive psychology. If dissociations of function arising from brain injury are helpful in developing models of cognitive function, dissociations occurring naturally in the course of development may be equally, or perhaps even more, valuable. Curiously, the potential usefulness of *developmental* fractionation does not seem to have been generally appreciated by either cognitive or developmental psychologists.

Short-term memory and cognitive development

Short-term memory (STM) must surely be one of the prime candidates for the type of analysis we are advocating. This is partly because there are a variety of well developed adult models, but also because it is increasingly clear that many developmental cognitive changes may be dependent upon changes in STM. For the sake of clarity, we shall use the term STM whenever we wish to refer to memory for temporary information over brief time intervals without making a commitment to any particular theory. Other terms will be introduced as and when we wish to refer to specific underlying mechanisms.

It is usual nowadays to insist on ecological validity in assessing the cognitive abilities of children and in this respect the standard procedures for assessing STM, such as memory span, are glaringly inadequate. However, it is worth remembering that, however we measure STM, the underlying mechanisms seem to have evolved to serve everyday human functions such as producing and understanding speech, planning actions and solving problems. All of these activities require temporary storage of information. There is already good evidence that temporary storage capacity is a crucial limiting factor on children's performance in a whole variety of cognitive tasks. Furthermore, as a number of researchers have suggested, quantitative changes in STM may result in qualitative stage-like changes in behaviour. The best known example of this derives from the work of Bryant and Trabasso (1971) who claimed that failure of transitive inference in 'pre-operational' children is due to inadequate memory capacity rather than to the absence of appropriate logical structures. This work has provoked numerous follow-up studies and considerable controversy (e.g. Mills and Funnell, 1983) but, whatever position one adopts, there is little doubt that poor STM could in principle result in stage-like changes in performance on this typically Piagetian task. A whole range of other qualitative changes in performance could be explained in a similar fashion (see e.g. Halford and Wilson, 1980). It has even been argued by Feldman, Klosson, Parsons, Rholes and Ruble (1976) that stage-like changes in moral judgements may be due to STM deficiencies in younger children since, when moral judgement problems are presented in a format which makes smaller memory demands, young children may display higher levels of moral development. STM also plays a central role in the acquisition and execution of basic educational skills. Baddeley (1979) has suggested that at least some varieties of developmental dyslexia may be economically accounted for in terms of deficits in short-term storage, particularly for the phonemic structure of individual words. It has also been suggested that short-term memory is involved in the interpretation of information beyond the single word level in reading comprehension (Fischer and Glanzer, 1986; Sanford and Garrod, 1981). Also Hitch (1978) has shown that errors of mental arithmetic can be predicted by assuming that they reflect the rapid forgetting of temporarily stored information. All this evidence suggests that STM is likely to be of central importance in understanding cognitive development, both from a theoretical and a practical point of view, and makes the development of STM abilities a prime candidate for analysis in terms of adult models.

Particularly strong claims have been made for the importance of a concept of STM abilities which includes central processing capacity in addition to temporary information storage. For example, Pascual-Leone (1970) proposed a stage theory of cognitive development which is closely related to Piaget's but assumes that increases in processing capacity, 'M-space' as he calls it, are a necessary condition for progress from one stage to the next. Thus the processes of concrete operational thought are supposed to require space for one more chunk of information in the 'central computing space' than the processes involved in pre-operational thought. Until this additional space becomes available the child cannot progress from one to the other. More recent formulations of stage-like theories (e.g. Case, 1984; Halford and Wilson, 1980; Halford, 1982) have adopted similar points of view and have tied stage transitions closely to changes in information-processing capacity. A related theoretical tradition has suggested that the major cognitive changes that occur in the course of development depend mainly on two factors: growth of expertise and increases in information-processing capacity (without assuming that this is directly related to stages of cognitive development). It is suggested that increases in domain-specific expertise make the items of information required to deal with a particular problem more accessible, more richly interrelated and co-ordinated into larger 'chunks' (e.g. Chi, 1978). As a consequence they make fewer demands on central processing capacity, so more items can be handled simultaneously. The reduced demands on capacity for solving a particular problem may also free spare central computing capacity for carrying out executive tasks which themselves aid the solution of the problem. Thus, for example, the well known finding that 7-year-old children, while capable of rehearsal in short-term memory tasks, usually fail to rehearse (Flavell, Beach and Chinsky, 1966) could be explained by supposing that they have little spare capacity for the executive programs necessary for such rehearsal. This type of account of the development of cognitive (information-processing) ability lays great emphasis on the role of STM and, it should be noted, assumes that the underlying system is capable of performing a number of functions other than the mere retention of information. What then is known about the development of STM?

There is of course a very large body of research on this topic and a review would be out of place here (see Kail, 1984, Ornstein, 1978); however it can be said that no real consensus has yet emerged. Consider the simplest and most universal finding: Galton (1883) in his pioneering studies of individual differences observed that children's digit span increased with age. The result has proved so reliable that it has been incorporated into a variety of intelligence tests, yet this venerable and robust effect has yet to be explained. In a recent review Dempster (1981) outlines some ten theories none of which he considers adequate to account for the experimental findings. While these theories differ along a number of dimensions they can be divided into two major groups. One attributes the increase in span across the age range to a developmental increase in the capacity of a short-term store; thus older children and adults are assumed to have a greater memory span partly or wholly because they have a larger short-term store. The other class of theory also assumes a short-term store, but maintains that its capacity does not change significantly; span improves because, as outlined above, increasingly efficient use is made of existing capacity. However else they may differ, theories of both types share one tacit assumption: that the short-term store is a single resource which can be adequately described by one parameter indexing its capacity. Such an assumption seems to us quite inadequate to handle the variety of functions that have been assigned to the system by developmental psychologists such as those discussed above; while to anyone familiar with the adult literature it appears a curiously out-dated approach, since cognitive psychologists nowadays tend to see STM abilities in terms of a rather more complex, modular system. It is possible therefore that the poor explanatory power of

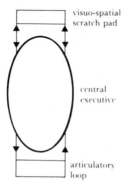

FIGURE 9.1   *A simplified representation of the working memory model (Adapted from Baddeley, 1983)*

current models of children's STM arises from too simple-minded an approach to the nature of the system and that the application of alternative adult models might be useful.

The working memory model

The model that we shall make use of is the working memory model of Baddeley and Hitch (1974), recently summarised by Baddeley (1983) and discussed at length by Baddeley (1986). This model has proved successful in accounting for data and generating research in adult cognitive psychology and in neuropsychology; it is now beginning to find an application in developmental psychology (Hitch and Halliday, 1983). The model emphasises the functional role of the working memory system in providing facilities for the temporary storage of small amounts of information in several aspects of cognition. These include such diverse activities as reasoning, reading and arithmetic. Working memory itself is conceptualised not as a unitary system, but as a set of separate, interacting, limited-capacity subsystems. In its present formulation, the model comprises an attentional *central executive* which serves a general co-ordinating function and two or more 'slave' subsystems which operate relatively independently but under the general control of the central executive. One of these subsystems, the *articulatory loop*, is concerned with the short-term retention of verbal material; the other, the *visuo-spatial scratchpad*, deals with visual material (see Figure 9.1).

The central executive, as its name implies, is held to be responsible for the organisation and monitoring of the other components and for communication with long-term memory and other elements of the cognitive system. It is assumed to play a major role in such tasks as comprehension of written text and reasoning and has been associated with the dual functions of temporary information storage and conscious attention. It is, however, unfortunate that the central executive, which is by any measure the most important component of the model, is also the least well understood. The related and widely used concept of a limited capacity central processor has been criticised on a number of grounds (see, e.g., Allport, 1980). It has even been suggested (Barnard, 1985) that the subsystems of working memory may be able to co-operate without the need for a central executive at all, although it is not clear how this might be achieved. Most investigators have concentrated on the more tractable study of the slave subsystems in the hope that by delimiting their functions that of the central executive will become clearer. The central executive is perhaps best described as the 'area of residual ignorance' within the model (Baddeley, 1983; though see Baddeley, 1986 for a summary of recent progress).

The articulatory loop

The articulatory loop is concerned with the short-term storage of verbally coded material and corresponds approximately to the entire short-term store as conceptualised in some earlier models of STM. It is assumed to comprise an active and a passive component. Information is coded in phonological form in the passive store, which is thought to be involved in the comprehension of spoken language, and decays in a matter of one or two seconds. The contents of this store can be refreshed by the active component of the system through subvocal rehearsal which uses an articulatory code. The articulatory loop has been investigated by means of a series of procedures which have come to be known as converging operations (Baddeley, 1983). (1) It has been known for many years that sequences of consonants or words which sound similar (e.g. b, g, c or cat, cap, hat) are harder to remember than equivalent dissimilar sounding sequences (Conrad, 1964). This is known as the phonemic similarity effect and is assumed to be due to the confusability of the traces of these stimuli in the passive phonological store. (2) Immediate memory for short words is better than for long words of similar frequency (Baddeley, Thomson and Buchanan, 1975). Even when number of syllables is equated, memory is rather better for words which can be spoken quickly, such as 'bishop' or 'wicket', than for words which take longer to say, such as 'harpoon' or 'Friday' (Baddeley et al., 1975). This word length effect is attributed to active rehearsal which is used to refresh decaying traces in the phonological store. There is a linear relationship between number of items recalled and the rate at which they can be articulated, the slope of this line giving a measure of the rate at which traces decay. (3) It has also been shown that if a subject is required to repeatedly articulate some irrelevant word such as 'the' both the phonemic similarity effect and the word length effect are abolished for visually presented materials (Baddeley et al., 1975; Murray, 1968). This procedure is known as articulatory suppression and is presumed to be effective because it blocks the active rehearsal process whereby the names of visually presented material enter the articulatory loop. (4) The presence of an unattended speech input disrupts immediate memory for visually presented materials and does so to a greater extent if phonemically similar to the memory materials (Salamé and Baddeley, 1982). This effect is assumed to reflect speech feeding automatically into the passive phonemic store. Although there are of course a number of difficulties and uncertainties about this account of the articulatory loop, it provides a reasonably convincing account of a wide range of adult data and is certainly specific enough to permit its application to development.

Developmental studies of the articulatory loop

We will begin by discussing an investigation carried out by Case, Kurland and Goldberg (1982) in which they attempt to account for the development of immediate memory in terms of changes in a single short-term store whose limited capacity resources can be assigned either to storage of material or to processing and executive functions. This type of explanation makes no appeal to the concept of an articulatory loop. Case et al. propose that the most important limiting factor on STM arises from the speed of item-identification processes whereby representations of the items are accessed in long-term storage. Developmental increases in memory span are supposed to be due, not to any increase in the overall capacity of the store, but to extra resources becoming available for storage as a result of a decrease in the capacity taken up by item-identification.

In their first experiment Case and colleagues measured auditory digit span in children aged from 3 to 6. They measured item-identification time in an auditory digit-naming task by taking the average time to initiate the naming response. The time changes in these two measures with age and were linearly related to each other, suggesting that age differences in the ease of item-identification might be responsible for the development of span (see Figure 9.2). The experimenters were, however, aware that their results could be due to some third factor which changes with age and affects both memory span and identification time. In their second experiment therefore, they attempted to reduce adults' item-identification times to the same level as 6-year-olds. They achieved this by using unfamiliar nonsense words

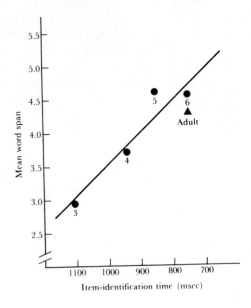

FIGURE 9.2   *Relationship between memory span and item-identification speed. Numerals denote age-groups from 3 to 6 years (Adapted from Case et al., 1982)*

instead of digits. The results showed that adults' memory span for these materials was now also at the 6-year-old level, (see Figure 9.2). This result evidently strengthens their interpretation quite considerably.

The working memory model could of course handle these results if the central executive is assumed to have both control and storage functions which interact in the same way as in Case's model. However, this would be highly unsatisfactory for the working memory account which maintains that verbal material is also stored in the articulatory loop. If the development of STM can be explained entirely without recourse to the articulatory loop, this is rather bad news for the working memory model. Interestingly enough, there are some studies which do implicate the loop in the development of STM. In the first of this sort, Nicolson (1981) investigated the word length effect in children aged from 8 upwards. When recall of visually presented words of different lengths was plotted against the rate at which they could be read aloud, a straight line function was found within each age group (see Figure 9.3). This shows that word length effects are obtainable in children as in adults, suggesting that children in this age range use the articulatory loop in much the same way. More interestingly, the recall data for all word lengths and all age groups up to and including

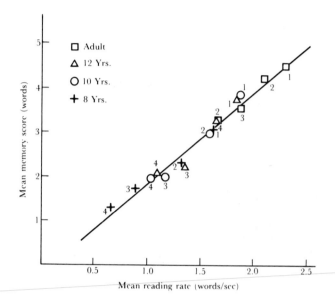

FIGURE 9.3 *Relationship between words recalled and the rate at which they can be read aloud for different word lengths at different ages. Numerals denote word length in syllables (Adapted from Nicolson, 1981)*

adults fell along the same straight line when plotted against reading rates. This suggests quite strongly that the trace decay rate which fixes the capacity of the articulatory loop does not change in the course of development, and that older children remember more because their faster subvocal rehearsal allows them to refresh more items within the critical time limit. Subsequent work by ourselves (Hitch and Halliday, 1983) has confirmed Nicolson's finding. Indeed, by using articulation rather than reading rate as a measure, and auditory presentation, Hulme et al. (1984) have even extended the finding down to children as young as four years of age.

A key question is how to relate this work on the articulatory loop to Case's findings implicating item-identification processes in the development of STM. Dempster (1981) has put forward the radical suggestion that the word length effect is not due to articulation but is because longer words take longer to identify. Such an interpretation would of course be inconsistent with the working memory model, which has to attribute the word length effect to the articulatory loop and differentiate it from item-identification effects which would be more plausibly attributed to the central executive.

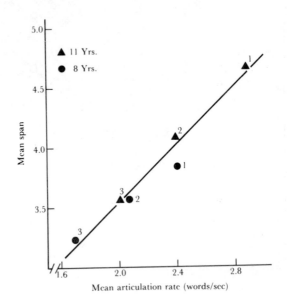

FIGURE 9.4a   *Relationship between memory span and articulation rate as word length is varied at different age levels. Numerals denote word length in syllables (Hitch et al., 1984)*

In order to test Dempster's suggestion we carried out an experiment in which 8- and 11-year-old children were tested on their short-term memory for lists of one, two or three syllable words which were matched for frequency; the words were presented in written form (Hitch, Halliday and Littler, 1984). We measured articulation rates, and we also measured item-identification time by using a voice key to measure how long it took to start to say each word in response to its written form. As expected in the light of the results just described, word length effects were found in both age groups and, when plotted against articulation rate, a single straight line described differences both within and between age groups (see Figure 9.4a). Thus nearly all the differences in memory scores could be accounted for in terms of how long it took the children to say the words. In contrast, while it was true that the older children were quicker to identify the words than the younger ones, there was no reliable relationship between word length and item-identification time within age-groups (see Figure 9.4b). Our results therefore argue strongly against the position taken by Dempster (1981) in showing that item-identification and articulation rate do not reflect the same underlying process. While it remains true that differences in item-identification time or articulation rate or indeed both may be responsible

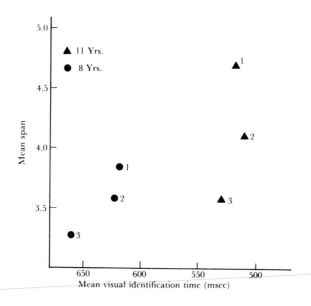

FIGURE 9.4b   *Plot of memory span as a function of item-identification speed for the recall data shown in Figure 9.4a*

for recall differences between age groups, it seems that a single store concept tied to a single measure of speed of processing is quite inadequate to account for STM in children.

Having made the case that the capacity and use of the articulatory loop remain surprisingly constant during much of development, we must now consider the boundaries of this generalisation. So far, our own researches have shown that the modality in which materials are presented is of critical importance in determining whether very young children use the loop. In the initial study suggesting this (see Hitch and Halliday, 1983), we investigated the word length effect in children aged from 6 upwards, comparing spoken with visual presentation. Thus children tried to recall a list of spoken words or a sequence of line drawings of the corresponding items. In the latter case they were dissuaded from naming the items aloud during presentation. Recall was always spoken, regardless of presentation modality. We found that older children showed similar word length effects for both methods of presentation, while the youngest children were sensitive to word length for spoken presentation but not visual. We therefore suggested that younger children do not use the articulatory loop to remember the names of drawings, despite the requirement for spoken recall and despite the evident availability of the loop for storing spoken inputs. Our data are consistent with Conrad's (1971) evidence that phonemic similarity of the names of simple pictures disrupts immediate recall in older children but not younger ones. Further data of our own (see Hitch and Halliday, 1983) shows that there is no effect of phonemic similarity or articulatory suppression in 5-year-olds' immediate recall of nameable line drawings, whereas both effects are present in rather older children. As we have already said, there is good evidence that the word length effect is present in children as young as four for auditorily presented materials (Hulme, Thomson, Muir and Lawrence, 1984).

The conclusion that even 4-year-olds make use of the articulatory loop to remember spoken materials is a radical one, given a large developmental literature suggesting that young children aged 6 and below do not rehearse subvocally in short-term memory tasks (see e.g. Kail, 1984). However, it is notable that almost all of these studies have used pictures or objects as the materials to be recalled. For example, in their widely cited study Flavell et al. (1966) presented children with sequences of nameable pictures of objects and animals to recall after a few seconds delay. The fact that little account has been taken of mode of presentation suggests that it has not so far been seen to be an important variable. According to the working memory model, however, spoken words have obligatory access to the passive phonological component of the articulatory loop but written words (and presumably the names of pictures) only have access via the active rehearsal process and this route is an optional one, though highly practised in adults. It is entirely possible that young children either fail to use this route or use it less effectively than adults, and in this case materials presented pictorially might not be retained in the articulatory loop system but elsewhere in working memory. This in turn might significantly alter prevailing views about the development of rehearsal strategies.

All in all this set of results is consistent with an interpretation in terms of working memory and would be difficult to explain in its entirety in terms of any other models of which we are aware. Thus a strategy of applying adult cognitive models to the study of development appears to have yielded dividends in this particular case. In addition we have an indication of a developmental dissociation in the encoding of pictorial material in younger and older children. This is, of course, precisely the type of result which allows developmental evidence to be brought to bear on the analysis of models of adult cognition; but the experiments described so far do not provide us with much information about *how* young children code pictorial material when they are not doing so verbally. The next section will discuss some experiments concerned with this problem.

Visuo-spatial scratchpad

The current concept of the visuo-spatial scratchpad (VSSP) derives chiefly from the results of experiments using selective interference techniques. Early work has shown that highly imageable verbal materials were remembered better when presented auditorily than visually, whereas the reverse was true for abstract, non-imageable materials (Brooks, 1967). Brooks suggested that this selective interference effect arises because visual perception involves a visuo-spatial coding system which is also involved in imagery. Baddeley, Grant, Wight and Thomson (1975) extended these findings by demonstrating that an irrelevant visuo-spatial tracking task disrupted performance on the imagery version of Brooks' task much more than the abstract one. It seems that the spatial rather than the visual component of tracking is responsible for this selective interference effect (Baddeley and Lieberman, 1980). Additional experiments (Idzikowski et al., cited in Baddeley, 1983) have shown that imagery can also be disrupted by making voluntary, task-irrelevant eye movements.

These findings have been interpreted as suggesting that the VSSP comprises a primarily spatial storage system and a rehearsal process which is also involved in controlling eye movements (Baddeley, 1983; 1986). Thus the VSSP is seen as having the same type of structure as the articulatory loop. The analogy has recently been developed further by Logie (1986) who has shown that exposure to 'unattended' visual inputs can disrupt the use of imagery. Logie has suggested that such inputs gain obligatory access to the visuo-spatial store in a similar fashion to the way unattended speech is thought to enter the phonological store.

Although the above experiments point towards a simple model of the VSSP, other methods of investigating the temporary storage and transformation of visuo-spatial information have suggested a number of differing interpretations. For example, Phillips (1983) reviewed studies of immediate memory for random chequerboard patterns which reveal a recency effect corresponding to better memory for the final pattern in a series. He suggested that this recency effect depends on an active process of visualisation, but its sensitivity to various types of post-list interference led him to propose that it draws upon general-purpose rather than modality-specific resources. In another line of work, Walker and Marshall (1982) studied stimulus repetition effects in serial choice tasks in which subjects are required to classify each member of a series of visual stimuli as rapidly as possible. Their basic finding was that a decision about a visual stimulus is speeded up if it was also presented on the preceding trial, but that there is no such facilitation if it was presented two or more trials back. Since this single-item visual recency effect is associated with incidental rather than intentional learning, Walker and Marshall interpreted it in terms of a passive visual store which is not dependent upon control processes. Furthermore, on top of these specific differences of interpretation, the current conceptualisation of the VSSP has not been clearly related to the extensive work on transforming and manipulating mental images (Kosslyn, 1980; Shepard, 1980).

To sum up, the precise nature of the VSSP has not yet been fully established, and this aspect of the working memory model is currently less well understood than the articulatory loop. Whereas the study of the loop and its properties has been greatly facilitated by the discovery and exploitation of experimental converging operations, a major obstacle to progress in understanding the VSSP is the difficulty of integrating evidence from different methods of investigation. This problem might reflect the fact that there are indeed many different visual stores. Alternatively, the tasks that have been used to investigate visual imagery and visual memory may encompass a variety of strategies, so that what we are seeing in the different paradigms is a system being used in a wide variety of ways. In this context, developmental studies seem capable of supplying valuable further evidence. Unlike adults, children younger than about 6 are generally thought to be relatively inflexible in their use of memorisation strategies (see Kail, 1984). Hence visual memory in young children may be less contaminated by strategies, and thus more likely to reveal the nature of a common underlying system. Indeed, we have already seen that young children's memory for pictures is far less likely to involve the possibility of verbal recoding effects than that of older children or adults. It was with these considerations in mind that we undertook our own investigations of the VSSP in children.

Developmental studies of the visuo-spatial scratchpad

The first objective in our investigations was to confirm our suspicion that young children do indeed use a visual coding system when remembering visual materials over short intervals. We used a converging operations approach whereby this hypothesis was subjected to a number of different tests. Given a positive outcome, we anticipated that the pattern of results would shed light on the nature of the VSSP as it is found in young children.

There was already some evidence showing that preschoolers' memory for visually presented materials is impaired when the items are visually similar to one another (Brown, 1977; Hayes and Schulze, 1977). However, it is possible that this effect originates during encoding, and is not indicative of visual storage. Our own investigation of visual similarity therefore included a rigorous attempt to assess if children tend to confuse visually similar items at initial registration (Hitch, Halliday, Schaafstal and Schraagen, in press). In the main part of the study, groups of 5- and 11-year-

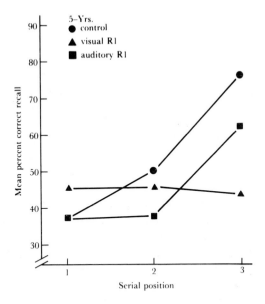

FIGURE 9.5a *Effect of visual and auditory RI on 5-year-olds' memory for drawings of familiar objects (adapted from Hitch et al., in press)*

old children were shown a short series of drawings of familiar objects and then attempted immediate spoken recall of the names of these pictures. The children were required to remain silent during presentation. One type of series comprised visually similar drawings depicting long thin objects in the same oblique orientation, another comprised visually dissimilar control items. The results confirmed that young children are disrupted by visual similarity, and showed that by age 11 this effect had disappeared. To assess the possibility of registration errors, other 5-year-olds were asked to name the drawings during the presentation phase of the memory task. The key finding here was that there were virtually no naming errors, strongly suggesting that the visual similarity effect arises in memory and not encoding.

In a further experiment we attempted to confirm and further investigate young children's use of visual coding by examining retroactive interference (RI) effects. Our reasoning was that RI should be greatest when the interfering material is presented in the same modality as that used for information storage. Five-year-old children were shown sequences of three drawings of familiar objects. Following presentation there was a 4s delay which was either unfilled, or filled by either a visual or a verbal RI task.

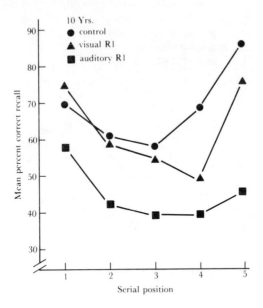

FIGURE 9.5b   *Effect of visual and auditory RI on 11-year-olds' memory for drawings of familiar objects (adapted from Hitch et al., in press)*

The child then attempted to recall the names of the drawings beginning with the most recent. We used this reversed order of report here to maximise the sensitivity of the experimental procedure to RI. The visual task involved asking the child to classify a further drawing by placing it against one of two comparison drawings, one showing an animal and one not. In the verbal task the experimenter pronounced a name and the child responded orally either 'yes' or 'no' according to whether it was the name of an animal. Thus the two tasks required similar decisions but contrasted visual-manual with auditory-verbal processing.

The results (see Figure 9.5a) show that there was a pronounced recency effect when the delay was unfilled, extending over one and perhaps two drawings. They also show that the recency effect was completely removed by visual RI, while auditory-verbal RI had a smaller effect, leaving recency intact. We interpreted these data as suggesting that a specifically visual form of storage contributes to the recency effect in young children's performance of this task.

We also tested 10-year-old children using an identical procedure save for changes in such details as the number of drawings presented and the number of stimuli making up the RI. The results conformed to quite a

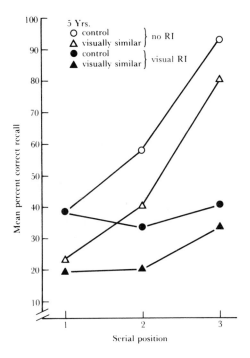

FIGURE 9.6   *Effects of visual similarity and visual RI on 5-year-olds' memory for drawings of familiar objects (adapted from Hitch et al., in press)*

different pattern (see Figure 9.5b). Firstly, the shape of the serial position curve showed primacy as well as recency. This is consistent with older children's greater use of verbal rehearsal, and is a familiar finding (see e.g. Hagen and Kail, 1973). Secondly, the recency effect was now more sensitive to auditory-verbal than visual RI. We therefore concluded that older children, unlike younger ones, are relying predominantly upon auditory-verbal information storage in this task.

   Having demonstrated that young children use a form of memory which is sensitive to visual similarity and visual RI, we carried out a further experiment to explore the relationship between these two effects. Using the 'backwards' recall task once again, we varied both the visual similarity of the drawings and the presence or absence of visual RI in a factorial design. The only major change was that the visual RI consisted of a simple visual matching task instead of the semantic classification task used in the previous study. Figure 9.6 shows the results, which demonstrate that visual similarity, unlike visual RI, impairs memory for all the items in a series.

Furthermore, visual similarity continues to impair memory even when recency is removed by visual RI. Thus it seems that similarity among the items and RI affect separate aspects of visual working memory in young children.

Our current interpretation is that similarity and RI affect different modes of accessing material in visual working memory. Specifically, we suggest that visual RI disrupts the use of a retrieval strategy like that discussed by Baddeley and Hitch (1977) and Hitch (1980), according to which memory traces are accessed via their recency of presentation. We further propose that traces in visual working memory contain sets of visual features and are subject to partial forgetting. Thus, the visual similarity effect is due to an increased difficulty of reconstructing the original items on the basis of partially forgotten traces. Unlike the first, this second mode of retrieval would apply equally to items at all serial positions.

Thus visual working memory in young children appears to be similar to the recency-sensitive systems identified by Phillips (1983) and Walker and Marshall (1982), but to involve modality-specific resources in contrast with Phillips' suggestion. We suggest that children's visual working memory does not involve active control processes in our tasks, since their memory for pictures is unaffected by having them perform an irrelevant concurrent task (Hitch and Halliday, 1983). In terms of the adult working memory model, our data encourage the reasonable speculation that we are looking at a point in development where the passive storage component is present, but where control processes for operating on the contents of the store are as yet relatively undeveloped. If so, they add significantly to what we know about the nature of this store. Furthermore, it seems likely that this information would have been much more difficult, if not impossible to obtain by testing adult subjects. We consider this and some further implications of our findings in the following sections, where we try to evaluate what we have learned from applying the working memory model in a developmental context.

Evaluation

Articulatory loop

Although we have couched our discussion largely in terms of the working memory model our broader aim is to show how the application of models of adult cognitive function can increase our understanding of cognitive development, and also to forward the claims of developmental fractionation as a tool of cognitive psychology. However, it is certainly worth noting that the working memory model in particular has served as a useful guide in investigating STM in children. It has drawn attention to features such as mode of presentation which have previously been overlooked and which, with the proper analysis, turn out to be important and revealing. At the same time the results on the whole emphasise continuity between cognitive function in children and adults, thus reducing the conceptual gap noted at the beginning of this chapter. One of the most striking examples of this continuity is the word length effect. The natural interpretation of this in terms of the working memory model, and the one that we have adopted above, is to suppose that the time-based capacity of the articulatory loop is roughly constant from the age of 4 onwards, but that the speed at which words can be rehearsed increases in the course of development. We have argued that this conclusion can be reconciled with the conventional wisdom on the development of rehearsal strategies between about the ages of 6 and 7 (e.g. Kail, 1984) by emphasising the difference between the effects of verbal and visual presentation in young children.

Inevitably, some doubts must remain, and these illustrate the way in which developmental data can help to refine a model of adult cognitive function. First, while our results and those of Hulme et al. (1984) strongly suggest that, with spoken presentation, children as young as 4 or 5 are using the articulatory loop to rehearse, we have no direct evidence, for example of the sort used by Flavell et al. (1966), to show that they do. Secondly, and more seriously, it is important to note that rehearsal, of the sort used by adults, is a fairly complex procedure involving as it does serial processing and grouping items during their presentation. These factors undoubtedly influence memory span in adults and must therefore partly determine the exact amplitude of the word length effect. However, the close numerical relationship that is observed between word length effects in adults and young children using spoken presentation implies that, although children are rehearsing more slowly, they are doing essentially the same thing as adults. That is, children as young as 4 are using rehearsal in the same strategic way as adults. However, it is one thing to suggest that young children may verbally rehearse spoken words but not pictures, it is quite another to claim that the form of this rehearsal process is effectively mature at the age of 4. Ornstein (1978), among a number of other workers, has carefully charted the development of rehearsal strategies and has shown that the skills involved emerge relatively slowly over a period of years. It passes belief that the dissociation between the systems involved in spoken and pictorial presentation is so complete that rehearsal strategies, which are available in something like the adult form when the input is spoken, need to be relearnt over a period of years when the input is in another modality.

One solution to this problem would be to abandon our interpretation in terms of the working memory model. We are reluctant to do this since it has suggested fruitful lines of research and since the results fit the model rather closely; certainly we know of no other model which would provide a better explanation of the data. An alternative would be to reconsider the relationship between the articulatory loop and the process of rehearsal. It has been universally assumed, though without any direct evidence, that the conscious process of subvocal rehearsal, the 'voice in the head' when we are trying to retain a telephone number, reflects the operation of the articulatory loop; if this is so then developmental changes in the nature of this rehearsal process should certainly be reflected in age related discontinuities in the word length effect. Suppose, however, that the articulatory loop of the working memory model is a more primitive and essentially automatic system; one might speculate that such a system had its origin in early childhood and served an important role in language learning. The conscious strategic process of subvocal rehearsal would then be seen as being superimposed on this more primitive system and might be thought to use different resources. If the word length effect was taken to reflect primarily the activity of the more primitive process then the developmental continuity of the word length effect would be compatible with the development of rehearsal strategies in childhood. Baddeley and Lewis (1981) have suggested that in reading there is a short-term phonological store which is independent of the articulatory loop and which allows rhyme judgements to be made even in the presence of articulatory suppression. It is at least possible that this store, which is supposed to be responsible for the 'voice in the head' when reading, is the same as the system used for the conscious process of subvocal rehearsal. This proposal is evidently highly speculative and is offered to show that developmental evidence can serve not only to confirm the working memory model but also to challenge some of its assumptions and suggest modifications.

Visuo-spatial scratchpad

Similar arguments apply in the case of the development of children's immediate memory for visual materials. Here, the working memory model was useful in suggesting that very young children might rely on a visual coding system. However, experimental techniques for investigating the visuo-spatial scratchpad in adults did not prove to be readily applicable to the study of children, in contrast to techniques for studying the articulatory loop. New methods had to be devised and they suggested some interesting comparisons between visual memory in young children and adults. We speculated that the major process in the development of visual working memory from age 5 upwards is the acquisition of the ability to execute control processes for maintaining and manipulating stored information, with the store itself undergoing little, if any, developmental change. If so, this would amount to a further example of a developmental fractionation. In this case the distinction between passive and active components of the adult system suggested by Baddeley (1983) is seen reflected in developmental differences.

Whether or not this is correct, we can identify two clear advantages from the study of visual working memory in children. First is the general advantage, shared with all developmental work, namely that we are investigating the adult system in a simpler, less mature form. Here, children appear to provide an opportunity for exploring the properties of passive visual storage without the extra complications that arise from the presence of flexible control processes and strategies. Second is an advantage stemming from young children's inability, or at any rate reluctance, to use verbal recoding strategies when remembering pictorial information. Investigations of visual memory in adults are bedevilled by the practical problems posed by the prevalence of verbal recoding and attempts to avoid it have included using meaningless visual patterns (Phillips, 1983) and requiring concurrent articulation (Broadbent and Broadbent, 1981). It appears that in young children these sorts of precautions are not so crucial as they are in adults, allowing visual working memory to be studied much more easily and in a potentially wider set of situations.

The study of visual working memory in children also poses some important questions which have yet to be explored. We speculated earlier on the possible functional significance of a passive phonological store in the child's acquisition of language; we must also ask what might be the functional significance of a passive visual store for the young child. One possibility, following Walker and Marshall (1982), is that such a system might keep track of the locations and identities of objects by preserving a record of the most recent changes in the visual environment. This is clearly a very basic function, and one we would expect to appear reasonably early in development. A second question concerns the developmental transition we have observed in memory for simple drawings. Our experiments suggest that older children tend to rely upon the verbal articulatory loop. Since we evidently do not wish to argue that older children are *unable* to use visual working memory, we must explain why there is no evidence for them doing so in our experiments. The whole question of what influences the development of strategies and whether this can be captured in the working memory model is obviously of major importance.

Developmental fractionation

Our investigations also raise the issue of the value of developmental fractionation as a general research strategy in cognitive psychology. Thus far we have been able to demonstrate evidence for such fractionation in the specific case of working memory. One important general question we can ask concerns the power of developmental fractionation for confirming or rejecting distinctions among components in adult cognitive models.

An interesting comparison can be made with the recent use of neuropsychological evidence in developing and testing models of normal adult cognitive function, as foreshadowed earlier in chapter 7 (see also Hitch, 1984). The general idea here is that patterns of impairment induced by brain damage, which Shallice (1979a) refers to as neuropsychological fractionation, will give clues to the organisation of cognitive function in the intact brain. The simplest case is a 'single dissociation', whereby brain damage of a certain type disrupts one group of cognitive functions (say 'A') but spares others ('B'). This suggests that A and B are mediated by separate neuropsychological systems, although an obvious alternative interpretation is that the spared functions are merely less sensitive to *any* sort of brain damage. More convincing evidence has come from 'double dissociations' of function, where in addition a second sort of brain damage is found to disrupt group B functions while sparing group A. Differential sensitivity of one group of functions to non-specific damage cannot account for this pattern of findings, which strongly implies that the two sets of functions are genuinely distinct (cf. Weiskranz, 1964). A familiar example occurs in adult memory, in the comparison between patients suffering from the amnesic syndrome and others classified as conduction aphasics (Shallice, 1979a). At a gross level of description, amnesics perform poorly on memory tasks involving long-term retention but normally on tests of short-term retention. On the other hand, conduction aphasics show the reverse pattern of performance. These observations have been taken as confirming a theoretical distinction between short- and long-term components of the memory system, originally proposed on the basis of other sorts of evidence (see e.g. Baddeley, 1976).

We have assumed that in normal child development the characteristics of different components of the cognitive system may follow different patterns of development. The most obvious case is where one component develops earlier or faster than another, as in our suggestion that the passive component of visual working memory develops before the active control element. The developmental fractionation of function in such cases is analogous to a single dissociation in adult neuropsychology, and hence open to similar sorts of objections. Such a fractionation would obviously have considerable value as a 'converging operation' for a distinction based on other types of evidence, but it would lack the logical force of a neuropsychological double dissociation of function. However, developmental dissociations of function have the important feature of arising 'naturally' and they presumably reflect the functional architecture of the system more directly than is likely with the unpredictable effects of nervous system insult. Neuropsychological patients are rarely 'pure' cases and commonly show multiple deficits which may have more to do with anatomical than functional relationships and which impede analysis. These problems are likely to be far less pervasive in dissociations arising in the course of development. In addition, because of the rarity of suitably pure cases, neuropsychologists are compelled to rely on a small number of critical single patient studies, with all the difficulties that this is likely to entail; children are, on the other hand, in plentiful supply. None of this is to decry the case study approach in cognitive neuropsychology, which remains promising (see Shallice, 1979b, for a thorough discussion). We do, however, suggest that far more attention should be paid to developmental evidence and developmental dissociations when constructing models of cognitive function. Far from being in opposition, the two methods are complementary to one another.

A further consideration is whether it might even prove possible to obtain the equivalent of a double dissociation of function in the study of development. If, as seems likely, there is considerable variation among the normal population and different components of the memory system develop in an uncorrelated fashion, then it is not impossible to envisage different individuals exhibiting complementary patterns of development. There may therefore be some value in undertaking longitudinal studies of individual differences in development in order to investigate this possibility. A promising place to look for such dissociations might also be in abnormal development such as that associated with deafness or blindness, but a discussion of the underlying logic of this sort of investigation is beyond the scope of the present chapter.

We have couched this discussion almost entirely in terms of the development of STM but the principles are generally applicable. One area in which this type of approach is beginning to bear fruit is in the study of reading. Over the past decade a number of models of the adult reading process have been developed (e.g. Carr and Pollatsek, 1985; Coltheart, Patterson and Marshall, 1980; Ellis, 1984) and some degree of consensus is being reached as to the main components of any such model. It is noteworthy that neuropsychological evidence has played a dominant role in these theoretical developments. Until recently these models have made little contact with the large literature on the process of learning to read which has followed rather a different course (e.g. Downing and Leong, 1982; Gibson and Levin, 1975). Thus, very much as in the case of memory, those concerned with learning to read have not found much use for adult models of the skilled reading process while the cognitive psychology of reading has paid rather little attention to the acquisition and development of reading skills. This situation has now begun to change; for example Marsh, Friedman, Welch and Desberg (1981) have proposed a cognitive-developmental stage model of learning to read which maps rather well onto models of skilled reading. It may also prove useful in the analysis of the varieties of developmental dyslexia (e.g. Frith, 1985; Seymour and MacGregor, 1984) and these studies in turn may well help to discriminate between and develop models of adult reading. We noted above the central role that neuropsychological evidence has played in the development of models of the skilled reading process, and in this context it is interesting to note that there has been a fairly active debate about the relationship between acquired and developmental dyslexia (e.g. Snowling, 1983). This has not, in our opinion, led to any very useful conclusions, but the argument has tended to take the form of a dispute about which type of acquired dyslexia is the best model of developmental dyslexia. We would suggest that this is the wrong approach and that, as in the case of working memory, developmental and neuropsychological data can best be brought into alignment through the effect that they have on models of adult function. Be that as it may, it is evident that there are many opportunities for the sort of approach that we advocate in reading research.

We turn finally to consider whether the strategy of developmental fractionation will be fruitful only for investigating certain specific topics, such as working memory, or whether it can be applied more generally to any aspect of the cognitive system. According to Fodor (1983), only certain parts of the adult cognitive system are organised in a modular fashion such that they are psychologically and physiologically separate from one another. Specifically, Fodor suggests that 'non-central' components of the cognitive system, such as subsystems for visual perception and language comprehension, are separable in this way, but that the central core of the cognitive system is non-modular. According to this analysis, we might expect developmental fractionation to be useful for distinguishing amongst peripheral components of the cognitive system, but to be inapplicable to central processes. This would be a severe limitation since the latter include such important and interesting activities as learning, reasoning and problem solving. Fortunately, Fodor's speculations about modularity may not be all that relevant here. The feasibility of developmental fractionation is dependent only on the general idea that the cognitive system can be analysed into simpler, more or less independent subsystems. Such subsystems as the articulatory loop and the visuo-spatial scratchpad are probably too small to qualify as modules in Fodor's sense, although they clearly share some of the properties he considers necessary. Since developmental fractionation appears to be fruitful at this finer level of analysis, it must remain an empirical question whether it can be equally useful in the study of other parts of the cognitive system and not one that can be answered on the basis of theoretical considerations alone.

Closing comments

We have suggested that an approach in which models of adult cognitive processes are applied in a developmental context can advance our understanding of both cognitive development and adult cognition itself. We have drawn attention to the theoretical significance of the developmental fractionation of cognitive function, and we have chosen to demonstrate this in the specific case of working memory. We would obviously expect the same strategy to prove useful in a range of other contexts. It is, however, appropriate to sound a note of caution. At the beginning of this chapter we commented that there was a danger that cognitive psychologists could be seen as attempting to colonise developmental psychology. To some degree, the way in which we have presented our case may have served to reinforce these fears. In particular, by emphasising the developmental fractionation of cognitive function we could be accused of using development as an analytic tool rather than as a subject of study in its own right. We have, after all, said little about the developmental process itself or the causes of development. Thus although we have provided a considerable amount of evidence about the way in which coding of information in working memory changes from the age of 4 or 5 and upwards, we have had nothing to say about why or how this development occurs. In contrast Piaget and the neo-Piagetians, whose approach we have largely dismissed, do offer truly developmental theories and provide some suggestions, however imprecise, about the causes of developmental change. We acknowledge the importance of these issues but would argue that questions of causation in development can only be approached when we have some real understanding of the phenomena to be explained. Without this the search for causes may be premature. It is precisely here, in providing a more adequate description of developmental differences and by so doing paving the way for tackling causal questions, that we see our approach as being most useful. However, until mechanisms of change have been investigated we cannot claim that there has been a proper integration of developmental and cognitive psychology within a common framework. To achieve this may well require radically different models from those current in the study of adult cognition (see, e.g., Rabbitt, 1981). We do nevertheless wish to claim that the approach we have described is one which can bring the desirable but elusive goal of theoretical integration somewhat closer.

References

Allport, D. A. (1980), 'Attention and performance', in G. Claxton (ed.), *Cognitive Psychology: New Directions*. Routledge & Kegan Paul: London.

Baddeley, A. D. (1976), *The Psychology of Memory*. Harper & Row: New York.

Baddeley, A. D. (1979), 'Working memory and reading', in P. A Kolers, M. E. Wrolstad and H. Bouma (eds), *Processing of Visible Language*, Vol. I. Plenum Press: New York.

Baddeley, A. D. (1983), 'Working memory', *Philosophical Transactions of the Royal Society Series B*, *302*, 311-24.

Baddeley, A. D. (1986), *Working Memory*. Clarendon Press: Oxford.

Baddeley, A. D., Grant, S., Wight, E. and Thomson, N. (1975), 'Imagery and visual working memory', in P. M. A. Rabbitt and S. Dornic (eds), *Attention and Performance*, V. Academic Press: London.

Baddeley, A. D. and Hitch, G. J. (1974), 'Working memory', in G. H. Bower (ed.), *The Psychology of Learning and Motivation: Advances in Research and Theory*, Vol. 8. Academic Press: New York.

Baddeley, A. D. and Hitch, G. J. (1977), 'Recency re-examined', in S. Dornic (ed.), *Attention and Performance*, VI. Erlbaum: Hillsdale, NJ.

Baddeley, A. D. and Lewis, V. J. (1981), 'Inner active processes in reading: the inner voice, the inner ear and the inner eye', in A. M. Lesgold and C. A. Perfetti (eds), *Interactive Processes in Reading*. Erlbaum: Hillsdale, NJ.

Baddeley, A. D. and Lieberman, K. (1980), 'Spatial working memory', in R. Nickerson (ed.), *Attention and Performance*, VIII. Erlbaum: Hillsdale, NJ.

Baddeley, A. D., Thomson, N. and Buchanan, M. (1975), 'Word length and the structure of short-term memory', *Journal of Verbal Learning and Verbal Behavior*, *14*, 575-89.

Baldwin, J. M. (1894), *Mental Development in the Child and the Race*. Macmillan: New York.

Barnard, P. (1985), 'Interacting cognitive subsystems: A psycholinguistic approach to short-term memory', in A. W. Ellis (ed.), *Progress in the Psychology of Language*, Vol. 2. Erlbaum: Hillsdale, NJ.

Broadbent, D. E. and Broadbent, M. H. P. (1981), 'Recency effects in visual memory', *Quarterly Journal of Experimental Psychology*, *33A*, 1-15.

Brooks, L. R. (1967), 'The suppression of visualization by reading', *Quarterly Journal of Experimental Psychology*, *19*, 289-99.

Brown, R. M. (1977), 'An examination of visual and verbal coding processes in preschool children', *Child Development*, *48*, 38-45.

Bryant, P. E. and Trabasso, T. (1971), 'Transitive inferences and memory in young children', *Nature*, *232*, 456-8.

Carr, T. H. and Pollatsek, A. (1985), 'Recognising printed words: a look at current models', in D. Besner, T. G. Waller and G. E. Mackinnon (eds), *Reading Research: Advances in Theory and Practice*, Vol. 5. Academic Press: New York.

Case, R. (1984), 'The process of stage transition: A neo-Piagetian view', in R. J. Sternberg (ed.), *Mechanisms of Cognitive Development*. Freeman: New York.

Case, R., Kurland, M. D. and Goldberg, J. (1982), 'Operational efficiency and the growth of short-term memory span', *Journal of Experimental Child Psychology*, *33*, 386-404.

Chi, M. T. H. (1978), 'Knowledge structures and memory development', in R. J. Siegler (ed.), *Children's Thinking: What Develops?* Erlbaum: Hillsdale, NJ.

Coltheart, M. (1982), 'The psycholinguistic analysis of acquired dyslexias: some illustrations', in D. E. Broadbent and L. Weiskrantz (eds), *The Neuropsychology of Cognitive Function*. The Royal Society: London.

Coltheart, M., Patterson, K. E. and Marshall, J. C. (eds) (1980), *Deep Dyslexia*. Routledge & Kegan Paul: London.

Conrad, R. (1964), 'Acoustic confusion in immediate memory', *British Journal of Psychology*, *55*, 75-84.

Conrad, R. (1971), 'The chronology of the development of covert speech in children', *Developmental Psychology*, *5*, 398-405.

Dempster, F. N. (1981), 'Memory span: sources of individual and developmental differences', *Psychological Bulletin*, *89*, 63-100.

Donaldson, M. (1978), *Children's Minds*. Fontana: London.

Downing, J. and Leong, C. K. (1982), *Psychology of Reading*. Collier Macmillan: London.

Ellis, A. W. (1984), *Reading, Writing and Dyslexia*. Erlbaum: Hillsdale, NJ.

Feldman, N. S., Klosson, E. C., Parsons, J. E., Rholes, W. S. and Ruble, D. N. (1976), 'Order of information presentation and children's moral judgments', *Child Development*, *47*, 556-9.

Fischer, B. and Glanzer, M. (1986), 'Short-term storage and the processing of cohesion during reading', *Quarterly Journal of Experimental Psychology*, *38A*, 431-60.

Flavell, J. H. (1985), *Cognitive Development*, 2nd edition. Prentice-Hall: Englewood Cliffs, NJ.

Flavell, J. H., Beach, D. R. and Chinsky, J. M. (1966), 'Spontaneous verbal rehearsal in a memory task as a function of age', *Child Development*, *37*, 283-99.

Fodor, J. A. (1983), *The Modularity of Mind*. MIT Press: Cambridge, MA.

Frith, U. (1985), 'Beneath the surface of developmental dyslexia', in K. E. Patterson, J. C. Marshall and M. Coltheart (eds), *Surface Dyslexia*. Erlbaum: Hillsdale, NJ.

Galton, F. (1883), *Enquiries into Human Faculty and its Development*. Macmillan: London.

Gibson, E. J. and Levin, H. (1975), *The Psychology of Reading*. MIT Press: Cambridge, MA.

Hagen, J. W. and Kail, R. V. (1973), 'Facilitation and distraction in short-term memory', *Child Development*, *39*, 113-21.

Halford, G. S. (1982), *The Development of Thought*. Erlbaum: Hillsdale, NJ.

Halford, G. S. and Wilson, W. H. (1980), 'A category theory approach to cognitive development', *Cognitive Psychology*, *12*, 356-411.

Hayes, D. S. and Schulze, S. A. (1977), 'Visual encoding in preschoolers' serial retention', *Child Development*, *48*, 1066-70.

Hitch, G. J. (1978), 'The role of short-term working memory in mental arithmetic', *Cognitive Psychology*, *10*, 302-23.

Hitch, G. J. (1980), 'Developing the concept of working memory', in G. Claxton (ed.), *Cognitive Psychology: New Directions*, 154-96. Routledge & Kegan Paul: London.

Hitch, G. J. (1984), 'Working memory', *Psychological Medicine*, *14*, 265-71.

Hitch, G. J. and Halliday, M. S. (1983), 'Working memory in children', *Philosophical Transactions of the Royal Society (London)*, Series B, *302*, 325-40.

Hitch, G. J., Halliday, M. S. and Littler, J. (1984), 'Memory span and the speed of mental operations', paper presented at the joint Experimental Psychology Society/Netherlands Psychonomic Foundation Meeting, Amsterdam.

Hitch, G. J., Halliday, M. S., Schaafstal, A. and Schraagen, J. M. (in press), 'Visual working memory in young children', *Memory and Cognition*.

Hulme, C., Thomson, N., Muir, C. and Lawrence, A. L. (1984), 'Speech rate and the development of short-term memory', *Journal of Experimental Child Psychology*, *38*, 241-53.

Kail, R. (1984), *The Development of Memory in Children*, 2nd edition. Freeman: San Francisco, CA.

Klahr, D. and Wallace, J. G. (1976), *Cognitive Development: An Information Processing View*. Erlbaum: Hillsdale, NJ.

Kosslyn, S. M. (1980), *Image and Mind*. Harvard University Press: Cambridge, MA.

Light, P. H., Buckingham, N. and Robbins, A. H. (1979), 'The conservation task as an interactional setting', *British Journal of Educational Psychology*, *49*, 304-10.

Logie, R. H. (1986), 'Visuo-spatial processing in working memory', *Quarterly Journal of Experimental Psychology, 38A*, 229-47.

McGarrigle, J. and Donaldson, M. (1975), 'Conservation accidents', *Cognition, 3*, 341-50.

Marsh, G., Friedman, M. P., Welch, V. and Desberg, P. (1981). 'A cognitive-developmental theory of reading acquisition', in T. G. Waller and G. E. Mackinnon (eds), *Reading Research: Advances in Theory and Practice*, Vol. 3. Academic Press: New York.

Meadows, S. (ed.) (1983), *Developing Thinking.* Methuen: London.

Mills, M. and Funnell, E. (1983), 'Experience and cognitive processing', in S. Meadows (ed.), *Developing Thinking.* Methuen: London.

Murray, D. J. (1968), 'Articulation and acoustic confusability in short-term memory', *Journal of Experimental Psychology, 78*, 679-84.

Nicolson, R. (1981), 'The relation between memory span and processing speed', in M. P. Friedman, J. P. Das and N. O'Connor (eds), *Intelligence and Learning*, 179-83. Plenum: New York.

Ornstein, P. A. (ed.) (1978), *Memory Development in Children.* Erlbaum: Hillsdale, NJ.

Pascual-Leone, J. A. (1970), 'A mathematical model for the transition rule in Piaget's developmental stages', *Acta Psychologica, 32*, 301-45.

Phillips, W. A. (1983), 'Short-term visual memory', *Philosophical Transactions of the Royal Society (London), Series B, 302*, 295-309.

Rabbitt, P. M. A. (1981), 'Cognitive psychology needs models for changes in performance with old age', in J. Long and A. D. Baddeley (eds), *Attention and Performance*, IX. Erlbaum: Hillsdale, NJ.

Salamé, P. and Baddeley, A. D. (1982), 'Disruption of short-term memory by unattended speech: implications for the structure of working memory', *Journal of Verbal Learning and Verbal Behavior, 21*, 150-64.

Sanford, A. J. and Garrod, S. C. (1981), *Understanding Written Language: Explorations in Comprehension Beyond the Sentence.* Wiley: Chichester.

Seymour, P. H. K. and MacGregor, J. (1984), 'Developmental dyslexia: A cognitive experimental analysis of phonological, morphemic and visual impairments', *Cognitive Neuropsychology, 2*, 43-82.

Shallice, T. (1979a), 'Neuropsychological research and the fractionation of memory systems', in L. G. Nilsson (ed.), *Perspectives on Memory Research.* Erlbaum: Hillsdale, NJ.

Shallice, T. (1979b), 'Case study approach in neuropsychological research', *Journal of Clinical Neuropsychology, 1*, 183-211.

Shepard, R. N. (1980), *Internal Representation: Studies in Perception, Imagery and Cognition.* Bradford Books: Montgomery, VT.

Siegler, R. S. (1976), 'Three aspects of cognitive development', *Cognitive Psychology, 8*, 481-520.

Siegler, R. S. (1978), 'The origins of scientific reasoning', in R. S. Siegler (ed.), *Children's Thinking: What Develops?* Erlbaum: Hillsdale, NJ.

Snowling, M. J. (1983), 'The comparison of acquired and developmental disorders of reading – a discussion', *Cognition, 14*, 105-18.

Sternberg, R. J. (ed.) (1984), *Mechanisms of Cognitive Development.* Freeman: New York.

Walker, P. and Marshall, E. (1982), 'Visual memory and stimulus repetition effects', *Journal of Experimental Psychology: General, 111*, 348-68.

Weiskranz, L. (1964), 'Treatments, inferences and brain function', in L. Weiskranz, (ed.), *Analysis of Behavioural Change.* Harper & Row: New York.

Young, R. M. (1976), *Seriation by Children: An Artificial Intelligence Analysis of a Piagetian Task.* Birkhauser: Basel.

Subject index

Author index